VIBRATIONAL ENERGY HEALING

by Bill Ellis

This book is dedicated to my wife, Sue, who has tolerated my absence from the domestic chore scene over the last few months.

People who require healing and my fellow healers at Holywell Spiritual Church in North Wales probably thought that I was cracking up when they saw some of the things I was trying out during healing sessions – such as Etheric Weavers and Touchstones.

Sorry to all of you.

I am most grateful to Alan James Fowler for his artwork illustrating the Healing procedures in this book.

Bill Ellis

Vibrational Energy Healing

Author

William R. Ellis

Broad Oak Cottage, Llyndir Lane, Rossett,
Wrexham, Denbighshire, LL12 0AU United Kingdom
Phone: (011) 44 1244 579 239
Email: "Bill Ellis" <feelwell2002@yahoo.co.uk>

Publisher

The Holistic Intuition Society

c/o Executive Secretary, John Living, Professional Engineer
RR# 1 Site 9 Compartment 6, Galiano Island.
British Columbia, Canada V0N 1P0
(250)539-5807   Canada & USA: 1-866-369-7464
Email: Intuit@in2it.ca

Check www.in2it.ca for any change in address

ISBN 978-0-9686323-7-6

INDEX

Appendices

List of Illustrations

Editor's Blog

I am most pleased to have been given the task of helping Bill Ellis to get his book published in print. Actually, it is a combination of three books that Bill has written about Healing - and so the order of presentation has been changed to give the methodology in a more easily readable format.

Bill has problems with his sight - so most of his preparation was dictated into his computer; this resulted in minor problems, which have been corrected. Some rather personal items have not been included, since they have no meaning for readers who do not know Bill's family and friends. What has not been changed is the wisdom that comes from Bill and his Healing Guides.

Bill's methods of using his Pendulum have varied over the years - and so varying signals were given for the same indicated meaning. I have added the following explanation of how a person works with a Pendulum, based on my personal experiences, which may assist you, the reader, in your own use of your Pendulum.

Making and Holding your Pendulum

You can make your Pendulum by having any form of weight suspended by a flexible connector that you can hold in your hand. You can tie a piece of string around a metal nut, for example, or a needle on a thread.

You can also use a crystal on a chain, a cross or other neck decoration, or a glass bead on a length of cord. Some people use specially shaped Pendulums - because energies are very responsive to shapes, to forms of structure.

But even so, the main movement originates from your Heart-Mind-Brain team via your nervous-muscular system - YOU are the most important part !

You will find it best to hold your Pendulum with the string, cord, or chain between your thumb and first finger, as illustrated.

A long length of string enables you to see the movement more easily, but the speed of movement is slow. A very short length moves very fast, but the amount of movement is less, making it more difficult to see - a real problem when you are starting !

Probably the best length to use when starting is about six inches (15 cm) - then as you get more experienced, you can reduce this to between 3 and 4 inches (7 and 10 cm), as you find suits you.

Some LOLs (Little Old Ladies) are absolute wizards at using a Pendulum; their friends may watch them, and try to do the same: *"It doesn't work for me !"* they cry. Why is this so ?

In most cases this is because they have not trained their system to give signals. This is like telling a five year old child *"Give me the first five numbers in the Fibonacci series"* - he does not have any idea of what is meant, which of his toys you want.

Now it may work if you ask your Heart *"Please give me a signal with my Pendulum that indicates YES"* and then watch to see if your Pendulum moves.

Repeat the question for NO, and for NOT AVAILABLE, and remember the signals. Then you can ask questions.

Signaling Systems

Basically, there are two major systems of signaling - perhaps best described as being Physical or Meta-Physical. The strength of the movement indicates the strength of the answer.

The Physical system is 'to and fro' indicates a joining (the food is good for you to eat), 'side to side' a separation (a barrier between the food and yourself - do not eat it, for whatever reason).

The Meta-Physical system is rotational:

> clockwise: YES, positive, male, inputting an energy, and sending Love;

> anti-clockwise: NO, negative, female, extracting an energy being . Note that there is no 'taking of Love' !

It may be best to decide which signal you want to use, and then train your Heart-Mind-Brain team and your nervous-muscular system to give these.

I find the following best:

WAITING	To and fro swing
YES	Clockwise circle
NO	Anticlockwise circle
NOT AVAILABLE	Side to side swing

So for each of these signals, make your Pendulum give the signal by using all your muscles in your forearm, wrist, and hand - exaggerating these movements (since you are in a training session).

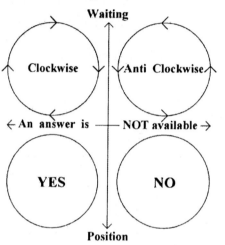

Then say *"This is a [to and fro swing], it signals [WAITING] !"* , and then holding your Pendulum still, and asking *"Please give me the signal for [WAITING]"*.

Repeat until each signal is clearly given when requested.

Pointing - with your Pendulum

One of the very good reasons for using a circle to signal YES or NO is that when you seek by asking your Pendulum to point towards something, you can check that it is giving a good signal.

Install a program to define the signals used by your Pendulum: *"When my Pendulum points to an item, it will first give a YES signal to indicate that it is the correct direction, or a NO signal to show that a problem exists"*.

A linear signal for YES or NO could be confused with the direction sought - the circular signals avoid this problem.

The skill of pointing with your Pendulum is most useful in selecting items from lists, books from shelves, checking on supplements for your use, and using Dowsing charts to identify causes of problems that need to be Healed.

Your Handy Chart

Since most of us have two hands, we can use the spare one (the one not holding your Pendulum !) as a chart for many purposes.

It is best to use signals that conform to indicators that you see often, such as the speedometer and charging gauge of your car - your Mind-Brain team is accustomed to the signals used.

This is a quick way to check on your health or vitality, if medications are beneficial to you, how many tablets should be taken (dose, doses per day - these may change with effect already achieved), percentage accuracy of a statement, etc.

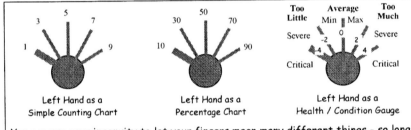

Left Hand as a Simple Counting Chart	Left Hand as a Percentage Chart	Left Hand as a Health / Condition Gauge

You can use your ingenuity to let your fingers mean many different things - so long as you have ensured that your Mind-Brain team understands the meanings to be signalled for each 'hand-chart' - and that you have specified to your Mind-Brain team which 'hand-chart' is being used for the Dowsing you are now doing !

Selection from Lists

You can use your Pendulum to select an item in a list, even to identify problems in a computer program.   You can do this by holding it to one side and see where it points, or use your other hand to point with a pencil or your finger to items until your Pendulum gives a YES signal.

When you get one selection, ask if there is also another to be found - you may have more than one error in a program, or need more than one supplement if you are checking what is needed for your good health.

Pendulum Power

When your pendulum makes a circle, the shape formed by the bob and string is a cone - a circular pyramid; and you know the powers attributed to pyramids !

The difference between an earphone and a loudspeaker is that the loudspeaker mechanism has a paper cone attached, which magnifies the vibrations.

In the same way, rotating your Pendulum magnifies your thoughts - the intent of your actions; this magnification (perhaps a thousand fold) makes the Healing action much more powerful.

How Healing Works

Bill was asking his Guides to explain how Healing works; he was told that Healing was done by 'Modular Node Waves' but did not understand - so asked me what was meant. I asked, got following from 'Upstairs' :

> Think about the Healee, get a good connection.
> Imagine/visualize Healee and what needs Healing
> 'See' the Healing take place.

> You and the Healee are Nodes.
> The wave between you is modulated
> by 'Upstairs' to be a carrier of
> Healing vibrational patterns, etc.

This may explain why you find that your Pendulum, when in Healing mode, automatically changes direction without your own impetus. Your Heart-Mind-Brain team, knowing your intent and working with 'Upstairs', knows when to change between input and extraction modes, and so changes its rotation.

I have also found that when in input mode, the rotation is supplanted by other shapes such as stars, asterisks, and cross-hatching that itself rotates - always reverting to a circular rotation when completed, and then stopping.

Asking Questions

Your Heart has neurons, similar to your Brain - people having a Heart transplant have often been found to have had their likes and dislikes changed to be more like those of the donor.

Your Brain seems to be the home of ego - so it is best to form the question in your logical mind, and then ask your Heart - <u>just as if it were an individual in its own right.</u>

Perhaps the reason is that your ego thinks it 'knows all' - so it tells what it thinks without checking ! So ask your Heart to get true answers.

How do you ask for a problem to be shown by your Pendulum ?

1. *"Signal YES if there is a problem here"* or
2.. *"Signal NO if the health here is not good"*

Case 1: A YES signal is the same as 'input' - OK if you put 'Healing Love' into a problem area before extraction.

Case 2: A NO signal can continue into extraction - which may be what you intend.

In both cases no signal should be given if all is well.

Working with Energies

Whenever you extract any 'Not Good' energies, make certain that you have defined that they do not come to you {or anyone else !) but are taken by 'Upstairs' to be Healed with Love and led to their rightful place.

Most of these energies have been hurt, and need Love and Healing. There are other energies that also seek Love and Healing - and seek a healer to help them !

Many Healers can feel the negativity from these energies, and think that they are being attacked. In most cases this is not so - they are being asked for help. Adopt a 'win-win' solution - if you have any suspicion that there are 'Not Good' energies around you, just ask 'Upstairs' to take them to be Healed, etc.

The strongest Love is 'True Holy Love, Namaste' ! Helping others for good without expectation of reward - just because you know it is the best way to 'Be'.

Further Study

In Walt Wood's 'Letter to Robin' he gives programming directions to improve your Dowsing skills and check that 'all is well' so that you have confidence in your Dowsing.

See also my book 'Intuition Technology' which covers some aspects of Dowsing and Healing not mentioned in Bill's book.

Namaste,   John Living

Introduction

As small parts of the Universe, we must submit to the Laws of the Universe. People use five senses to perceive the material world around them. However, our material world consists of more subtle occurrences than can be perceived by the five senses, and if we become attuned to the higher dimensional worlds, we can more easily comply with the Laws of the Universe.

In other words, by developing your ability to sense energetic fields, you will perceive the world around you with a more complete perspective that includes a newly developed bio-energetic ability.

A definition of a healer is: 'A person who was sick and is now healthy'. A definition of a good healer is: 'A person who was very sick and is now healthy'. That's right, every person's being heals itself.

A person who is sick does not have the ability to draw in sufficient 'life force energy', Prana, to enable the body to heal itself. This is where a 'healer' steps in to supply such energy. A 'healer' is a person who has the ability to 'channel' such energy and pass it to the sick person.

The work of the healer is now complete. The extra energy is now used by the sick person's body to heal itself.

This book presents some revolutionary new methods of bio-energy healing - of energetic cleansing, balancing, normalizing, and healing that can be utilized by anyone to heal the self and others; that can be performed by anyone, on anyone, and at any distance.

At birth, we are all given the unique ability to feel our own bio-energetic field and that of others, as well as the energy field of any living matter. People hold powerful energetic strength and potential, inside and out.

This book will give you special techniques to open and develop bio-energetic ability and use it for your own health and balance. You will not only be able to help yourself be healthy, you can help family, loved ones, and pets as well.

By learning to control and direct your own energy, or even the energy of anyone else, you will learn how to achieve optimum health for yourself and others.

Developing bio-energetic abilities is a fascinating and evolving process. Once you have started to develop your energy and healing abilities, it is not possible to stop, turn away, or forget the experience. Once you start, you will never stop learning.

It all began when a man asked me to assess the energy state of another person who was far away. His photo was not available, and the man had never seen the person he was asking about, but he wanted to help his friend's loved one.

So how, then, could I start to assess this person, let alone give healing at a distance ?

Then I remembered the work done by Michael Nudel and Eva Nudel Ph.D. and their ability to work with the 'etheric image' of a person. So I got a photocopy of a human body form and asked the man to visualize his friend and to project the image of his friend into the form on the paper.

When I held my pendulum over the image, I discovered energy in it. I noted all known identification details, the name, birth date and post code on the drawing to determine the person's energy. With the aid of a pendulum, I assessed the unknown person's energetic state.

People are energy beings. The roots of human problems are energy problems. Thoughts, emotions, feelings, and actions are energy operations. You influence other people with your bio-energy, and other people in turn influence you. Energy fields interact when people stay close to each other.

When an influence is positive and peaceful, you gain positive energy and balance. On the other hand, when people are faced with an angry communicator or prolonged stressful event, they are involved in a negative energetic influence.

In many cases, people's energy may be blocked, become unbalanced, stagnant or stale.

This book will teach you how to release energy blocks, whether they be emotional, mental, or even spiritual blocks, and to release bio-negativity in bio-energetic and chakra therapy. You will be able to open your chakras and make them working and functional. Functional chakras bring vital energy to the chakra and energy system.

In addition, you will learn how to prepare your mind and your bio-energy to perform the bio-energetic healing work and maintenance of physical, mental, emotional, and energetic health on an everyday basis.

You will learn how to achieve a meditative state of mind - an important healer's tool in energy healing. You will learn how to develop visual memory and the ability to visualize. A vast amount of healing work is performed with the help of visualization.

Visualization may be healing in its nature, just as positive thought may be healing. Nevertheless, you will learn to use your newly developed ability to visualize.

Finally, you will learn how to achieve an energetic balance in order to prevent physical illnesses, to perceive positive healing information, and discharge unwanted energetic information or harmful bio-negative energy from human energetic systems. You will be able to relieve imbalances and discomforts on the energetic and physical level.

You do not need to be a specialist, psychic, or healer to gain awareness from this book. Nevertheless, you may grow spiritually and energetically. The teaching will give you the possibility of self-awareness, personal growth, wisdom, new understanding, and maturity.

This book will help you to be healthy and to live a highly energetic, distress-free, balanced life. You will improve your relationships and communication, learn to be more successful with high self-esteem and inner-self knowledge, and be happy and positive-minded.

This book explains:

- Knowledge regarding the use of techniques and strategies to relax the mind and body, 'How to' diagnose and 'heal' with a dowsing tool, and 'how to' protect oneself and your client during a healing session.

- Pranic Healing and applies it's principles to new methods of 'Distant Healing'.

- Introduces you to the most modern thinking on how a 'healer' is able to channel 'life force' energy and how some 'healers' are able to intensify this 'life force' energy and then transform this energy into a further energy with immense healing power.

This 'new' energy has been known about for one hundred years or so but it's effect on life and it's part in healing has only recently been recognized.

Another 'new' healing is also introduced, called 'Focal Touch'. You can now be attuned into this energy - we show you how to create this energy and apply it 'hands-on' or at a distance.

Diagnosis and Medical Systems

In some jurisdictions diagnosis is unlawful by anyone except a medical doctor.

It may be best to avoid saying *"You have [cancer, or any other problem]"* and instead say *"My Intuition indicates that you may have a problem in your [location of problem]"* - which is meant wherever diagnosis is mentioned in this book.

Never, ever, raise fear in a patient. Explain that you will just do your best, with the help of non-physical Beings, to identify problems, locate their causes, and heal the energies involved as best you can - even in a case that may appear to be untreatable or terminal; you may be wrong - as are some physicians on occasions !

Everything is energy - so energy work may completely change the apparent circumstances. There is always hope !

Most doctors entered medicine with the intention to be Healers - but so much of the medical system is manipulated by the pharmaceutical companies that they became prescription writers.

If these doctors were trained in Metaphysical Healing methods such as are mentioned in this book - and were free to use them without persecution by medical authorities - then the public health systems would cost less and be more effective in improving the health of people.

Chapter One
Mental Tools To Aid The Healer

In order to grow spiritually, achieve deep understanding of your life purpose, maintain bio-energetic health, work with human energy, and help yourself and others, you need to improve your subtle bodies, especially the mental and intuitive bodies.

Preparing For Visualization

To develop understanding of our energetic being and energetic health and the ability to work with bio-energy (perceive and interpret energetic information), we will need to use our highly developed mental and intuitive bodies.

One of the most effective methods for developing the third eye and the intuitive body is visualization. An ability to visualize images at will and retain visual memory can be developed by practice.

When you are relaxed, you may visualize colour and hear its correlating sound (the seven colours of the spectrum have seven musical notes correlating to these colours). Later, you may practice the visualization of colour combination, seeing geometric or voluminous figures. A highly developed third eye leads to the ability to observe radiation of the subtle bodies or coloured aura.

Visualization, like intuition, is a type of thinking which is used for making contact with the inner-self, rather than with the outer world. Employing images in our mental work to remember information preceded communication with words. Communicating with the inner-self using mental images requires our full attention to imagery.

Visualization means creating a mental picture or image as in your night dreams. These created images have the energy to influence you, and they can be animated by your mental energy.

Mental images, being your energetic children, work for your wellbeing, bringing energetic and physical health. You, by managing energetic images, can help the healing process to occur. By visualizing the perfect consequence, your consciousness will be programmed to achieve it in reality.

Mental Imagery

For healing purposes, you should use mental imagery. This is different from visualization in that it induces deep physical relaxation in addition to the process of visualization.

The deeper the relaxation, the more vivid and controllable are the images, and the more they may be healing in their nature. Becoming relaxed, you may stimulate and facilitate vibrant mental healing images.

Relaxation of the physical body allows you to 'tune-in' to the inner-self, and mobilizes the body's resources for inward activity.

The effects of relaxation include reduced heart rate, blood pressure, and sweating, increased functioning of the gastrointestinal tract, relaxation of muscles, and an increase of oxygen and blood flowing to the brain. One of the characteristics of the relaxation response is the rapid shifting of the brain-wave patterns from low-amplitude, rapid beta waves to higher amplitude, slower, more strongly rhythmical alpha and theta waves.

Beta waves occur mostly in the waking state, whereas alpha and theta waves are found in such states as meditation and contemplation.

The first and most important step in the process of visualization, mental imagery, or any energetic work is preparing the mind. As your physical body, your mind has to be calmed down, quieted, and eased into the special condition of the alpha and theta state.

The Meditative Mind State

Researchers have discovered that the human brain is powered by electricity. Scientists have found that the human brain has a tendency to produce brain waves of four frequencies, which they have termed beta, alpha, theta, and delta.

Beta waves are the most rapid waves. Beta waves are present when we are in a 'normal' state of mental arousal - talking, and performing everyday tasks. These waves are dominant in our brains because of their association with alertness, arousal, concentration, and cognition. When beta waves are dominant, we keep our attention externally.

<u>Alpha waves</u> are the next most rapid. Alpha waves appear in the brain when we close our eyes and relax our bodies.

Bodily and mental passiveness or an unfocused state brings brain-wave activity down, causing the brain to produce dominant alpha waves, otherwise known as the alpha state.

The alpha state is a neutral brain state, which can be achieved by people when they are without stress, are healthy and in a relaxed state. People with stress, mental or physical illness, or anxiety may have difficulty to achieve the alpha state because of a lack of alpha brain activity.

<u>Theta waves</u>, the next frequency, occur when calmness and relaxation deepen into drowsiness. The very slow theta waves are often indicative of deep reverie, mental imagery, and the ability to access memories. In the theta state ('hypnagogic,' or 'twilight'), we are able to have daydreams or visualize unexpected dreamlike mental images, and have vivid memories, like of childhood or other pleasant memories.

Through theta activities we can access our unconscious being, insight, and creative thoughts. In our active and busy times, adults produce the theta state rarely or not at all, whereas children are in the theta state almost all the time.

It is the most mysterious state of the brain. However, it may be kept for any lengthy period of time only by experienced people because of the tendency to fall asleep when large amounts of theta waves are generated.

<u>Delta waves</u> are the slowest, which the brain generates when falling asleep. When delta waves become the dominant brain waves, it means that we are either asleep or unconscious.

<u>The meditative state</u> of brain in its peak is characterized by the brain-wave activity throughout the whole brain (both left and right hemispheres).

Sitting with closed eyes in a relaxed, passive state, we may achieve the alpha and theta, or meditative state. Ideally, in achieving the meditative state, we should aspire to reach its peak.

How can you achieve the meditative state of mind that will be needed for your bio-energetic work ? The ability to stay focused on a single thing may be achieved by frequent practice.

At first, choose a quiet place where nothing will disturb you. Relax your body, and release any tension from your body by tightening different groups of muscles for a moment, then relaxing them.

Skilled meditators diffuse their vision and consciousness, becoming oneness with the universe. They have clear consciousness as long as they need it without the help of concentration on the object or any activity. For beginners, having a lot of thoughts and few moments of clear consciousness is normal; nevertheless, keep practicing to gradually master and control the consciousness.

Meditation alone may be helpful in everyday life. During meditation you cannot worry, fear, or hate. Your body can learn to rid itself of anxiety, depression, hostility, or any stressful or habitual emotions.

Nowadays, meditation is used in the prevention and healing of high blood pressure, heart problems, migraines, and arthritis.

To perform any bio-energetic work, which you are learning, you will always need to enter into the meditative state of mind.

Depending on what you are going to do, you will need to empty your mind either of having any thoughts or of mental intention.

How Bagha Yoga Accelerates the Meditative State

Thanks to Burt Goldman - The American Monk.

Sit in a comfortable chair, close your eyes and take a couple of deep breaths. Now take your mind back to a time when you were deliriously happy, comfortable and contented.

Any time will do - you just passed an exam, driving test, got a great job. Anyway you are very happy ! Avoid any 'short term' happiness that 'turned sour'.

Hold that image in your mind for a minute or two. Now, with your mouth closed, just place the tip of your tongue to the roof of your mouth just behind the teeth and hold it there for three seconds, one - two - three. Then lower your tongue.

You have just been initiated into Bagha Yoga. In future if you want to reach the meditative state instantly, just close your eyes and place the tip of your tongue to the roof of your mouth for three seconds only. Try it now - great, wasn't it !

After a days practice, you can do it with your eyes open, even while driving - good for relieving road rage anger.

Intention as Mental Command

The second step in preparing our minds for the visualization process and bio-energetic healing involves learning to give yourself intentional mental commands. An intentional mental command is a mental command that directs our consciousness, attention, and mental actions to visualize.

The process of visualization may be enhanced greatly when you send intentional commands about how the process must proceed.

You give mental commands about what you wish to achieve in order to receive it in reality. You need this ability in bio-energetic healing as well, which can help to increase the possibility of healing and shorten the time of healing.

Before imagining, it is always necessary to define and clarify what you are going to visualize. You can tell this instruction aloud or mentally. When you know exactly your goal in the visualization process, and give your will or thought direction, you will increase the effectiveness of your work greatly.

In all this work, the key is to give a mental command or have it programmed, and then relax to 'let it all happen' - without any effort to force things. This is meant whenever the word 'try' is used !

Performing inner mental control over the self, you can become a master of your life. If you learn how to turn your will towards your inner-self, you will take advantage of your life, be your own authority, control your healing, and maintain physical, emotional, energetic, and spiritual health.

Development of Visual Memory

Bright visual memory will be helpful and important in the process of imagery. Using visual memory (right hemisphere), humans reflect received information not only with words but with images, and they continue to see and work with images as they want.

The ability to perceive the world with visual images is given to everybody because of the universal ability of seeing colourful and visual dreams.

However, only the very young have such memory. In school, children develop logic memory, which is directed by the left hemisphere. As time passes, the left hemisphere becomes overwhelmed with stored information, and the ability to memorize drops down sharply.

The human brain consists of two hemispheres: the right hemisphere - visual (emotions), and the left hemisphere - logic (mind). The brain is supposed to memorize colour, smell and sound with these two hemispheres. Perceiving information in this way, the brain composes an image in the right hemisphere and puts the image into words in the left hemisphere.

Image information is memorized easily, and may be kept forever. However, in the civilized world any information is perceived in a curtailed way. People begin keeping such information in the left hemisphere, while nothing is kept in the right hemisphere. In this way, children's visual memory may be lost.

The lack of visual memory causes feelings of missed information; the mind artificially fills in the unrecalled details to get the whole image. Visual memory demands the understanding of stored information, creativity, self-confidence, absence of stress, and a healthy psyche.

Like achieving a meditative state of mind, where both hemispheres have to increase the whole brain's power, perceiving information with both hemispheres and with all senses is our goal in visual memory.

Exercises for Developing Visual Memory

Before every exercise, you may envision the process of visualizing that you are going to perform with the intention of a needed result.

Any mental exercise without intention is less effective. Mental intention can increase the effectiveness of your intellectual and physical exercises within two to three times.

1. Empty your mind of thoughts. Thought is energy. When your mental energy is not calmed, it is in chaos. In this condition, it is not possible to achieve a positive result in your imagery work, and you will tire easily. The total abstinence of thoughts gives you a sensational feeling of lightness and freedom. When you visualize, use all five senses for more effective visualization.

Next, find any object, and look at it for 3 - 5 seconds, trying to picture it on the inhalation. Close your eyes, and try to recall the visual image on the peak of breath in 3 - 5 seconds. On the exhalation, try to diffuse the image mentally (fading, throwing away). With practice, change the method of picturing and diffusing, velocity, and rhythm.

2. Empty your mind, and gaze on the chosen object (for example, any body part). Keep your eyes directed on the object's centre and try to look at the whole thing in 3 - 10 minutes. Then, close your eyes for 3 - 4 minutes and try to recall the colour image as brightly and clearly as possible. Repeat a few more times, and compare the original with the image.

Perform the exercise in a different way each time, and try to find new details. A new way of performing the exercise will lead to a condition of astonishment and lift your whole condition to a new qualitative level. Try to do this exercise with all your body parts.

3. Gaze at an object in the same way as in the previous exercise for 3 - 10 minutes (or until the first thought). Turn around and look at a piece of white paper. Try to recall the image and place it mentally on the paper.

4. When you are out walking or standing in a queue, you may perform the following exercise. Take a look at someone or something, close your eyes, and try to visualize the image in 3 - 7 seconds. When your eyes are closed, you may still move. Gradually master in the act of recalling this clear and bright 'momentary photo,' and keep it in your mind as long as you need.

When you have practiced for a while in performing this exercise with closed eyes, you may then try visualizing with open eyes. In this case, you look at a 'photo', and see a memorized visual image with opened eyes while turning around to 'see' any scene.

5. Choose a subject, take a look at him or her, and close your eyes. Now you hold a 'momentary photo' image mentally. Try to continue the situation in mental visual images rather than stop it.

Mentally pretend and follow the subject's moving or direction, then compare your result with reality after opening your eyes. With more practice, you will be able to animate a 'picture' and reduce the quantity of mistakes in comparison with the subject's real actions.

6. Start as in exercise 4 - with one exception: the 'momentary photo' now needs to be moved, overlaid, and changed in its form in a determined direction. Keep manipulating the 'mental photo' as many times as you need until you do it easily, without any strain.

7. Now try this method of mental animation: Imagine any animal, and let it live its own life and move in your imagery. Vivify objects in your imagination.

This exercise is performed with closed eyes in the beginning of practice - and then, as you master it, with opened eyes. You may imagine that you are touching the object and it becomes vivified.

Try visualizing actions with objects or live creatures upon your will.

It is necessary to achieve a relaxed meditative state when working with images, so that you are able to freely manipulate any imagined objects. Your imaginary work must be done effortlessly and creatively.

Visualization as Mental Healing

Now you have a powerful tool - your imagination, whose power far exceeds the power of will. The power of your will can also be helpful in the process of visualization.

Visualization takes place in your mind reality, not in the physical reality. Visualization works with your inner subjective reality, and through this reality it changes physical existence.

When you have improved your imagination, you are able to manage your thoughts and images in a right way for you, increase your mind power greatly, and help your physical body's healing.

Keeping visualization as an everyday practice, you will be able to help yourself relax the body, relieve any pain in your body, and free yourself of bad habits or addictions. You will find visualization of healing your organs a powerful aid in self-healing.

Visualizing White Light Healing Energy

With the following exercise, try to direct the healing energy of White Light to your physical body. Stay focused, and practice this exercise - believing in successful results.

Sit on a chair and relax your body, keeping your spine straight. Try to achieve full relaxation - just let it all happen without any force or effort. Mentally imagine how a flow of White Light enters the crown chakra and then spreads throughout the whole body.

Almighty White Light fills the diseased organ and dissolves toxins and ill cells into subtle substances, which speed away with White Light's flow to your feet. Then, they are expelled from the body into the ground.

Visualize White Light entering the crown chakra and acquiring an auric egg form. Imagine the self inside this auric egg. The energy of White Light starts circulation in your auric egg or energy system, and your breathing becomes even and calm.

Mentally, create bubbles from White Light. These subtle balls surround your chakras and penetrate them, entering your physical body.

Beginning at your brow chakra, imagine how a bubble of White Light enters and surrounds your head. Imagine similar light balls entering all other chakras from the head to the root chakra.

Try to observe this process with your inner sight. Your blood flow is recharging now with vital energy, and your nervous system is stimulating.

In the process of meditation, your inner voice announces: *"I am surrounded by White Absolute. Every cell of my body is like an antenna receiving energy and giving it to my whole physical body"*.

Increasing the Field Flow

You will need to develop two skills: to activate the movement of your body's energy in and out as well as up and down; and to raise and lower your field's frequencies.

To improve the flow in and out and up and down we use the breathing exercises progressing from feet to head.

1 Starting at the feet, imagine that you are on each breath inhaling energy through your feet up to your abdomen; immediately exhale pushing the energy back down your legs and out your feet.

Take normal rather than exaggerated deep breaths and focus your attention on how your legs feel as the energy flows up and down.

Do this about ten times or more if you are habitually ungrounded, or until you feel you have established a circuit that will continue.

2 Now focus your awareness on the inside front of your knees, and imagine breathing through this area. As you inhale feel the energy entering your knees and rising into your abdomen. As you exhale, experience the energy flowing downward and out the knees. Repeat ten times or until you are aware that the circuit has become automatic.

3 Next focus awareness deep in the pelvis, slightly anterior to the rectum (the root chakra). Again pull energy inward with each inhalation up to the abdomen and outward on exhalation.

4 Now become aware of a location in the lower abdomen just below the navel (sacral chakra). Again breathe in toward the spine to the abdomen and then out from the spine, allowing the energy always to move upward on inhalation and downward and out from the lower abdomen on exhalation.

These exercises will increase the amount of energy flow and also indirectly will increase circulation of the blood and lymphatic fluid.

5 Now move your awareness to the solar plexus or your stomach above your waist, which is called the emotional chakra (solar plexus chakra). Because this area of the field is frequently sluggish, you may have difficulty visualizing breath entering easily and smoothly. More than ten breaths may be required to establish a free flow.

6 Next place your attention on the middle of your body at the heart level. As you breathe through the heart chakra, your chest will fill as the energy moves downward into your abdomen.

This chakra is the one that is usually most open and free. Ten breaths may be adequate to increase the energy flow here. If you feel that your heart chakra is closed, the sensation generally comes from problems in the emotional chakra not in the heart.

7 Now focus on the throat chakra in the middle of the 'V' above the breast bone. Throat chakra stagnation in adults has been associated with blocked creativity. As you breathe through this chakra be aware of energy going both ways, down on inhalation and coming back up to the throat on exhalation.

8 Focus your attention on the brow chakra, located on your forehead just above and between your eyes. Breathe deeply but smoothly through this spot, feeling the air go into the centre of your head, then downward filling the chest and abdomen without strain. Exhale through the brow chakra and repeat ten times.

9 And last, focus on the spot on the top of the head, above your ears. Imagine inhaling air down through this crown chakra into the body and out the crown chakra on exhalation. Repeat ten times.

The energies should now be flowing in and out so that your field is expanded by many inches or even feet around your body.

10 Before you leave this imagery exercise, repeat taking one breath through each chakra into the chest and abdomen. But instead of exhaling back down and out the same chakra, exhale the energy up and out the crown chakra. This way the energy is flowing from each chakra up and out the crown.

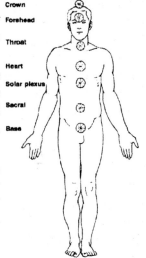

11 If your mind starts wandering during any of these exercises, go back to the knees with a few breaths. This will ground you rapidly.

12 Now focus on the feeling in your feet, the insides of the knees, the bottom of the pelvis, the sacral chakra, the emotional chakra, the heart chakra, the throat chakra, the brow chakra and the crown chakra.

Spend a few minutes now settling in, observing and being aware of what your bio-electro-magnetic field feels like when it freely flows in and through your body in all directions.

The Seven Major Chakras

Increasing Energy Frequencies

You should learn to increase your vibrations in all ranges: high, low and in the middle ranges to stabilize the field before attempting deeper meditation.

We no longer emphasize just going up in vibrations but rather in filling a wide range of frequencies from low to high with all in between. With health, happiness and successful meditations your range of frequencies expands. With disease and emotional disturbance the range decreases.

To expand your frequency range it is helpful to imagine each chakra spinning clockwise while visualizing a corresponding colour. We will be spinning clockwise only the following chakras:

1. Root chakra   Red
2. Sacral chakra   Orange
3. Solar Plexus chakra   Yellow
4. Heart chakra   Green
5. Throat chakra   Sky Blue
6. Brow chakra   Indigo
7. Crown chakra   White

The auric field contains the complete spectrum of frequencies of light from red to blue violet to white.

The lower chakras are marked by colours lower in the light spectrum and therefore lower frequencies. Higher frequencies and colours higher in the spectrum characterize the upper chakras.

Spinning Chakras

1 Start by focusing on the root or the deep pelvic chakra, colouring it a rich red. If you don't see red, imagine a red apple, a red dress or a tie. See the energy spinning clockwise. Spin the chakra for at least ten complete revolutions.

If it moves smoothly and easily in a complete circle a few repetitions will suffice. If it is stuck and resistant or moves in a lopsided circle, if it doesn't move or it goes counter-clockwise, or if the colour fades, you need to spend more time and focus your awareness on this chakra, for there is a block in the vortex of the field.

2 Next move to the lower abdomen, the sacral chakra. Colour it orange and spin it clockwise ten circles, while you observe the spinning. In our culture this chakra is often weak with a poor flow.

3 Now focus on the solar plexus, the emotional body; colour it yellow like a lemon. Spin it clockwise ten times.

4 Next be aware of the heart chakra; colour it green - a rich, vibrant green, like new growth in the Spring. Spin the chakra ten times clockwise.

5 Now be aware of your throat; colour it a rich yet light blue, like a clear sky. Spin it clockwise ten times. As you progress upward in the body, the colours become lighter and more vibrant, approaching the frequencies of white.

6 Next focus on the brow chakra; see it as indigo. Spin it clockwise ten times. You will note as you move up the body the vortex becomes smaller and it spins faster.

7 Finally pay attention to the crown chakra, visualizing it as a crystal clear white, like water or ice. Imagine spinning the chakra clockwise with the vortex going deep down into the body. Spin it ten times or until it spins freely.

8 Because all momentum slows down over time, go back to each of the chakras in sequence, visualizing the corresponding colour and spinning them several times.

Start with the red root chakra, then on to the orange kundalini, the yellow emotional body, the green heart chakra, the blue throat chakra, the indigo brow chakra and the white crown chakra.

9 Now lie there quietly and visualize energy flowing from your feet upward in each chakra toward the crown, where it flows up and out and spills down around your body in a white light.

You have now expanded your 'field' significantly and also increased the frequency of your 'field' significantly.

Protection During Energy Field Healing

It is of vital importance that you protect yourself and your Client during Energy Healing. This is done to stop any negative influences attaching themselves to you or your Client.

<u>(1). Putting on a Bandhan</u>

A simple exercise for protecting your subtle body and for preserving the state of meditation is to put on a 'Bandhan', a technique from Sahaja Yoga. This exercise can be done before and after healing.

Whilst sitting or standing, place the left hand at your side at the level of the waist with the fingers slightly open and palm pointing upward.

Putting on a Bandhan

Using the right hand, describe an arc, starting at the level of the left hip, going over the head, down to the right hip and back again. This movement should be done seven times.

<u>(2). Bio-Energy Defence</u>

Before working with bio-energy fields, it is important to learn how to protect yourself and to use it every time you work with bio-energy. Self protection must be done to avoid any energetic interfering of bio-systems at energetic contacts, especially their bio-negative influence on each other.

There is an opinion among energy healers that in order to avoid being contaminated with negative energy during energy healing, after a close encounter, one must stay emotionally uninvolved in the bio-energetic process.

However, this is not enough ! Bio-energy fields interrelate even without intentional cooperation. Someone's negative attitude or constant thoughts may depress your energy system and enervate it if this person is constantly close to you.

When you are involved in the bio-energetic processes of healing, besides the possibility of becoming enervated, there is a possibility to acquire the same energetic and even physical problems as your patient. Because of this threat, you need to perform bio-energetic defence.

Dealing with an etheric body image may be the safest method of energetic assessment and healing, because much of your work is done with energetic information on the 'energy informative' level.

Nevertheless, make it a rule of thumb to perform bio-energetic defence when you work energetically to avoid problems with energy fields interfering.

Here is a method of self-defence called the 'Yoga Lock' for working carefully on the energetic level.

Put the fingertips of one hand on the fingertips of another, but in the reverse order (one thumb is put on the little finger, another thumb is put on another little finger, and other fingertips are put accordingly).

One palm faces your chest, and the other palm faces away from the body. While keeping the lock, tell yourself mentally: *"My illnesses do not transfer to you, and your illnesses do not transfer to me."*

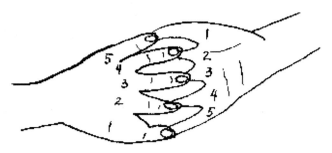

Yoga Lock for Energetic Protection.

Chapter Two

Physical Tools To Aid The Healer

The universe, including galaxies, is composed of spinning wheels and spirals of energy. Energies pass in the form of waves in space. Chakras are spinning and energy spirals through chakras while they are in good condition. Kundalini rises spirally to the crown chakra.

We cannot see these energy movements, but we can see its manifestations. We can evaluate our chakras and measure their openness and their health. A chakra's spinning or stopping, as we will observe, can tell us about its condition. Furthermore, chakras' spinning can be measured as patterns of bio-energetic activity and the energetic flow of Prana (healing, flowing energy) entering chakras.

As Prana is considered bio-positive energy, everything that prevents the bio-energetic balance (any congested, stale, stagnant energy or energetically harmful information) in the energy system is bio-negative energy.

In energy field healing, bio-negative energy may be recognized in the forms of energetic signals such as tingling, coldness, heat, subtle heaviness, or any other signals. Unusual signals or negative energy in this case shows imbalance in the bio-energy system.

Using the Pendulum

To assess degree of flow, its bio-positive or bio-negative direction, and to determine its quality and strength of energy, we use a pendulum. With the pendulum's help, we can grasp energy flows around the chakras.

The pendulum is used as an assessment and diagnostic tool in energetic healing. It gives clear evidence of energy flowing through the chakra system. It moves as energy spins and spirals in the chakra.

When holding a pendulum, we can feel the degree of movement, its velocity, and the smoothness or ease with which it spins or swings around. All these characteristics describe energy flow in the chakras or bio-energy systems.

In this way, we may determine the quantity and quality of energy flows in the chakra by observing the direction and 'shape' of pendulum movement, allowing for assessment of a human organism on the energetic level.

An advanced healer always feels any sluggishness or subtle hesitance of pendulum movement over chakras, which can tell a lot about the energy flow. With more practice with the pendulum in the chakra healing method, you will also be able to feel any subtle uncertainty of the bio-energy flow showing an imbalance in the system.

Of course locating the chakras through dowsing is by itself rather meaningless: you need to be able to interpret the responses. In order to be able to do this more fully we need to understand the functions of each chakra. When you dowse a chakra you are liable to encounter:

Clockwise: Open and Functional, feelings governed by the chakras are integrated and balanced, physical system should be functioning.

Counter-clockwise: Closed, feelings governed by the chakra are not assimilated, physical systems not fully functional.

Horizontal oscillation: Holding energy, a strong block, noticeable resistance to the feelings associated with the chakra, physical symptoms are likely to be due to repressed emotions.

Vertical oscillation: Energies being focused from the personal towards the spiritual, some physical disturbance is likely.

Erratic or Elliptical movement: Energies in chakra are unbalanced and feelings governed by the chakra are erratic.

Standstill: No energy being circulated, will lead to physical symptoms.

Other variations are possible, but these are the most common.

Our Energetic Environment

In our present society the shroud of mystery has been lifted from many subjects that once were considered mysterious.

Nowadays many intelligent people are searching for ways to bridge the gap which has existed between science, religion, and occultism, and it is acknowledged that there is only a thin dividing line between physics and mysticism.

The oneness of life is beginning to be recognized and it is becoming evident that universal laws govern our world at all levels.

The personal consciousness which we feel as uniquely our own is but a part of the larger collective consciousness of humanity. It would seem that the individual experiences and wisdom that each of us collects during a lifetime becomes a part of the collective consciousness.

The brain cells, which are being passed on to each succeeding generation through the hereditary process, seem to be encoded with this inherent information.

Though not consciously remembered, the information is there as an existing potential. Each new generation has the possibility of carrying the torch of human understanding a little further.

The mastering of the pendulum is exciting, for it allows the pendulist to tune into the storehouse of the collective consciousness.

In this way, information is available from an inexhaustible source and not confined to the knowledge of but one individual, no matter how well-informed he may be.

In theory, the pendulist may receive verifiable information on almost any subject that has been known to other men throughout the ages. However, certain prerequisites are required. This is a precise science dealing with facts which can be verified, and as such it requires a serious approach.

The answer which is sought must be useful, non-egocentric, and reasonable. The question must be a 'right question' concerning factual matters; there is, for instance, no use asking the colour of the hair on a tortoise !

Dowsing is a form of intuitive and psychic sensing which bridges the usual gap between the personal and universal consciousness. We all contribute to the universal collective consciousness, which is the sum total of all human experience.

The pendulist, if sufficiently sensitive, is able to tune into this reservoir. In this way the pendulist can detect the radiations from objects and conditions in the human body, thereby bringing together physics and metaphysics.

Conditions Affecting the Pendulum

Let me take a moment to explain that there are certain circumstances when you may not get accurate results. Sometimes the pendulum will not respond to questions, will act as if it is sluggish, will barely move, or will simply hang still.

Audible music, especially 'heavy' popular 'noise' seems to confuse the readings. You will find it much easier to work when you turn it off.

Be aware that your re-actions are governed by your beliefs ! If you believe something, then that is true - for you !

The pendulum may not work if there is an electrical storm, an earthquake, tidal waves, volcanic eruptions, or atomic testing in your area, as these events may well disturb the electro-magnetic energy field of the earth. There may be a time period during and after any such disruption in which you can not get accurate readings.

If you are extremely tired, very ill, or have a high fever you may have difficulty. You are working through the nervous system in your body, and when you are exhausted or out of balance you may not get accurate readings. You would be forcing yourself to really concentrate, so work when you are fresh and alert.

However, when you feel an illness coming on it is still possible to use the pendulum and get a few quick answers to help yourself. But any prolonged work would not be advisable.

Another time when you will find it difficult to take readings on yourself or another is after a laying-on-of-hands treatment. This can put so much energy into the body that it is not possible to get a steady reading.

This is due to the fact that the healing energy is still working and conditions are changing. This can last as long as three days in the case of psychic surgery. The pendulum will actually show this by changing its way of swinging, indicating the changing conditions in the body.

The most accurate readings are obtained when you work through your heart, which by-passes ego - and be sincere, similar to a state of prayer. Your mind has wonderful abilities, but it must be guided by your heart.

Misuse of the Pendulum

Before discussing some of the infinite uses of the pendulum, I should mention another area that one should avoid because it does not deal with facts; that is predicting the future. If you misuse the pendulum in this way you are going to be on the Ouiji board level: you will be engaged in trying to find out when you are going to die, whether you should marry someone, and other types of fortune-telling.

If you play with the pendulum, as a game, the results will be superficial and you will only get what is in your own subconscious.

When used properly, the pendulum tunes into the universal consciousness where the energy of intelligence will bring forth the right information.

Those who work at predicting the future know that the time element is the most difficult to forecast. The only time the pendulum can tell you something in the immediate future is when the information is already present in the human consciousness, as for instance during an election.

You can not get an accurate reading before people have made up their minds, but when the votes are in but have not yet been counted or announced, the answer is there and the pendulist can pick it up accurately.

You can test this also at a trial when the jury is working towards a decision; but again, you will not get an accurate reading before the members of the jury have made up their minds. Then you are picking up what is already known, but you are not really predicting.

Thus if you want to know your own subconscious it is easy, but then you are dealing only with the content of your own consciousness, and not with objective knowledge; it would act as a sample which the operator would detect instead of being the medium between the pendulist and the sample.

When the pendulist works objectively, new facts can be discovered that were previously completely unknown to him.

Hints for Using the Pendulum

Some pendulums have a screw top and are hollow so that a sample can be placed inside that is similar to a material for which one is searching.

The pendulum should be light, not too heavy or cumbersome, round or pear-shaped, and pointed at the bottom.

Almost anyone can learn to use a pendulum to some extent, provided they practice, apply self-discipline, and remain aware of what they are doing. It will, of course, take some people longer to learn than others, because they may need more guidance and practice. As in anything else, some people will become more adept, since talent is always an important factor.

Most people, however, can learn to use the pendulum for quick, simple, precise, factual answers, even if they do not wish to make a lifetime study of all the possibilities and uses described in this book.

Every object, animate or inanimate, gives off radiations, and our senses can feel and measure these to some extent. Our bodies receive these radiations just as a radio or television set receives its signals, the recipient of information not available in any other way. The pendulum acts like the loudspeaker attached to your heart-mind-brain radio transceiver.

The positive and negative poles of a magnet have their counterparts in the human body: in most people the left side of the body is negative and the right side positive, with a neutral space in the centre. And that is exactly how your mind has to be: neutral, quiet, in a questioning state, never letting thought or desire interfere with or influence the answer you seek !

This is the most important thing to remember when you use a pendulum: have your mind in an 'I don't know' attitude !

If a condition was negative yesterday, I really don't know about it today; it may be the same, it may have improved or regressed. Whenever you work, only you will know whether you are doing this.

You must be aware of your emotions and of what your mind is doing at the time you question. Any thoughts about a possible answer, any personal desires, and any ego involvement or tendency to show-off will influence your work.

But if you question in complete objectivity the answer can and must be trusted. If you are not sure of the result after taking a reading, or your mind says *"I thought this would be the answer"*, you may have influenced it. Go back and do it again; test it in another way, verify your answer. You can learn to be objective.

After you have worked with the pendulum a while you will gain confidence. Start with some of the simple exercises given here and then move on to more complex work; then when you finally proceed to areas where you may be emotionally involved, you will find that you can work on them objectively as well.

Approach the pendulum with enthusiasm and with the confidence that you are able to do it. A half-hearted or doubtful attitude will only result in uncertain findings.

Always work in quiet surroundings by yourself if at all possible, away from sceptics, negative thoughts, or anyone trying to influence you.

When Dowsing you may get a thought that 'pops' into your head - pay attention to such a very first thought; any second thoughts may be coming from ego, and not from your heart.

The Spectrum of Consciousness

I speak of positive and negative conditions that relate to work with the pendulum, so I will clarify these. Though there are positive and negative poles in a magnet and the body itself has its own magnetic field, I will be using the terms positive and negative to identify certain segments of the spectrum of consciousness.

As I see it, consciousness extends over a vast spectrum. Each of us as an individual has a personal frequency in which we live. We can function within a certain frequency range in the overall spectrum of consciousness.

To remain in a state of health one must stay within one's optimum range. Certain conditions around us (which include food, clothing, and shelter) can change our frequency to such an extent that a condition of disease occurs.

In other words, things in our environment sometimes lower our frequency below our level of tolerance, thereby creating an unhealthful state.

It is wise to check out the environment in which we spend most of our time, as well as the various types of food which make up the bulk of our diet.

Once it has been established, we can stay within our healthy frequency range without having to constantly check everything out.

The Language of the Pendulum

The language of the pendulum may differ depending upon the person from whom you have learned the technique. Different people interpret the various signals differently. Your pendulum will work well for you as long as its meaning of its signals are clear.

The degree to which the pendulum rotates will indicate the extent of your answer. It may show you a small negative circular motion, as if it is saying, *"Don't worry too much about this condition"*, while a large circular motion might mean, *"Watch out, trouble"*. It might show a small YES swing or a very large *"Hallelujah, everything couldn't be better"* 100% swing. The larger the swing the faster the pendulum seems to rotate, as if emphasizing the answer.

This is a tool that you will have for life. If you are not sure if a vitamin is good for you for example, hold the vitamins in your non-dominant hand, and dowse over it. Ask: *"Is this good for me ?"* You will get a YES or a NO signal.

Various Uses of the Pendulum

There are basically five different ways in which to use the pendulum:

1. The pendulum is held directly over an object or body and questions asked concerning this object or body.

2. The pendulum is held over an object (like food or a remedy) which is held in your left hand and questions asked regarding the object's relationship to yourself.

3. The pendulum is held over a person, photograph, drawing or anatomy chart and the pendulums motions observed and noted. The observations are then analyzed using the pendulum motions given in the Chakra Chapter e.g. clockwise, counter-clockwise, etc.

4. The 'Witness Method' is used which makes it possible to work for yourself or for someone else who may be present or at a distance. Witnesses (described later) are used for questioning and working in greater detail by using lists of words.

5. The pendulum is used as a Healing Tool.

Each of these uses is discussed in detail in the following chapters.

The direct method is the simplest way to start using the pendulum and to get used to it, gaining confidence as you work.

Start by holding it over objects around your house and checking to see whether they give off positive (clockwise) or negative (anticlockwise) vibrations. Try any rocks, artifacts, or ancient relics to see if they show any negativity.

You may decide not to wear old jewelry anymore or perhaps not to keep some old pot, painting, or treasure around any longer.

Anything which gives off positive vibrations is good to keep close to you in your surroundings.

Try checking the difference in the degree of the swing when you hold it over a plant or flowers, some of which may be doing better than others. A just-opened flower will give a stronger reading than one which is beginning to wither.

It is very important to check your household products, your cosmetics and soaps, your cleansers, and anything with deodorants in it. So many of the products we use today contain harmful chemicals and could be the causes of allergies, rashes, or even low energy.

Animal Tests

You can test animals as well, using the pendulum over your pets. On one egg ranch in Southern California the pendulum is used over eggs to see whether the egg is fertile or not, and also whether it contains a male or a female chick; in this way the egg production at the ranch has been increased tremendously.

Sex Determination

In a similar way, the sex of an unborn child or animal can easily be determined by using the positive swing for male, the negative swing for female. In the case of multiple birth, it is also possible to find out by careful questioning how many males and females are in an animal's litter; first establish how many there are in all by asking if there are 1, 2, 3, etc., then how many males, and how many females.

Direction Finding

When you are outdoors, your pendulum can be used to tell you where north is. Simply ask this, point your arm, and turn slowly around in a circle. The pendulum will then oscillate until you notice a large swing indicating north and a shorter one pointing to the south.

You can then check the exact direction by asking for the largest positive swing. This can be very helpful when you are out camping or in a strange environment, but test it before you get lost !

The pendulum indicates direction because you are working with the electromagnetic energy of the earth, which runs from north to south.

Harmful Radiations

You will find it very interesting to test your television set to see how far it gives off harmful radiations. Turn it on and start right at the screen to pick up your negative swing, then see how far out it goes before the pendulum shows neutral again. It may extend as far as several feet, depending on the size of the set and the strength of the tubes.

Also check at each side to see how wide the negative angle is. Don't sit within that negative zone close to the set, or let your children or animals sit within this area - because they are going to pick up the harmful radiations.

It also happens that some places or houses, or even whole streets, give off harmful radiations due to a certain kind of subterranean water or a noxious field. This situation may result in the inhabitants picking up harmful emanations which cause illness and lack of sleep.

More Dowsing Techniques

Dowsing is called 'Radiesthesia' in Latin-based languages; it is the human body's perception of, and reaction to, fields of energy. Radionics is a method of influencing such energy fields, mostly with the detection and Healing of disease in human beings. Dowsing is often associated with the detection of underground water, oil, minerals etc.

Each aspect of dowsing, every use to which it is put, has its own set of rules. All these constitute the discipline of the operator and the more he is able to master the rules, the more successful he becomes.

Slipshod, careless and inattentive work is not rewarded with good results in dowsing.

Needless to say, dowsing should not be attempted when one is tired physically and mentally.

Magnet Dowsing

This is a special case of dowsing used by some people, which has become subject to a number of beliefs - and special rules formulated to handle the circumstances observed. They may not be relevant for each dowser - so check if they are relevant to you !

The operator of magnet dowsing has to face one direction, namely West if he is right handed. But if the operator by any chance is left handed, then he should face East in order to get results from magnet dowsing.

The operator should sit on a chair and a small table should be in front of him where charts, phials, photographs, etc. should be kept for the purpose of examination.

The feet should be placed firmly on the ground and the legs should not touch each other or cross each other. The right and left legs have their own polarity, and they have their own positive and negative character, and if by any chance they touch or cross each other tests will be vitiated.

The right hand should hold the pendulum with two fingers only, namely the thumb and the first finger. These two fingers should not come in contact with other fingers nor should touch them.

Good care should be taken of this because if other fingers touch the two holding the pendulum, all tests will be vitiated. It may be noted here that every finger of the hand has its own polarity and if the unwanted fingers touch the thumb and the first finger with which the pendulum is held it is quite reasonable that the tests will be invalidated.

There is always a right and wrong way of doing things, and here in magnet dowsing the wrong way should be avoided.

The left hand should hold the magnet to magnetize the body and mind of the operator. This magnet should be of moderate strength. For all practical purposes a pocket horseshoe magnet is found to be suitable for dowsing purposes. Care should also be taken that the two hands do not touch or cross each other.

The left hand holding the magnet may be raised and kept at a distance from the right hand holding the pendulum, or it may remain hanging on the left side of the body.

If the left hand magnet remains too near the right hand or the chart on the table, it may have adverse action on the tests.

The table on which the charts or medicines are placed for the purpose of magnet dowsing, should be clean and should not have any other articles thereon because otherwise the tests may lose their precision. Nothing extra should be on the table because everything has its own vibrations and these may vitiate the tests undertaken by the operator.

Before sitting for work, it is advisable to wash the face, hands and feet with water. This will keep the operator clean and his mind will be at ease, and these would help him in dowsing correctly.

There are many days which should be avoided for the purpose of magnet dowsing, because these days are inharmonious for testing purposes. These days are usually connected with the sun and the moon, and when their magnetisms are at variance magnetic influences on earth are also at fault.

Therefore, it is desirable to avoid certain days for testing purposes. These are the Full Moon and New Moon days, the 1st, 8th and 14th day of the Moon for every fortnight. Thus four days only in a fortnight should be regarded as prohibited days for magnet dowsing.

The time when the sun is rising or setting is not good for testing, and therefore sunrise and sunset time should also be avoided. These are the few rules to be remembered by the operator and if he follows them he is likely to get quick mastery over magnet dowsing.

All the questions asked should be asked separately as definite statements. The first question should be *"Now I will get correct answers to my magnet dowsing"* - If the pendulum moves up and down (the YES signal for magnet dowsing) then the statement is correct; but, if it moves horizontally (the NO signal) then the statement is false - so wait about 15 minutes before re-checking.

For example, a statement may be made such as: *'This person requires more than one colour"*. If the pendulum moves up and down, the statement is correct. But, if it moves horizontally, then the statement is false, and the person requires only one colour.

If the statement is found to be correct, it means that the patient has a colour hunger for more than one colour, hence, the next statement should be that *"He requires more than 2 colours"* and so on till the pendulum signals NO. After knowing the exact number of colours required by the person, the first colour should be found out, then the second and so on.

Now the above may be illustrated by means of a few drawings in order to show the correct position of the hands and the pendulum, and the manner of dowsing with the help of charts and medicine phials, just to help the operator for the work of dowsing.

The Magnet Pendulum is shown here suspended by means of a black string about 3 inches long. The string is tied to the centre of the bent side of the horseshoe magnet. This pendulum should be held over charts and photographs, and operated in the manner previously indicated.

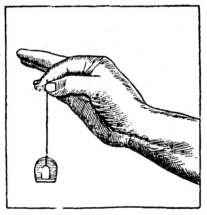

The picture also shows how the magnet pendulum should be held in the right hand with the two fingers, namely the thumb and the first finger.

Holding the Magnet Pendulum.

It is to be noted that the two fingers holding the pendulum do not touch any other finger of the right hand.

Holding the Magnet

The horseshoe magnet required for magnetizing the operator's body and mind is held in the left hand as shown.

The magnet should always be held with the keeper removed from it.

The left hand may be held aloft at a distance from the right hand pendulum, or it may be kept hanging on the left side.

This magnetization is very important in all kinds of magnet dowsing, whether crude or advanced, because if the body and mind are not magnetized the results arrived at may be wrong and undependable.

When it is a question of selection of medicine from among many, the method of magnet dowsing should be as shown below.

Here on the table a number of medicine phials are placed, arranged in a semicircle equidistant from the centre where the magnet pendulum is held and operated.

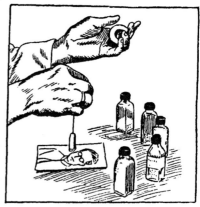

Dowsing For Correct Medicine.

The left hand carries the magnet to magnetize the body and mind of the operator. The magnet pointer is suspended from the right hand over the photograph of the patient placed on the centre of the semicircle or rather its base line. The stage is now set for magnet dowsing the correct medicine with which the patient is in harmony.

With the right hand a circular amid gentle rotary movement is given to the magnet pendulum and soon it begins to move by its own motion.

As it moves slowly from one point to another, the movement of the magnet pendulum should be watched with care. Later the movement of the magnet pendulum becomes constant and points to one or another of the five bottles placed before it in a semicircle.

The experiment should be repeated at least ten times before a decision can be taken and the right medicine is fixed for that particular person whose photograph is placed on the chart, as shown.

This simple experiment will be found useful for all who have anything to do with healing.

That medicine which has cosmic harmony with the patient in question is the best medicine for the time being.

It should however be remembered that the magnet pendulum will show the strongest amid the most appropriate medicine amongst those placed before it, but it cannot obviously point to the medicine most suitable and curative unless it is placed before it. It is because of this that some magnet dowsers fail to get the very right medicine and are often disappointed.

Using Charts

The strength of the selected medicine may he further ascertained by the Percentage Chart. Hold your pendulum over the 'Rising Sun' and see where it points. If the selected medicine shows 75% then it should be concluded that it is not the curative medicine, the search for which therefore should be continued. The indicated medicine must show 100% before it can be administered.

The following charts are from spiral bound chart books prepared by Juanita Ott - these are just illustrative samples of the many charts that Juanita has kindly made available.

You can purchase these books from Juanita's web site:

www.mirrorwaters.com

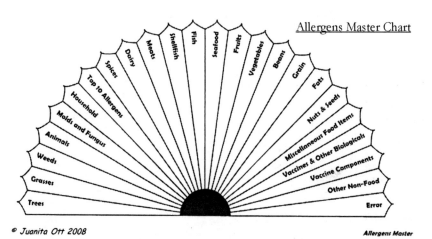

Allergens Master Chart

© Juanita Ott 2008　　　　　*Allergens Master*

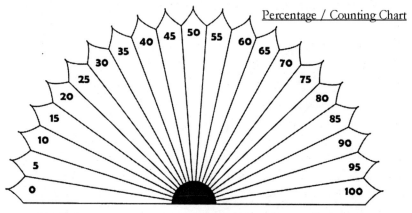

Percentage / Counting Chart

© Juanita Ott 2008　　　　　*Percentage/ Probability*

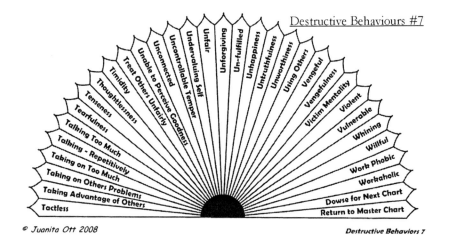

Destructive Behaviours #7

© Juanita Ott 2008

Destructive Behaviors 7

Chart available from the Holistic Intuition Society

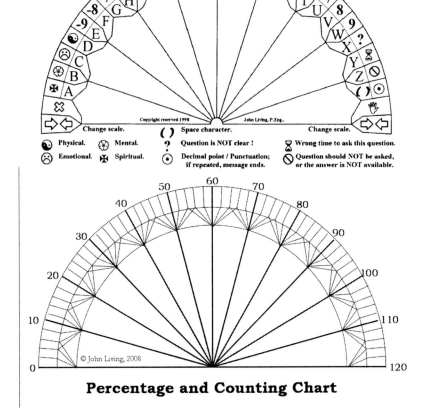

Pendulum Dowsing

Message Chart

✖ "Big Kiss" means 'I Love You'.

Last character is NOT correct.

Change scale.

( ) Space character.

Change scale.

🌑 Physical.   🕸 Mental.

? Question is NOT clear !

Wrong time to ask this question.

☹ Emotional.   ✠ Spiritual.

⊙ Decimal point / Punctuation; if repeated, message ends.

Ø Question should NOT be asked, or the answer is NOT available.

Copyright reserved 1998   John Living, P.Eng.,

© John Living, 2008

Percentage and Counting Chart

Chapter Three

Subtle Anatomy

Human beings are complex energetic systems. People receive energy from the cosmos and give it out in the form of thoughts, emotions, and actions. People have electro-magnetic fields surrounding them - a network of high and low bio-energy fields.

These energy fields are both material and nonmaterial - as particles and waves or quanta. These fields consist of different energies, from dense physical energy to subtle energies which control many of the physical body's activities, characteristics, actions, feelings, or emotions.

Slow-vibrating matter is considered to be physical matter, whereas the sub-atomic vibrating at the speed of light (or higher) is subtle matter, or energy. The physical body is penetrated by subtle vital energies as well as slow-vibrating matter.

All living things are surrounded with their own 'atmosphere', which we refer to as the bio-energy field or aura. The bio-energy field, or aura, is different from any other known fields in physics.

The aura is the summary of energy fields around the human body or any live object, and manifests as any radiation or radiance around material objects. Insects, plants, animals, and humans all possess their own special aura, including the bio-energy field.

There is no dead material; all objects live, breathe, move, 'laugh', and suffer. The bio-energy field cannot be seen around a dead body, because all subtle bodies, from which the bio-energy field consists, leave a body at death - but the very lowest auras of material can still be seen.

Humans radiate energy waves. When the mental activity of someone changes, these waves change also. Such modifications can occur with a speed of thought sent by a human. The aura or bio-energy field is a summary of human electro-magnetic fields, all subtle bodies with their energetic potentials that give strength and power to the biological field.

The aura plays the role of an energetic reservoir. Our energetic potential depends on conditions of physical, emotional and spiritual health. The bio-energy field consists of a few subtle energetic bodies; these layers protect us as atmosphere protects the earth.

The subtle bodies that make up the bio-energetic field are complex structures as compared to the physical body.

Besides our physical bodies, we possess seven more 'invisible' subtle energetic bodies, all with their own individual 'colour' of energy that gives a personal tone of the aura to everyone. These seven subtle bodies are called the Etheric, Astral, Mental, Karmic, Intuitive, Nirvana, and Absolute auric bodies - sometimes these are given other names as labels.

The Etheric, Astral and Mental bodies are the main bodies of interest to the Energy Field Healer.

The Etheric Body

The etheric body is an energetic matrix of the physical body. This duplicate or 'double' of the physical body is a subtle body of energetic vitality that evenly doubles the form of the physical body.

The etheric body feeds the physical body by vital energy. Without the etheric body, the physical body cannot exist.

Moreover, the etheric body may be considered as a model from which the physical body is constructed. The etheric body, like the physical body, has each of our vital organs in an energetic form interacting with the physical organs to help keep them healthy.

If any physical organ or extremities are lost, their ethereal counterparts do not change and still exist; the etheric body remains whole.

The theory of the etheric body stems primarily from the Eastern esoteric teachings, in which the emphasis is placed upon the subtle nature of man. The oriental understanding asserts that the objective physical body is but the outward manifestation of inner subjective energies.

This body, consisting of fine energy threads or lines of force and light, is the archetype upon which the dense physical form is built.

It can best be described as a field of energy that underlies every cell and atom of the physical body, permeating and interpenetrating every part of it, and extending beyond to form a part of what is commonly called the health aura.

The Bible speaks of it as the 'Golden Bowl'. To those with deeper vision it is often seen as a web or network animated with a golden light.

This etheric framework consists of material drawn from the four ethers, which is built into a specific form. The network of fine tubular thread-like channels, commonly known as the nadis, are related to the cerebro-spinal and sympathetic nervous systems.

These channels, depending upon the quality of energy they carry, pass to certain areas of the body via the chakras, or centres of force within the etheric body.

The integral unit formed by the etheric and physical bodies is basically the most important vehicle of man, as it connects the physical world with the subtle worlds. Through it the five senses are able to function on the physical plane, and progressively it is able to register the impact of energies flowing to it from the higher realms.

Seven grades or sub-planes of physical matter form the physical - etheric unit. They may be tabulated as follows:-

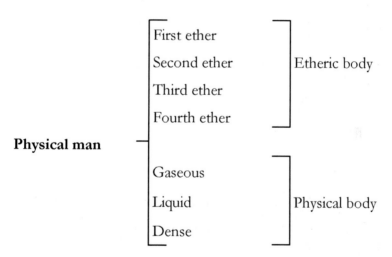

Physical man	First ether	
	Second ether	Etheric body
	Third ether	
	Fourth ether	
	Gaseous	
	Liquid	Physical body
	Dense	

These grades of matter should not be thought of as existing in separate layers, but as a homogenous force field containing a variety of high frequency energies, which are held in one cohesive unit under the direction of the soul.

Each of the four types of attenuated matter or ethers are peculiarly specialized according to the level upon which they are found.

Dr. Guenther Wachsmuth, in his study of the etheric formative forces, lists the four ethers under the following headings:

Warmth ether, Light ether, Chemical ether, Life ether.

Each ether is said to have its own form-building tendencies, and the following basic geometric shapes indicate the workings of these ethers.

- Spherical forms
- Triangular forms
- Half moon forms
- Square forms

These basic forms, expressed in nature, indicate the predominant etheric formative forces that are active. The structural shapes of the vegetable kingdom vividly portray this process, as do the organs of the human body.

For example, we can see the chemical ether as the predominant force in shaping the half moon shapes of the heart valves, and the valves of the blood vessels. The leaves of the plants and trees and the shapes of crystals all illustrate the workings of the etheric formative forces. The flow of these etheric forces will be discussed in more detail later when dealing with diagnosis and treatment of disease in the etheric body.

There is in the human body a symbol of the distinction between the higher etheric and lower physical levels. It is quite simply the diaphragm, which separates the upper cavity of the body, containing the organs concerned with activities analogous to those of a spiritual nature, from the viscera which are concerned with the more mundane but necessary pursuits of a material nature.

The etheric body has three basic functions, all closely interrelated. It acts as a receiver of energies, an assimilator of energies, and as a transmitter of energies. If each of these functions is maintained in a state of balance, then the physical body reflects this interchange of energies as a state of good health. The key to health lies in the correct reception, assimilation and distribution of energies.

There are a number of factors which disturb the even circulation of energies throughout the etheric body, and these must be divided into two main categories: the objective and the subjective factors.

The objective factors are those within the substance of the etheric vehicle itself, preventing the even flow of energies to the various parts of the organism. They may be likened to large boulders jutting up from the bed of a stream, hindering the passage of the water as it returns to its source.

Such obstacles either dam up the water, creating congestion, or the water flow is increased as it forces its way by.

These objective blockages are miasms, toxins, physical anomalies, and diseased or traumatized areas. The miasms and toxins are perhaps the most dangerous elements to be considered, as their presence in the etheric substance undermines health in a most insidious way, often leading to gross organic pathology.

Miasms may be classified under three major headings: syphilitic, tubercular and cancerous. They may be acquired during the lifetime of the individual, or hereditary.

When a human being incarnates, it is said that he draws the material for his etheric body from the etheric vehicle of the earth, and the substance for his dense physical body comes from the earth itself.

This matter, polluted by countless diseased bodies over millions of years, carries within it the seeds of the three major diseases. As the individual appropriates materials for his bodies, he may, if his present experience calls for it, acquire those elements which predispose him to certain disease patterns.

It is hard to put a clear definition to the word 'miasm', but it may be thought of as a para-physical disease pattern, residing on etheric levels, in varying degrees of intensity and activity. This pattern is inevitably found upon the fourth or life ether. Its presence alone, undermines health.

If the life of the individual transgresses the natural laws, then to that degree the miasm may be activated. Bad falls or emotional shock frequently precipitate the miasmic pattern from the fourth ether, so that it brings about gross pathological changes.

How often we see in the case history of a patient that their health deteriorated following a fall or other type of shock !

Toxins, like miasms, hinder the flow of energies through the etheric body. Such toxins may be of a bacterial or chemical nature. Childhood diseases leave toxic residue patterns which may upset the individual's health for years to come. Drugs leave their residues, as do chemical poisons which pollute our food and general environment.

All of these disturb the function of the etheric body, and their removal is essential to optimum health.

There is a deep esoteric relationship between the etheric body and the kidneys. Both are concerned with reception, assimilation, and transmission of energies, the kidneys expressing the more physical aspect of these processes. I believe it is significant that kidney diseases are on the increase, as this reflects the tremendous stresses that our etheric bodies are under in this modern civilization.

Congestion of the etheric body is a major cause of disease. This congestion may be objective, that is miasmic or toxic, or it may be due to subjective factors found in the chakras or centres of force within the etheric body. Where there is an incorrect flow of energy through a chakra, congestion can occur, and this may be found in the etheric or astral bodies.

Over-stimulation of the etheric body and its chakras is another prime source of disease, and the causes must always be sought out and corrected if health is to be reinstated.

Lack of co-ordination between the etheric body and the physical body can bring about poor health. This is frequently the case with trance mediums when the etheric body is easily drawn out of the physical, in order to let a discarnate entity utilize the dense vehicle.

Epilepsy, debilitation, impotence, obsession and laryngitis express varying degrees of poor co-ordination between the physical and etheric bodies.

In summarizing, it suffices to state that the etheric body is the instrument of life, which produces and sustains the physical form. It is the true intermediary or unseen link between the physical world and the subjective realms of the astral and mental levels.

Upon its correct reception and distribution of energies, depends the health of the physical body. As healers we should note that it is a potent receiver of impressions, which are conveyed to the consciousness via the chakras.

The Astral Body

The astral body is connected with the physical body during its normal waking state. It is separated by death or a deep sleep.

The astral body is represented by an egg-form cloudy mass containing a core of even more dense 'material and energy' in the middle.

This core has the shape of the physical body. The egg-form surrounding the core is called the 'astral aura', which extends out from people up to 1.5 feet.

The astral body (the 'body of desires') possesses extraordinary mobility, and depending on the emotional state, it can manifest different shapes and sizes at once. When professionally trained, an individual may move instantaneously in the astral body in the area of the moon gravitational field (out-of-body experience) with an unbelievable speed. The astral body belongs to the astral world.

Physical manifestations of the astral body include vivacity, activity, vitality, cheerfulness, laughter, and the ability to feel joy. A highly developed astral body results in the ability to deeply identify with an image of an another individual besides one's self, actor's mastery, and inspiration.

Higher Level Bodies

These are described by most clairvoyants as being egg-shaped; each surrounds and inter-penetrates the bodies of lower levels.

A good overview, based on information gleaned from many clairvoyants, is given in the book 'Intuition Technology' by John Living, available from the Holistic Intuition Society.

The best detailed views are presented by Barbara Ann Brennan in her books 'Hands of Light' and 'Light Emerging'; these include many illustrations of problems associated with the various auric bodies.

Assemblage Point

The first person to publicize the Assemblage Point was Dr Jonathan Whale - in his excellent books 'The Catalyst of Power' and 'Naked Spirit', which describe how the location and the angle of entry are closely inter-related with human health and behaviour.

These short notes are based on the websites of Dr Whale: www.whalemedical.com/ap1.html and www.nakedspirit.co.uk - see these for more information - or better still, buy his books !

The epicentre of the human energy field is called the Assemblage Point. The location and entry angle of the Assemblage Point with respect to the physical body dictates the shape and distribution of the human energy field.

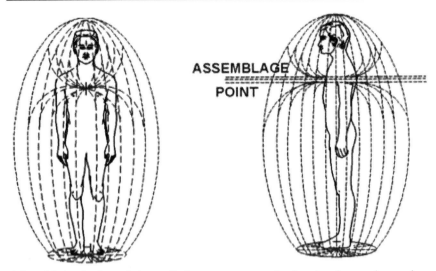

The biological activity of the organs and glands determines the position of the Assemblage Point, and thus the shape and distribution of biological energy throughout the physical body.

The location and entry angle of the Assemblage Point regulates how we feel and behave. Disease also dictates the Assemblage Point location and entry angle. Any type of severe trauma can cause an involuntary shift of the Assemblage Point to a dangerous location.

An unstable and displaced Assemblage Point may occur if we had a consistently negative home relationship. Genetic reasons or disease can similarly produce abnormal and unstable Assemblage Points.

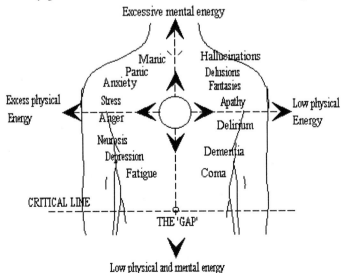

Chapter Four
Chakras: The Energetic Force Centres

Having outlined the basic picture of the etheric body, it is now possible to enlarge upon it by giving a more detailed description of the chakras or force centres that occur in certain areas of the etheric vehicle.

These chakras are of vital importance to the practitioner, because they are the focal points which receive energies for the purpose of vitalizing the physical body. It is through these centres that the healing energies are directed towards the diseased areas of the body, in order to bring about a state of equilibrium or health.

The force centres or chakras are located upon the surface of etheric body, and appear as rotating vortices of subtle matter. Each centre is composed of concentric, interblending whorls of energy, the rotations of which are speeded up and intensified commensurate with the inner development of the individual, until the chakra becomes inter-dimensional and capable of receiving and transmitting in a harmonious manner.

A chakra may be defined as a focal point for the reception and transmission of energies. These energies can originate from a variety of sources, some cosmic, others from the collective 'us' of a nation or humanity at large, or from the physical, emotional and mental worlds of the lower self.

All make their impact upon the unit of human consciousness we call man, galvanizing him into action and determining his moods and characteristics.

The chakras in the etheric body come into being where the strands of energy cross and re-cross each other. The seven major chakras form where these lines cross each other twenty one times.

The minor chakras, of which there are twenty-one, occur where the energy strands cross fourteen times. Where the lines of energy cross seven times, lesser focal points are created, and there are said to be forty-nine such points. Beyond this there are many tiny force centres, which probably correspond to the acupuncture points of Chinese medicine.

The chakras have three main functions.

1. To vitalize the physical body.
2. To bring about the development of self consciousness.
3. To transmit spiritual energy in order to bring the individual into a state of spiritual being.

These centres are in the nature of distributing agencies, providing dynamic force and qualitative energy to the man. They produce definite effects upon his outward physical appearance, and through their continuous activity his character tendencies emerge.

It is important for the centre therapist practitioner to have a clear understanding of energy flow, as related to the function of the force centres. He should never forget that 'ENERGY FOLLOWS THOUGHT', and that a clearly visualized picture of the route taken by the healing energies, to their destination via the chakras, to the organ systems of the body, will in the final analysis increase the beneficial action of his work.

The incoming energy, which is designated as the primary energy, may be a healing rate, a colour, or a homoeopathic potency radionically broadcast. It enters the chakra situated in the etheric body and is transmuted at this point by a process of differentiation into the secondary energies of the primary energy involved.

This occurs automatically, the speed of the transformation and effect upon the physical body being determined by the condition of the chakra.

Having passed through the centre, the secondary energies play upon the nadies, causing the nervous system to respond, and in so doing pass the impulse on to the endocrine gland associated with the chakra. This effects a release of its hormones into the bloodstream, thus conditioning man and making him what he is at any given time.

Much of the ill health we see today can be traced directly to the condition of the chakras, as they determine the proper functioning of the aforementioned systems. Perfect co-ordination of the nadis, nerves and endocrine glands results in freedom from disease.

Most of the early Westernized literature concerned with the chakras pays very little attention to their relationship with the endocrine system, and the affect of that relationship upon the health of the individual. This important factor cannot be overlooked if we are to gain a clear and practical picture of the etheric mechanism.

Basically the centre therapist is concerned with energy flow and distribution.   It is his task to diagnose the imbalances that occur in the reception, assimilation and distribution of energies as they enter and circulate throughout the etheric body. The normal flow of energy entering a chakra and flowing unimpeded to its destination is illustrated.

The chakras in the etheric body are to be found in various states of activity. They reflect the physical, emotional, mental and spiritual quality of the individual, and may be found in any one of the following conditions represented by the following five symbols.

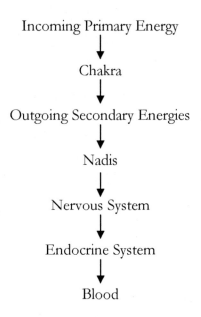

Incoming Primary Energy

↓

Chakra

↓

Outgoing Secondary Energies

↓

Nadis

↓

Nervous System

↓

Endocrine System

↓

Blood

Circle: The chakra is simply a saucer-like depression, closed and inert, or rotating very slowly. There is no real intensity in its action, and the energy within it is just perceptible as a dim glow. The symbol further stands for the human body viewed from an etheric point of view. It symbolizes the single cell within the human body, or the atom of the physicist.

Circle with the point in the centre: The chakra is opening with signs of pulsation. It has a glowing point of energy in the middle of the saucer-1ike depression, and its rotation is becoming more rapid.

Circle divided into two: Here the activity of the chakra is quickening and alive. The point of energy at the centre is extending outward towards the periphery, it burns more brightly and due to its rotary action casts off energy in two directions, thus creating the appearance of a divided circle. The depression is becoming a vortex of energy, more brilliantly lit.

Circle divided into four: This represents the chakra which is radiantly active and seeking to blend with other chakras. Not only is the circle rotating but the cross within it rotates as well, creating an effect of great beauty.   It indicates a high point of inner development, and is the true circle of matter, the equal armed cross of the Holy Spirit.

Swastika: Indicates that the point of energy at the centre of the chakra has extended to the periphery and is circulating around the periphery. This fiery wheel signifies the highest activity of matter, blazing and radiant throughout. Such a chakra becomes fourth dimensional and is better described as a sphere than a wheel. It is functioning in perfect unison with the other chakras.

During the course of making a diagnosis it will be found that each chakra of the patient falls into one of the first four categories. Because of these imbalances, due to the inability at this time to exert proper control over the energies flowing through the human form, disease and suffering become manifest.

In a Spiritual Master such as Jesus all seven major chakras were perfectly balanced, correctly awakened, and energized, making him an expression of perfected man. This is the example and promise that he held out to us, that each may become as perfect as him, and ultimately express the Divine Purpose.

Determining the condition of each major chakra is the main work of the centre therapist. These force centres must be working properly in order to supply the physical body with the right amount and quality of energy. Any deviation from normal creates an imbalance which may ultimately lead to organic pathology.

Damage to Chakras

Chakras can be damaged by traumatic accidents, and especially by sudden, dramatic, emotional shocks. Nagging fears or anxiety can, through constant wearing activity, disturb the functional balance.

Chakras are frequently found to be blocked, either at the point where energy enters, or at the point where it exits to flow into the etheric body.

If a blockage occurs at the entrance, the energy flowing in is frequently driven back to its point of origin on the astral or mental planes. This brings about psychological problems and endocrine dysfunction.

If the blockage is at the exit, the energy builds up until enough pressure enables it to burst through to stimulate the appropriate endocrine gland.

This causes erratic endocrine function with attendant physical and psychological problems. These blockages are of a subjective nature, as opposed to the objective nature of the blockages caused by miasms or toxins.

It should always be remembered that each chakra, although only present in subtle matter, externalizes itself on the physical plane as an endocrine gland, just as the nadis materialize as the nervous system.. It cannot be too strongly stated that the subtle anatomy directly relates to the physical. Acting as though they were separate factors only leads to a distorted view of the total man.

As previously mentioned there are twenty-one minor chakras. These centres are, in the average and advanced person, governed by the action of the major chakras, and are treated via the nearest major force centre. However in cases where the major chakra is normally inactive, it may be necessary to treat the minor chakras directly.

They are to be found in the following locations: one in front of each ear, one above each breast, one where the clavicles meet, one in the palm of each hand one on the sole of each foot, one just behind each eye, one related to each gonad or ovary, one near the liver, one connected with the stomach, two superimposed, connected with spleen, one behind each knee, one near the thymus gland, and one near the solar plexus.

The Seven Major Spinal Chakras

Literally translated, the word 'chakra' means 'wheel'. It expresses the focalization or multi-concentric manifestation of the dynamic life principle in space.

Ancient Eastern texts speak of the universe as a gigantic mandala, containing many other mandalas, or concentric force fields.

In the human body, the chakras or psychic centres signify the spatial un-foldment of the macrocosmic universal power on the level of the microcosm, thus bearing out the truth of the ancient Hermetic axiom, 'As above, so below'.

The ordered descent of the soul through successive gradations of subtle and physical matter provides a remarkable picture of the workings of Nature and the continuity of relationships between the subtle and physical anatomy. Let us trace this descent.

The soul upon incarnating draws to it enough of the universal 'chitta' or 'mind stuff' to form the mental body. Next, the less refined matter of the astral plane is used to form the emotional vehicle. Following this, the etheric structure is built from matter more coarse than that of the astral or mental planes. The subtle nervous system of the nadis is built from matter of the etheric levels, and this web gives rise to the physical nervous system.

The next step down brings about the formation of the endocrine system. It is not suggested that each vehicle is built in that order, but that it represents a progression of appropriation of matter by the soul.

Now we can consider the concentric centres of force in the etheric body, and their relationship to this progression.

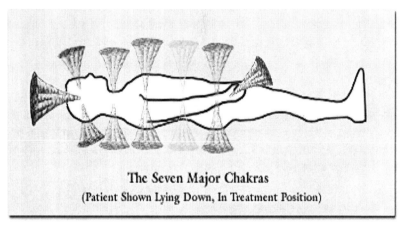

The Seven Major Chakras
(Patient Shown Lying Down, In Treatment Position)

Muladhara (Root Chakra)

The first chakra is Muladhara, located at the base of the spine. Energy wave fluctuations of this base chakra correspond to the colour red. Red has the lowest vibration rate in the visible spectrum, thus it affects the most dense or material matter in our organisms. Muladhara affects and is most affected by the physical body.

Nevertheless, it gives an awareness of eternal life and the divinity of individuals. Many researchers think that this chakra of the physical plane belongs to the etheric body. It plays a connecting role between the centre of physical energy (Ajna chakra) and the centre of psychic energy (Sahasrara chakra).

The Muladhara chakra is responsible for the normal condition of the five senses, sex, and physical growth. The root chakra is associated with survival, stability, structure, manifestation, and patience.

Physical Correlation of root chakra - penis, groin, testes, vagina, anus, bladder, coccyx (tailbone), bones, and the sexual and reproductive systems.

Such malfunctions as obesity, hemorrhoids, constipation, physical weakness, arthritis, prostate enlargement, bladder problems, reproductive problems, and menstrual cramps are correlated with a dysfunctional root chakra.

Open chakra - sense of being grounded, survival instinct, ability to let go of the past and emotions, the ability to stand on your own two feet.

Closed chakra - poorly developed sense of reality.

Blocked chakra - insecurity, depression, inability to release the past.

Malfunction - tendency to haemorrhoids, constipation, sciatica, prostate problems in men.

Svadhisthana (Sacral Chakra)

The second chakra is named Svadhisthana and is located in the sacrum (lower abdomen). Energy wave fluctuations correspond to the colour orange. The sacral chakra corresponds to the ether body. Many researchers think that the chakra of the physical plane (Muladhara), along with Svadhisthana, are comparable belongings of the ether body. Certainly, they are similar to each other by their energetic functions. Nevertheless, the sacral chakra is more complex than the root chakra. Muladhara absorbs electromagnetic fields from the earth (through the ground chakra) that are necessary for the physical body.

Svadhisthana, which produces an internal energy, utilizes the Prana of food matter, which it distributes along meridians to the organs of the physical body and to the other energetic centres and subtle bodies. The sacral chakra controls our energetic states. The health of our physical bodies depends on this chakra's activity. As the entire ether body, the sacral chakra is important for our wellbeing and vitality, and is associated with abundance, pleasure, and the inspiration to create.

Svadhisthana is responsible for prosperity, desire, sexuality, and accelerating the healing process.

Interactions of Svadhisthana with other chakras determine the influence of food intake on our energetic manifestations (Manipura chakra), sexuality (Muladhara chakra), and emotional sphere (Anahata chakra).

Physical system - reproduction.

Body parts - womb, kidney, bladder.

Psychological keyword - relating.

Physical correlation of sacral chakra - spleen, ovaries, adrenal glands, uterus, kidney, urinary tract, lower abdomen, large intestines, appendix, sacrum, sexual system, and energy level. Kidney illnesses, spleen problems, impotence, frigidity, uterine bladder problems, food cravings, toxins in large intestines, and gas pain are correlated with dysfunctional sacral chakra.

People with a low energy level have a dysfunctional sacral chakra.

Open chakra - ability to relate to others, ability to share, self-confidence.

Closed chakra - selfish, self centred, unfeeling.

Blocked chakra - inability to sustain relationships.

Malfunction - tendency to menstrual problems, impotence, frigidity, kidney or bladder problems.

Manipura (Solar Plexus chakra)

The third chakra is Manipura, located on the fifth lumbar (abdomen) vertebra. The chakra's energy corresponds to the energy of the colour yellow. Manipura is related to the astral subtle body; through the solar plexus chakra, a connection between the chakra's system and astral body's energy and substance is kept.

The solar plexus chakra controls our emotional states, and emotions are directly linked with our sense of well-being and health. Manipura also accumulates and distributes energies which are produced in other chakras. It governs personal power, self-worth, self-confidence, self-esteem, decision-making, metabolic energy, and insight.

Physical system - digestion.

Body parts - stomach.

Psychological keyword - direction.

Physical Correlation of solar plexus chakra - musculature, pancreas, stomach, liver, gallbladder, small intestines, blood sugar, lower, middle, and upper spine, diaphragm, upper abdomen, solar plexus, and digestive system.

Ulcers, diabetes, hypoglycemia, digestive problems, liver problems, hiccups, and burps are correlated with dysfunctional solar plexus chakra. People with digestive problems have a dysfunctional solar plexus chakra.

Open chakra - sense of direction in life, willingness to take personal responsibility for actions, a controlled will, self-determination.

Closed chakra - sense of powerlessness, lack of self esteem, lack of direction in life.

Blocked chakra - weak, easily swayed by others, no sense of self.

Malfunction - tendency to ulcers, eating disorders.

Anahata (Heart Chakra)

The fourth major chakra is Anahata. It is located on the fifth thoracic vertebra (on the chest). Anahata's energy colour is green. It relates to the mental body. The heart chakra is the entrance to higher consciousness and spirit, and it keeps the balance between the three lower chakras and the three upper chakras.

Anahata chakra helps in the mastery of language and poetry. As the mental body, its chakra determines mental creativity, logic, memory, velocity of the thought process, eagerness to philosophical and scientific knowledge, and self-control.

It brings a balance of action and joy, promotes wisdom, intelligence, and inner strength. Anahata chakra affects our actions, behaviors, and thoughts, and keeps the balance within the physical body.

Physical system - circulation.

Body parts - heart, lungs.

Psychological keyword - compassion.

Physical Correlation of Heart chakra - lungs, windpipe, breast, chest, ribcage, bronchi, heart, circulatory and lymph systems, blood pressure, esophagus, shoulders and shoulder blades, mucous membranes, immune system, and thymus.

Asthma, high blood pressure, breathing allergies, cough, lung's illnesses, heart problems, and immune system illnesses are correlated with dysfunctional heart chakra.

Open chakra - transpersonal love, compassion, openness, acceptance.

Closed chakra - lack of emotional depth.

Blocked chakra - inability to empathize.

Malfunction - tendency to hypertension, angina.

Vishuddha (Throat Chakra)

The fifth chakra is Vishuddha, located on the first thoracic vertebra on the thyroid level (throat). The energy colour is blue. This chakra connects to the karmic body. The throat chakra brings knowledge, creativity, communication ability, purity, calmness, and mastery of the individual's entire self.

At this level, an individual expresses the entire self and his or her ego verbally, and shows the inner-self to the outer world. Here, emotions may be expressed in forms such as painting, singing, or writing. The throat chakra controls and expresses both thoughts and emotions.

The throat chakra gives energy to the voice and desire to express the individual self. Voice power shows the throat chakra's strength, whereas a weak voice shows the throat chakra's imbalance. Differences in the voice reflect the state of the moment: emotions, sexual arousal, love, or a thought state. It brightly shows the interconnection between chakras.

Physical system - respiration.

Body parts - lungs, throat.

Psychological keyword - creativity.

Physical Correlation of Throat chakra - throat, vocal cords, ears, nose, mouth, jaw, neck, shoulder clavicles, sciatic nerve, legs, feet, knees, arms, elbows, hands, thyroid and parathyroid, skin, respiratory system, colds, and sinus allergies.

Problems with arms, hands, legs, feet, mouth, thyroid, flu, neck ache, headache, allergies, skin problems, sore throat and sinuses, ears problems, and nausea are correlated with dysfunctional throat chakra.

People with throat problems who get regular colds have a dysfunctional throat chakra.

Open chakra - good powers of communication, self-expression, creativity.

Closed chakra - inability to express inner self, sense of frustration.

Blocked chakra - cannot express emotions or ideas verbally.

Malfunction - tendency to sore throats, losing voice unexpectedly.

Ajna (Brow Chakra)

The sixth chakra is named Ajua (the brow chakra). It is located on the second cervical vertebra (on the neck), and on the forehead between the eyebrows (on the front, or medula plexus).

The forehead location is called the 'Third Eye', and it is connected to the intuitive body. The energy colour is dark blue (indigo). Ajna is the centre of physical energy, and the transformer of universal energy or energetic information to the physical body and to other chakras as well.

Through the third eye chakra, a universal energy is channeled to the physical body. The chakra governs growth and co-ordination on the physical level, and it allows mastery in spiritual and emotional growth as well.

Moreover, through Ajna chakra, we are able to open ourselves to the universal creative energy, or energetic information. The Ajna chakra perceives energetic information and commands where the information should proceed in the system.

The third eye is a source of super-consciousness (the unconscious sphere of consciousness), spiritual wisdom, clairvoyance, imagination, and intuitive insight. With a developed third eye, we may become perceivers of past, present, and future.

The Third Eye is a place where the balance between mind, emotions, spirituality, and the physical body may be achieved in order to create, heal, and perceive universal and divine information.

We may achieve and control our balance and awareness in a state of enlightenment; this is why thought can be creative and healing.

Thus, through our imagination, wisdom, and creative abilities, we can lead ourselves to healthy, happy, and fulfilling lives.

Openness to spirituality may significantly change our understanding of our inner selves and our connections with an outer world and other people. Through the third eye chakra, we may transform ourselves into spiritual beings and control our minds as spiritual masters do. The healthy chakra, with its highly developed intuition, leads to overall well-being and happiness.

Through the Ajna chakra, one reveals the divine within the self and reflects divinity within others. An opened and functional third eye chakra dissipates ego, duality and reveals the sense of oneness with the Universe and unity with the cosmic laws.

Intuition, inner vision, insight, divine wisdom, spiritual and emotional growth come into reality in the third eye chakra. At the Ajna level, one may express theories, ideas, and ideologies.

<u>Physical system</u> - mentation.

<u>Body parts</u> - the brain and eyes.

<u>Psychological keyword</u> - intuition.

Physical Correlation of third eye chakra - eyes, sinuses, headache, forehead, autonomous nervous system, pituitary gland, cerebrum (the part of the brain responsible for senses, visualization, and verbal/auditory), cerebellum (the part of the brain responsible for motor coordination, reality contact, balance, dizziness, and the epilepsy center), brain stem, and the hypothalamus (the part of brain responsible for stress response).

Blindness, eyes' problems, headache, migraine, colds, brain-physical and brain-psychological problems, addiction and obsession, brain stem problems, and nightmares are correlated with dysfunctional third eye chakra. People with regular headaches have an unbalanced or dysfunctional third eye chakra.

Open chakra - imaginative, creative, visual, has lucid dreams, intuitive.

Closed chakra - fantasies without meaning, dependence on rationality.

Blocked chakra - lack of imagination, prosaic outlook.

Malfunction - tendency to headaches, fuzzy thinking, mental confusion.

Sahasrara (Crown Chakra)

The seventh major chakra is Sahasrara, located on the top of the head. The colour is white. Through Sahasrara chakra, we receive universal cosmic energy and energetic information from God or the Divine Centre. Sahasrara represents the highest aspect of the Self as a cosmic organism. It is linked to the Absolute body (the conclusion of the development of all seven subtle bodies of a cosmic organism), and it relates to the whole being.

Sahasrara chakra is a centre of psychic energy. The crown chakra is the most purified and evolved energy level in the bio-energy system, a balanced and perfected universal wisdom.

The goal of a human is to improve one's own karma by living a 'good' life, and a healthy Sahasrara chakra regulates human behavior and personal characteristics to live a life in accordance with karmic law. Sahasrara chakra is a centre of spirituality, refinement, and magnificence. Through the crown chakra, human spirit connects to Universal Spirit, and the spiritual being moves toward Universal Consciousness - the individual self is fully dissolved here.

At the crown chakra level, the cosmic self opens to the Source, unites with cosmic principles, and governs the entire universe within the body.

The crown chakra is associated with universal knowledge and spiritual understanding, and is the only chakra that follows the subtle body in cosmic spheres after death.

Physical system - not relevant.

Body parts - not relevant.

Psychological keyword - awakening.

Physical Correlation of crown chakra - central nervous system, pineal gland, hair, head top, cerebral cortex (the part of the brain responsible for thinking), and mind agility. Depression, distress, alienation, confusion, mind agility, and hair problems are correlated with dysfunctional crown chakra.

Open chakra - aware of human potential growth, consciously on path of self realization.

Closed chakra - unaware of potential, dependence on a physical explanation of reality.

Blocked chakra - alienation, isolation, a closed mind.

Chakras' Performance

The human organism, its functioning, and the condition of its subtle bodies depends on the chakras' work, or spinning. When the chakras are spinning effectively, they bring balanced functioning to the organism, a free flowing of energies, and harmony between consciousness and sub-consciousness and between inner and outer worlds as well.

Chakras show patterns of electro-magnetic activity. When all chakras work properly (spinning not too slow or too fast), a physical organism is in perfect health and powerful energetic shape.

When the chakra is opened and functional, it can perform its work perfectly, process Prana energy, bring energy to the physical organs and subtle bodies, and remove used stale or stagnant energy from the system.

When the chakra is closed or blocked, it stops spinning and becomes dysfunctional. Chakras may become closed when they are congested with stale or stagnant energy. One way they can close is during an instance of fight-or-flight response of the organism.

This response is a natural way for the organism to become alert and prepared to any danger or unusual situation. However, if this stressful condition of the body is left uncontrolled and continues for a long time, the chakras may stay closed and dysfunctional.

When the physical body stays in prolonged stress (distress) or depression, the chakras cannot spin and work properly; they become unbalanced, blocked with stale and stagnant energy.

Our thoughts and attitudes can block energy flowing through the chakras as well. Unexpressed emotions can cause the chakras to be overcharged, leading to their closing or blockage. Personality problems both cause and are caused by energy imbalances.

Imbalances in the chakra system of the physical body reveal themselves through both negative personality and physical illness; dysfunctional chakras cause imbalances in the subtle energetic bodies, and imbalances in the subtle bodies then manifest in personal, psychological and emotional problems.

When chakras are closed, energy cannot be transformed and released to the physical body. If energy is not flowing freely through energetic systems, physical problems may develop in specific areas, and discomfort or illness can occur in the organism.

When a chakra is blocked, it needs healing by uncovering and removing whatever is blocking it. The clearing of congested energy from the human energy system becomes a necessary prophylactic way for keeping the organism healthy.

Because the chakras work together as a system, a block in the functioning of one chakra may affect the activity of another.

These chakras are especially inter-related:
>   (a) the root chakra and the third eye,
>   (b) the sacral chakra and throat chakra, and
>   (c) the solar plexus chakra and heart chakra.

If one chakra is not functioning, it must be cleansed, balanced, normalized, and healed together with the associate chakra.

Chakras are interrelated not only with parasympathetic and sympathetic autonomous nervous systems, but endocrine systems as well. Chakras transform vital energy to the endocrine glands:

root chakra (Muladhara)   - testicles
sacral chakra (Svadhisthana)   - ovaries
solar plexus chakra (Manipura)   - adrenals and pancreas
heart chakra (Anahata)   - thymus,
throat chakra (Vishuddha)   - thyroid and parathyroid
third eye chakra (Ajna)   - pineal gland
crown chakra (Sahasrara)   - pituitary (master) gland.

Chakras feed the life-force into our endocrine systems, which regulates our hormonal balance.

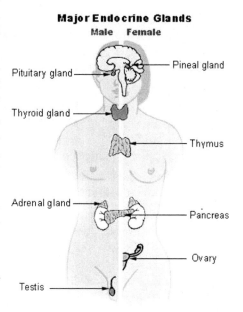

Major Endocrine Glands

Male   Female

Pituitary gland

Pineal gland

Thyroid gland

Thymus

Adrenal gland

Pancreas

Ovary

Testis

Healthy chakras spin in a clockwise direction in a front of a body and in the same way in both sexes, whereas closed, unbalanced chakras spin in a counter-clockwise direction, stay still, spin in eclipses, or move unevenly.

The energy balance of the bio-energy system, which is very important to our general well-being and health, can be achieved by energy that is in a constant smooth flow, refreshed and vitalized, aided by constantly spinning chakras.

Physical Manifestations of Opened and Closed Chakras

The Root Chakra

When the root chakra is open and functional, it provides vital energy, stability, survival, solid structure, security, patience, and manifestation.

When closed, it causes fear, frustration, lack of fulfillment, restlessness, and a feeling of disconnection. Energy deficiency or depleted energy through a closed or blocked first chakra causes terminal illnesses, and vice versa.

The Sacral Chakra

When the sacral chakra is open and functional, it provides a good appetite, genteel taste, desire, pleasure, vitality, pride, emotion, sexual satisfaction, and prosperity.

When closed, it causes greed, manipulation, sentimentality exhaustion, and guilt.

The Solar Plexus Chakra

When this chakra is opened and functional, people are able to make decisions and understand personal power and the inner-self.

A working solar plexus chakra brings nourishment, balance, intelligence, personal power, self-confidence, and self-respect.

When the chakra is closed, it causes unworthiness, fear of failure, inability to make decisions, lack of confidence, low self-respect, apathy, and inflexibility.

The Heart Chakra

An opened heart chakra means the beginning of higher consciousness and light. It brings a strong feeling of acceptance, empathy and joy. It shows individuality, unity, adaptability, generosity, purity, innocence, gentleness, dignity, and nobility.

The closed chakra may cause abhorrence, avarice, selfishness, meanness, malice, and anger.

The Throat Chakra

When the throat chakra is opened and functional, it shows willpower, creative visualization, skillful communication, orator mastery, artistry, spirituality, truthfulness, independence, and self-expression.

The throat chakra may become dysfunctional through blocks of emotional energy or suppressed anger and tears. The closed chakra may cause addictions, suppressed feelings, untruthfulness, dependency, lack of creativity and mastery, uncertain communication and gossip.

The Brow Chakra

When the third eye chakra is opened and functional, it brings spiritual perception, intuition, inner-sense, sense of unity with the universe, creative energy, an ability to bio-energy healing, and even telepathy and clairvoyance.

When the chakra is closed it causes iciness, pragmatism, meanness, mental tension, tightness, inability of spiritual perception, and tartness.

The Crown Chakra

When the crown chakra is developed, it leads to openness to the Divine Source, a feeling of unity with the universe, spirituality, faith, peace of inner-self, and enlightenment.

When it is not well-developed, the crown chakra may cause hopelessness, depression, alcoholism, egoism, an inability to understand the inner-self, and disconnection with the spiritual world and Divine source.

Chapter Five

Dynamics of Energy Field Healing

Akasha is the primary and basic material from which all in the universe is formed, including God, humans and earth; it is the bridge between being and non-being. Everything is included in Akasha: subtle 'invisible' occurrences are represented in the aspect of vibration, whereas the solid or 'visible' by human sight is represented in the aspect of physical matter.

The universe is filled with a subtle, vital force named Prana.

There is an instant and constant flow of this cosmic energy into humans. Without Prana activity, Akasha stays as a shapeless and lifeless dark space. We cannot see Prana, but we can see its manifestations. Electricity is one way to observe Prana's manifestation.

Prana is a vital force, like a gas of great power, penetrating everywhere, coming from the Great Unknown. Prana submits to human consciousness and follows thought and mental control. Prana can be both creative and destructive energy. As healthful energy, Prana possesses tremendous strength and is necessary for our well-being bringing vitality. If blood has little Prana, illness will occur.

Yogis determine Prana flow as healing energy. If one is aware that Prana submits to mental direction or thought energy, one can utilize enormous amounts of the vital energy using visualization and meditation. An individual trained and able to direct Prana abundance around ill people becomes a healer. The warmth of Prana energy radiating from a healer's hands is a real sign of his or her ability to heal.

Energy healing and balancing involves cleansing the energy system of bio-negative energy, allowing bio-positive energy to flow freely in the system in order to restore energetic balance and health.

With energy balancing, you will be able to heal physical problems in the physical bodies as well as imbalances on the energetic level. In bio-energetics, any illness is perceived as an energy imbalance. When the energy is balanced, this influences the physical body positively.

Bio-positive energy is an essential element in maintaining physical, spiritual and energetic health. However, in current practices, healers often do not pay attention to the directions of movements, aspects of bio-positive and bio-negative energy, and the withdrawal of weak energy. Weak and stale energy must be relieved in order to let vital energy flow in and out of a freely balancing energy system.

Later you will be able to correct physical problems and illnesses using methods of energy cleansing, balancing, energizing, and healing. Energy field healing is the art of correcting energetic defects in the energy field. In energy field healing, the healer seeks to restore the flow of the energy to its strong, natural and healthy state and correct any defects that are present, thereby helping to restore and maintain health to the body, emotions, mind and spirit - to all levels of the being.

The healer, in doing this, treats what may be the ultimate cause of disease. By treating ill conditions in the energy field, the healer may work to assist in the resolution of a disease condition which has already manifested in the physical body, or in the mental and emotional life of the patient.

The activities of the healer may also serve to prevent future disease, by treating faulty energetic conditions in the patient's energy field which might otherwise result in illness in the future, should they remain untreated.

Additionally, the activities of the healer are beneficial simply because they enhance the entire life process of the patient, even if disease is not present, enhancing functioning of body, mind and spirit and enabling the patient to live a healthier, more balanced and fulfilling life.

As an energy field healing treatment is performed, the healer conducts an extra measure of the universal life energy into the patient. This serves to supplement and enhance the overall health of the energy field.

The healer also expands his or her awareness for the purpose of gaining information regarding the condition of the energy field of the patient, to detect energetic anomalies of various kinds.

The healer then treats these faulty conditions by using various special techniques, to work with the field in various ways to correct the undesirable conditions that may be present.

A skilled healer is therefore capable of supplementing and enhancing the health of the vital energetic life processes of the patient, upon which physical, emotional and mental health depend.

Instrumental in the healer's art is the acquisition of expanded awareness, for it is the healer's expanded awareness that makes it possible for the healer to become fully aware of the condition of the energy field, and to acquire and use the various abilities and techniques that are useful in healing.

To do this, the healer heals not from any specific state of mind, but from a wider realm of awareness - from the whole being. As afflictions of body, mind and spirit begin in the wider realm of consciousness, the whole being, so does the healer heal from that level.

The healing provided is not merely a physical 'curing', but an emotional, mental and spiritual healing to the very core of the person's being

The first step in becoming an energy field healer is learning to channel the energy in a simple way. You will acquire the ability to conduct this energy into your patient for the purpose of supplementing and enhancing your patient's life processes, at all levels.

Principles of Energy Field (Pranic) Healing

Certain basic concepts are easier to understand and remember if they are labeled.

<u>1 Principle of Life Force</u>: For physical life to exist, it must have life force or vital energy. Life force is essential to physical life. It is also necessary for the existence of more subtle life forms

This life force has been called by various names Prana, Ruah, Chi, Manna, and many other names. Rapid healing is brought about by increasing the life force or Pranic energy level of the affected part or the whole body

<u>2. Principle of Pervasiveness</u>: Life force or vital energy is all around us. It is pervasive; we are actually in an ocean of life force.

Based on this principle, a healer can draw in Pranic energy or life force from the surroundings, and give it to the patient without exhausting himself or herself

3. Principle of Diseased Energy: Disease not only exists in physical form but also in energy form. Disease in energy form is called diseased energy or diseased bio-plasmic matter.

Clairvoyantly, diseased energy is seen as greyish or dark.

4. Principle of Transmittability: Life force or vital energy can be transmitted from one person to another person or object, or from one object to another object or a person.

5. Principle of Contamination: Diseased energy is transmissible. It could be transmitted from a patient to another person or to a healer.

The diseased energy of a subject could contaminate a person, an object, an animal, or a plant. Therefore, to avoid contamination, it is extremely important for healers to flick their hands when sweeping and after energizing, and to wash their hands and arms after cleansing and energizing.

6. Principle of Controllability: Life force and diseased energy can be controlled and directed through the will or through 'mind intent'.

7. Principle of Cleansing and Energizing: In healing, giving life force is not enough; it is also necessary to remove the diseased energy. Removing the diseased energy is called cleansing. Giving life force to a patient or an object is called energizing. The rate of healing can be accelerated by applying the principle of cleansing and energizing.

8. Principle of Radical Reaction: When energizing is done without removing the diseased energy, a crisis may take place in the form of temporary worsening of the condition. This is called radical reaction. This could be avoided or minimized by thorough cleansing.

9. Principle of Receptivity: A patient has to be receptive or at least neutral in order to receive the projected Pranic energy.

Being relaxed also helps increase the degree of receptivity. Without receptivity, the projected Pranic energy will not be absorbed, or only a minimal amount of it will be absorbed.

Patients may not be receptive because: they are biased toward this type of healing, they do not like the healer personally, they do not want to get well, or they are in general not receptive about anything.

10. Principle of Stabilizing: Projected Pranic energy tends to leak out if it is not stabilized.

Stabilization is done by energizing the treated part with light whitish-blue Prana, or covering the treated part with pastel blue Prana with a 'wiping' motion of the hand. Symptoms tend to recur if stabilization is not done.

11. Principle of Releasing: For healing to take place, it is necessary for the projected Pranic energy to be released. Otherwise, a substantial portion of it will return to the healer.

Releasing is done by being detached and by cutting the etheric link. The healer can be warm and caring but at the same time detached. Here, being detached does not mean being cold.

12. Principle of Correspondence: What affects the energy body or the etheric body will tend to affect the physical body - and what affects the physical body will tend to affect the energy body. When the energy body is healed, the physical body will also be healed.

13. Principle of Interconnectedness: The body of the patient and the body of the healer are interconnected with each other since they are part of the Earth's energy body.

On a more subtle level, it means that we are part of the solar system. We are interconnected with the whole cosmos. This principle of interconnectedness is also called the 'Principle of Oneness'.

14. Principle of Directability: Life force can be directed. It follows where your attention is focused; it follows thought.

Distant Pranic healing is based on the principle of directability and the principle of interconnectedness.

Polarities

All energy is either positive (+ve), negative (-ve), or neutral.

Chemical elements that enter our physical bodies via food products cause negative polarity in our vital strength. These elements can be solid, fluid, or gaseous elements of nature matter.

The Earth is a giant reservoir of negative polarity. Negative elements and chemical compounds enter into the human bloodstream and into the heart. The heart, working as a pump, delivers them into the lungs, where they unite with Prana, the solar energy of positive polarity (+ve). These positive-negative forces penetrate the blood as dew penetrates the earth.

These vital forces belong to the etheric body, whereas oxygen belongs to the physical body. In this way, positive-negative forces enter the organism and charge every cell by vital energy.

The polarity of positive and negative is a balancing force between all forms of energy and matter, and it is a necessity for every structure to exist. Foods also have polarities. Everything in the cosmos is characterized by positive, negative, or neutral energy.

We cannot identify positive and negative as good and bad in the physical bodies because both these kinds of energy are necessary to maintain life and the vital flow of energies.

When the human physical body sleeps, positive-negative forces regenerate damaged cells. This process is as natural as any of the body's functions: transforming food energy into vital energy, regenerating blood cells in red marrow, the regulating of heart pulsation and breathing, and so on.

An even flow of positive-negative current brings a sedating effect on the nervous system; the nervous system regenerates itself when Prana flows freely. Constancy of the ether flow balances vital energy for the organisms. Illness occurs when positive-negative polarities are not balanced.

Polarity not only affects all processes in the physical body, but also relationships between physical bodies and subtle bodies, and between the universe and humans. Physical bodies and subtle bodies are kept close by the polarity of positive-negative. All bodies interact with each other because of their differences in densities of energy fields.

Physical bodies consist of the densest, or slowest energy and are considered negative; whereas subtle bodies, in order of descent from the physical body, become more complex and faster in energy, and are considered positive. Polarities interacting between all these bodies must stay in balance all the time.

Thus, an imbalance flowing from the highest energy fields to the lower brings illnesses on the physical level. Bringing energy in without the cleansing of energies may cause even more imbalance.

Nevertheless, any energetic movement may also be directed in the reverse way in order to achieve the balance between the energies again. Later you will learn methods of cleansing and balancing the bio-energy fields.

When we determine the balance of body/emotion/mind/soul, we are referring to the balance of polarities in each aspect.

The body is a negative pole, emotion and soul are neutral, and the mind is a positive pole. On the physical level, an energetic imbalance can occur because of improper foods or poor diet, bringing an acid/alkaline imbalance and toxins into the body. On the emotional level, unbalanced emotions bring negativity instead of peace.

An acid/alkaline imbalance, toxins, unbalanced emotions or negative thought patterns affect the harmony of the whole bio-energy system. Patterns of negative energy cause abnormalities to all normal processes in the physical bodies.

If negative, harmful energy and abnormal processes continue to exist, they finally destroy the physical body. This is why people need to heal any imbalances in their bio-energy systems.

When we use the term 'bio-positive energy', we mean the pure healing energy (Prana) coming from God when positive energy flows freely in energy systems, bringing vitality and health.

Without bio-positive energy, there is no life. Bio-negative energy, however, is trapped, disharmonious, stale, or stagnant energy that blocks pathways and prevents vital energy from freely flowing in the energy systems. Negative energy brings imbalances into energetic systems and causes illnesses and emotional trauma.

Vitality through Pranic Reception

In this section we will deal with the very important topic of vitality.

One of the most frequent complaints we hear from patients is that they are chronically tired. Clinical evidence suggests that providing patients live sensibly, energy healing treatment can do much to improve their vitality, thus enhancing their ability to throw off disease.

Vitality is closely linked to the correct functioning of the spleen chakra, so it is necessary in any diagnosis of the chakras to determine the condition of this centre. Prana or vital force is distributed from the spleen chakra to all of the other major chakras, and from there sent to the organic systems of the physical body.

'Prana' is a Sanskrit term, which broadly translated means 'life-energy'. It is the life essence which works through the four ethers, and manifests in the activity of matter; without Prana there would be no physical manifestation.

This form of energy is responsible for maintaining the integrity of the physical-etheric vehicle. Its presence in correct proportions is essential to health, and it is for this reason that the energy field healer must give it careful consideration.

There are various types of Prana, but our main concern is with that form of Prana which emanates from the sun. Solar Prana radiates through our entire solar system, and is assimilated by all forms, be they planetary, human, animal or vegetable. Each form absorbs this Prana, circulates it, and keeps what is required to maintain its integrity.

The excess, now saturated with the distinctive qualities of the form it has passed through, is discharged back into the etheric force field of the earth to be utilized by other forms of life.

To these individual qualified Pranic emanations are given the names, planetary Prana, human Prana and so forth. On the microcosmic level the human etheric vehicle assimilates a mixture of solar and planetary Prana, and then discharges the qualified excess back into the etheric body of the earth, to mix with the Prana found therein.

The plant and animal kingdoms function in a similar manner, so that a vast interchange of energies can be seen to go on, using the etheric web as a medium for transmission.

It is the human Prana which manifests as the health aura. When being discharged this blends with the Pranic excess radiating from the atoms of the dense physical body, and produces an area of radiation that is commonly mistaken for the etheric body.

The health of the etheric body, and hence the dense physical, depends upon Prana, and the healing arts are moving towards a recognition of this fact. For example it is now understood that sunlight plays an important part in the building up and maintaining of health.

By virtue of this fact sanatoriums are often placed in the countryside, close to the sea, or on mountain slopes where the air is clear and heavily charged with the life-giving Prana. In such conditions patients are able to rebuild their depleted systems far more rapidly than in the contaminated environments of our cities.

Another point of consideration relative to Prana, is the fact that in recent years the practice of yoga has become popular in the Occident, and people are doing breathing exercises designed to increase their intake of Prana.

These exercises, known as pranayama, are aimed at cleansing the body of impurities and filling it with Pranic currents, thus increasing vitality and instilling a feeling of well being. It should be pointed out, however, that many of these exercises, if practiced without due care and diligence, can be very dangerous to Western man - and may bring about over-stimulation of the etheric body with subsequent psychic and physiological disturbances.

Frequently the type of patient who asks a healer for help will be one who is familiar with such exercises, and may in fact practice them. For this reason it should be kept in mind that pranayama incorrectly practiced may be a root cause for etheric dysfunction.

Pantanjali, the Indian philosopher, lists five differentiations of Prana in the human body. The healing rates of these Pranic forces are very useful to the practitioner who consciously works on the etheric levels, and they may be directed through the appropriate chakras to the areas concerned. The list is as follows:

- <u>Prana</u>, extending from the nose to the heart, and having special relation to the mouth and speech, the heart and lungs.

- <u>Samana</u>, which extends from the heart to the solar plexus. It concerns food and the nourishing of the body through the medium of food and drink, and has a special relation to the stomach.

- <u>Apana</u>, which controls from the solar plexus to the soles of the feet. It concerns the organs of elimination, of rejection and of birth, thus having special relation to the organs of regeneration, and of elimination.

- <u>Upana</u>, which is found between the nose and the top of the head, and has a special relation to the brain, the nose and the eyes.

- <u>Vyana</u>, which is the term applied to the sum total of Prana in the human body.

The implications inherent in these differentiations of Prana and energy healing measures are self-evident.

For example in cases of hay fever or chronic sinus trouble, treatment of the Ajna chakra with upana and the required colour is going to be significantly useful.

Energy healing for samana directed via the solar plexus chakra will help a patient to absorb nutrients more fully, and the energy for apana directed by way of the sacral chakra may prove most useful in treating a patient during childbirth, as complementary to regular medical care.

Certain manifestations of Prana may be observed directly by the human eye. Atoms that have become heavily charged with Prana manifest as brilliant white dots of light that dart and spin through the atmosphere. It is especially easy to see them on a clear sunny day against a blue sky, by simply focusing the eyes at a distance of about six feet and observing them move through the intervening space in a silent erratic dance.

The esotericists give to this energy dot the name of 'vitality globules'; such particles of matter are being continually taken up by the etheric body, so that they can play their role in vitalizing it.

Having briefly sketched in a description of the Pranic forces and their role in vitalizing the human form, we can now consider the way in which Prana is taken into the etheric body.

Vitality of the patient is always of concern to the energy-healing practitioner, for he recognizes that the body's ability to restore normal function depends in great part upon the vitality levels of the various systems.

The Pranic Triangle

The spleen chakra, which is that centre of force so closely related to vitality, is not a major spinal chakra. Its role is to supply vital energy to all the chakras on all levels of the personality or lower self. It is not directly related to those energies, which sweep man into a state of spirituality by way of the major centres.

Its role is one of vitalizing the etheric body.

It must be understood that the seven major chakras appeared during the course of man's early evolution, as a response to the impact of the seven major streams of energy that are said to comprise the evolutionary scheme of things in which we live and move and have our being.

They are not however directly related to the process of vitalizing the etheric body with solar and planetary Prana; a separate group of chakras are responsible for this function.

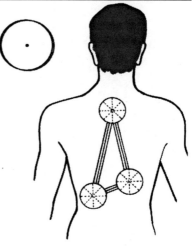

The receptive apparatus for Prana consists primarily of three force centres. The best known one is the spleen chakra; in addition to this there is another chakra situated just below the diaphragm, and a third lies between the shoulder blades just above the heart chakra.

The Pranic Triangle

Like the other chakras they appear as rotating saucer-like depressions in the surface of the etheric body, and are linked by a triple thread of energy to form a triangle of force known as the pranic triangle.

Prana enters the etheric body through minor force centres found throughout the upper part of the torso. It is then drawn down to the spleen chakra, and enters to circulate through the triangle formed by the three chakras.

Before being discharged from the spleen centre to vitalize the etheric body, the Prana is subjected to a process that regulates its potency.

If the organism is a healthy one, the vibratory rate will be stepped up. If the health of the individual is poor, then the rate of potency will be stepped down, so that the vitalizing effect of the Prana will not disrupt the etheric body.

Assimilation takes place after the Prana has been circulated through the triangle of force set up by the three Pranic chakras. It permeates the etheric web and creates a state of vitality in accordance with the ability of the organism to receive Prana.

Thus the dense physical body and the etheric vehicle are maintained in one cohesive unit, and will remain so until the silver cord is loosened, and contact with the etheric body is broken, resulting in death and finally disintegration of the earthly vehicle.

From the orthodox point of view the distinctive function of the spleen remains unknown. To the student of subtle anatomy it provides an interesting correspondence to the placenta and the umbilical cord, which connects the foetus to the mother for nutritional purposes. This cord, as we well know, is cut when the birth of the child is complete.

Similarly the etheric silver cord is cut when the physical and etheric bodies are separated at death, and the inner man is 'born' in full consciousness, into the world of a higher and more subtle dimension.

In assessing the vitality index of a patient, the energy field healer must determine whether the Pranic energies are being received, assimilated and distributed properly by way of the spleen chakra.

The other two centres in this Pranic triangle should also receive attention, particularly the one between the shoulder blades, as it is profoundly affected by distortions or subluxations of the dorsal spine, tensions in the upper and mid-dorsal musculature and general poor posture. All of these factors disturb Pranic circulation and utilization and ultimately lead to a state of fatigue.

If, as energy field healers, we understand the nature of vitalization of the human form by solar energies, we are going to be in a better position to help our patients.

Chapter Six

Identifying Energy Problems

Do you remember the fourteen principles of energetic (Pranic) healing from Chapter Four ?   They are so important that I will reiterate three of them again.

9. Principle of Receptivity: A patient has to be receptive or at least neutral in order to receive the projected Pranic energy. Being relaxed also helps increase the degree of receptivity.

Without receptivity, the projected Pranic energy will not be absorbed, or only a minimal amount of it will be absorbed.

Patients may not be receptive because: they have not given permission, they are biased toward this type of healing, they do not like the healer personally, they do not want to get well, or they are in general not receptive about anything.

13. Principle of Interconnectedness: The body of the patient and the body of the healer are interconnected with each other since they are part of the Earth's energy body.

On a more subtle level, it means that we are part of the solar system. We are interconnected with the whole cosmos.

14. Principle of Directability: Life force can be directed.   It follows where your attention is focused; it follows thought.

Distant pranic healing is based on the Principle of Directability and the Principle of Interconnectedness.

From the above three principles we see that:

(a). unless you have permission from the proposed recipient, healing will not work either face to face or at a distance.
(b). all life forms are connected as we swim about in the sea of consciousness.
(c). by 'intention', Pranic energy can be directed any where, whether the recipient be in the same room or thousands of miles away.

If you are still not convinced, let us try an experiment.

When you take a piece of white paper and hold the pendulum over the paper, the pendulum does not move because the paper does not signal energetically or even contain any energetic information.

Nevertheless, when we 'place' an energetic image (energetic matrix) of a visualized person on this paper, the pendulum starts moving, perceiving the bio-energy of the etheric body image.

The pendulum is very sensitive to bio-energetic fields. When we visualize a live person and 'put' the image on a white paper, the pendulum will spin clockwise. In a case of visualizing a dead person, the pendulum spins counter-clockwise, indicating a lack of life or balanced energy.

To ask questions regarding this person (who can be anywhere at the present time) you hold your pendulum over the paper and just ask YES/NO type questions. To receive correct answers, you have to keep the whole person's visual image in your mind during the procedure, reduced to the paper size. This is a phenomenon of mental energy. You ask questions and receive answers in YES/NO fashion from the person's energetic informative field.

The person you are talking with is somewhere far away right now; nevertheless, his or her subtle energetic bodies are answering your questions. This phenomenon is as opening doors to other bio-energetic phenomena, which are connected not only with human's bodies and bio-fields, but with their energetic 'phantoms', or etheric double images, as well.

Now we come to the 'nitty gritty'; we have found out about subtle anatomy, energy fields, bio-positive and bio-negative energy, and how this bio-negative energy can cause pathology in the physical body. What follows now is how we can detect these energetic problems and later, how to eradicate them.

Problems in the Subtle Bodies

The human form presents an amazing complexity and variety of parts. There are billions of cells, each performing a role aimed at integrating the diversity of structures into a smoothly functioning organism. Each part is dependent upon another for its existence.

Stop the heart and the whole organism fails; destroy certain brain cells and a part falls useless or the personality of the individual is radically altered.

All of these functions and processes are revealing their secrets to the march of medical science, so that today there is an ever growing mass of information about humans as a highly complex and co-ordinated series of organ systems.

In contrast there is little to be found in the scientific texts about man as a 'force field' system.

In 1935 Northrop and Burr put forward their electro-dynamic theory of life. This revolutionary concept of life as force field systems, while not immediately accepted with open arms by the more orthodox scientists of the day, has subsequently proved to be one of the greatest steps forward in the study of life from the angle of energies and force fields.

To progress, Energy Healing must move towards a recognition of man not simply as an electro-magnetic force field, but as something more. As science spends more time investigating the energy fields of life it will confirm the early work of energy healing pioneers, and will be able to accept the basic concepts of this method of diagnosis and healing.

However, the spearhead of any investigation energetically carried out must always be ahead of the prevailing thought of the day. For this reason the next step ahead for energy healing is the development of diagnostic techniques based on the subtle force fields of man. Not the electro-magnetic fields but the etheric force field with its centres of dynamic force that feed and maintain the physical organism.

Regular physical body diagnostic procedure is a long and detailed process, something entailing protracted periods of tiring work, which frequently leave the practitioner drained of energy; often many expensive laboratory tests are done.

These physically orientated methods, dealing as they do with the organic systems, cannot in the final analysis arrive at the cause of disease. It is essential to determine the conditions existing in the force centres and the subtle bodies in order to get near to the cause of imbalances in the human force fields.

The technique of diagnosis as utilized by the centre therapist is directed straight at the etheric body with its seven major force centres. This phases out the irrelevancy of the billions of cells which make up the physical form with its organic systems, and concentrates upon the energy field that activates them. It must ever be kept in mind that the life processes of the physical body depend upon the activity of the underlying force fields - which we call the etheric, astral and mental bodies.

The diagnostic procedure in centre therapy is quite basic and simple in conception. It determines the condition and activity of each major chakra and the spleen centre, and the state of the etheric body and the presence of miasms or toxins in that vehicle.

Please note that the following methods can be carried out with the patient present or at a distance. The latter is the object of this book.

Method 1 - Simple Body Scan

This method was given by Joe Smith in a workshop course.

You start out with a drawing of the human form. Next and up most is to get permission ! Don't scan some one without it.

We will call this person Mary Whatshername as our target for today; she said "OK" to me. Write her name and all you know about her on the top of your sheet - this is of vital importance.

Tell your pendulum that you wish it to remain still during the scan, then to rotate clockwise (Positive) at a problem location. Then start with your pendulum at the feet and work slowly up the legs search for past and present problem spots. Your pendulum will circle in those spots. Mark them with an 'X' or check mark or circle. Go right up the body, then the arms, hands, head area; then do the back side since it might show something else.

For instance if you had a circle in the heart area, the power of the swing is the first indication of how serious it is. A small swing might be normal, but a large one needs looking into.

Ask on a scale of 1 to 10 what condition is Mary's heart - 10 being good, anything under 5 needs attention. If you pick up something in the arteries above the heart check their cholesterol. They could be partially blocked.

This scanning has no limits in what you can find. You can even go to a more advanced book to further search, like a Body Atlas; but the simple body scan will give you a lot of information. If you find something in the liver area ask a series of questions to pin point it. Like they say, *"ask the right questions and get the right answers"*.

Now that you have got this information, what do you do with it ? You are not a doctor and you cannot diagnose. For instance if you found a spot on the person's breast, do not run out and tell her she has cancer ! Merely say *"I found an area of concern on one breast"*.

Use a little common sense with this, tell them to see a doctor; but you can still send them 'Healing Love' !

Method 2 - Using a Witness

I will now explain the equipment, or materials, used in the 'Witness' method, which is the most complex. The materials required include a Pointer, Witnesses, a Case Sheet, Anatomy Charts, and a Percentage/Counting Chart.

You will then have at your disposal a most interesting and rewarding method, one in which the pendulum can be your informer and you can utilize it to its fullest potential.

A primary witness is something that ties the pendulist in with the person for whom he is working, be it yourself or someone else. It can be any object which has been handled by the person, such as a photograph (a negative is even better), a signature, preferably in pencil (ink has a strong vibration of its own), a bit of clothing, some hair, a Body Scan with identity details, an anatomy chart with identity details etc.

The very best primary witness is a spot of blood, since it keeps its vital radiation for many years and is as personal as a fingerprint. However, the pendulist is not analyzing the blood of a person when using a blood-spot as a primary witness, it merely ties him in to all that is going on in the being of that person.

I personally prefer to use a blood-spot, and it is also most useful for use in 'Broadcasting', which will be gone into later. To make a blood-spot-witness, prick a finger and put a drop of blood on a small absorbent paper such as rice paper, tissue, or paper towel.

This should be placed immediately in a small cellophane envelope (available in stamp shops) and taped shut with scotch tape. If you do not have any cellophane at hand, you could fold the blood-spot in a small square of wax paper or plastic, but do not put it in any material that is too thick. You can also have the person initial it, since all blood-spots tend to look alike.

A more lasting way is to keep it in a file with the person's name, together with other charts you might make for him. A paper clip will easily keep it inside an ordinary manila file.

A secondary witness is used to work on a specific problem for the primary witness (yourself or another person). Secondary witnesses are the names of things: diseases, conditions, harmful materials in the body, or the names of a part of the body, or of a system or function that needs specific attention.

Furthermore, secondary witnesses are also the names of colours, remedies, or procedures which are indicated by the pendulum, and which are used to counteract a specific negative condition and help to change that negative condition to a positive one.

Such secondary witnesses can be made simply by writing the necessary word in pencil on a slip of paper. They are usually written up specifically as needed in your investigation - it is helpful to always keep slips of paper at hand for this purpose.

A tool that you will require is a Pointer. A wooden Chinese chopstick sharpened to a point is ideal. You will also need a drawing of the human form showing front and back views. Draw the chakras in position as small circles.

Again add all details of this person, full name, date of birth, post (zip) code, e-mail address, and any other identification you can think of. This is to ensure that you are working on the right person.

Hold the pendulum in the active hand over the drawing until you get a confirmatory YES signal to indicate a good connection. Now hold your pointer on the persons name with your non-dominant hand.

First the vitality index of the patient is determined by mentally asking for the vitality level of the patient, and measuring it off on the measuring chart: 0 – 100% (of that person's maximum, or the level for a normal person of that age, sex, etc). This is noted on the case sheet, 75 to 80 of personal maximum being normal for most operators.

Then the spleen chakra is checked - the practitioner asks mentally if it is over-active, under-active or normally active, because the state of this chakra has a direct bearing on the vitality of the patient. According to the condition of the chakra, the case sheet is marked with the appropriate symbol: +, -, or N.

If the spleen chakra is under or overactive, it should be checked for blockages at the entry or exit points. If a blockage is found it should be entered on the case sheet.

Next check the condition of the other two Pranic force centres in a similar manner, and write down your findings.

Having ascertained the condition of the Pranic centres and the vitality index of the patient, attention can be turned to the seven major spinal chakras. The procedure for their analysis is similar to that applied to the spleen centre.

Beginning at the crown chakra and working down to the base, each centre is checked in turn by pointing at the chakra on the drawing. The practitioner asks mentally if the crown chakra is over-active, under-active or normally active, and marks it down.

It should be understood that in seeking to determine the state of the chakra, the practitioner is not trying to determine a fleeting condition, but the absolute basic condition of that chakra.

For example one may find a patient with a solar plexus chakra that gives a reading of under-active. A sudden fright would certainly bring about a great deal of solar plexus activity, but it would be temporary and not reflect the true state of the chakra.

The basic state of a chakra does not change day by day, from one condition of activity to another - it remains steady and tends to change slowly under the impact of treatment or the alteration of character traits by the patient's own efforts.

Where there is a condition of over or under-activity, the degree of imbalance, as a percentage, is measured (by numbers as before) and noted. The progress of this reading towards zero imbalances following treatment may be used as an indication of progress towards normal balance of the chakra.

If the crown chakra reads + or - then it must be checked for blockages which may be present and causing the imbalance. With the degree of imbalance registered, the practitioner mentally asks if the chakra is blocked.

If a positive response is indicated by the pendulum, then it must be determined if the blockage exists at the point where energies flow into the chakra, or where they exit to make their impact upon the endocrine gland, in this case the pineal body.

The following symbols are used to denote a blockage.

> Incoming/Entry blockage.   I
>
> Exit/Outgoing blockage.   E

Where a blockage is indicated, these symbols are entered upon the case sheet.

This procedure as outlined for determining the condition of the crown chakra, is then repeated for the ajna, throat, heart, solar plexus, sacral and base chakras, and the findings listed.

Having analyzed the state of each chakra, the practitioner then turns his attention to the etheric body as a whole, and seeks out those factors which may be inhibiting the flow of energies throughout the etheric vehicle.

First the presence of miasms must be accurately determined. There are quite a number of different labels for the miasms, but the centre therapist is concerned with the three major ones. These are:

- Syphilis, a disease which comes to mankind by courtesy of the Lemurian civilization,
- Tuberculosis passed on by the Atlanteans, and
- Cancer which is the disease of the present Aryan civilization.

It is interesting to note that both syphilis and tuberculosis have been brought under control, representing as they do the physical and emotional aspects of man's evolutionary development.

But the permissiveness of today is releasing certain energies in various sections of society, with the result that the syphilitic expression of disease or energy imbalance is on the increase.

For the most part, individuals in the present age are concerned with the development of their mental bodies. This activity carried forward consciously or unconsciously, with too much emotional suppression, produces cancerous conditions. The miasms then are syphilitic, tubercular, or cancerous. It is said that under these three headings all disease can be categorized.

Patients may have one or more miasms in combination which undermine their health in general. The reader is well advised to spend some time studying literature on the miasms, because these factors, if present in the etheric body, contribute much towards ill health, and their removal by homoeopathic or energy healing means is essential to health.

Toxins from bacterial, chemical or drug sources may be sought out and noted. Little attention need be given to them, as it has been found that treatment of the chakras eliminates them anyhow, without them having been identified in detail.

Miasms and toxins along with the intensity should be entered on the case sheet.

Case Sheet for: *Mary Whatshename*   Date: *2008 FEB 30*
Address: *211 Mangrove St, Banyan City, Coromondel*
Phone H: *(515)279-8313*   C: *(515)709-6623*   W: *n/a*
DOB: *1972 JUN 31*   Other Data: *mary@unintel.com*
Past Problems: *Sinus trouble, poor visibility, digestive disorders.*
          May have suffered abuse.
Present Conditions:
Vitality Index: *55*   Spleen Chakra: *25-O*

Chakra	+N-	Blockages	Astral	Mental
Crown	*N*			
Ajna	*57 -*	*E*		
Throat	*40 +*			
Heart	*10 -*			
Solar Plexus	*N*			
Sacral	*N*			
Root	*N*			

Miasms, Toxins, Physical Anomalies: *Syphilitic*

	ETHERIC	ASTRAL	MENTAL
Congestion			
Over Stimulation	*Y*		
Lack of Co-ord.			

Next the overall condition of the etheric body is determined. Here three factors are of importance:

1. Congestion of the etheric body.
2. Overstimulation of the etheric body.
3. Lack of co-ordination.
    a. Between the physical and etheric bodies: P/E
    b. Between the etheric and astral bodies: E/A

If any of these conditions are identified, they should be measured for their intensity (again numbers and questions), and the appropriate notes made on the case sheet.

This concludes the diagnosis of the etheric body and its chakras. Treatment is determined upon these findings.

The Case Sheet that I use is shown (Adapted from a sheet by David V. Tansley). Some results are indicated to give you some ideas.

The patient is thirty-five years of age, with a history of sinus trouble and poor vitality, accompanied by digestive disorders, especially of the stomach.

First the spleen chakra is functioning very poorly, and this would in part account for the lack of vitality.

The spleen chakra is underactive (-) by 25% and has a blockage in the outlet (O).

The vitality index at 55 is too low for a person of that age.

Of the major chakras, three show an imbalance. The ajna is under-active, and this, because it governs the nasal area, will have a direct bearing on the sinus problem. The fact that it is both under-active and blocked will create a situation in which the individual will have difficulty in expressing self as a personality.

This can lead to unconscious feelings of self pity which frequently occur with sinus and catarrh conditions.

The block at the exit of the ajna is naturally going to create an endocrine imbalance, the pituitary is going to function erratically. Among other things the pituitary manages the function of the pancreas, so there is a link here between the stomach disorder and the ajna chakra.

The throat chakra is overactive, therefore the thyroid is going to be in a similar condition. The patient is burning up an excess of energy and yet the spleen being under-active is not really supplying anywhere near the amount needed.

This indicates that the spleen chakra is going to need direct attention to stimulate its function.

The heart chakra is under-active, but not too badly. This may point out circulatory trouble and disturbed vagus function, an important point to consider, keeping in mind the profound effect this nerve has on body functions.

The etheric body contains a syphilitic miasm. This miasm tends to affect the throat (thus relating to the throat chakra problem), the eyes (bringing in the ajna chakra and the sinus area again), and the brain with its relationship to the vagus.

The etheric body shows a condition of over-stimulation, energy is circulating too rapidly and is discharged before it has a chance to be absorbed and utilized . . . yet another factor in the fatigue problem.

Usually the miasm is the cause for this condition of the etheric body. Remember a miasm can speed up or slow down the circulation of energies.

This briefly then is an interpretation of the preceding analysis of the chakras and the etheric body in relationship to the health of the person concerned. The analysis is simple, quick and gets right to the point, covering the main factors concerned, without going into endless details regarding the physical organic systems.

Upon the basis of this analysis an effective programme of treatment can be quickly assessed, and we will follow this through in the next chapter so that a clear example is available for reference.

Method 3 - Visualizing the Etheric Body

An individual's etheric body contains his or her complete energetic information including all organs, parts, and systems of the physical body. Whether healers perceive energy in a patients bio-energy field at a close distance or any long distance, they 'deal' with the etheric body.

Performing bio-energy healing, healers work with the etheric body, at first perceiving its energetic information and imbalances, and then cleansing, balancing, energizing, and stabilizing the energy fields. Healing and stabilizing imbalances on the etheric level brings health, vitality and balance to the physical body.

When performing a distant energy healing or assessment, healers keep the visualized patients energetic image before their eyes.

Then the healer can transfer the visualized patients energetic image onto a drawing or copy of the human form in order to perform energetic assessment and healing.

In order to complete the connection between patient and healer, all personal details of the patient must be written on the image sheet.

Details would include full name, date of birth, post code (Zip), email address and any further individual details known. These details are very important !

There are many people on the earth with the same names or birth dates; nevertheless, you have exactly the same person whose energetic information you wrote and whom you want to assess now.

Some healers prefer to make their own drawings of the human form whilst holding the visualized image of their patient in their mind. This is not really necessary as the connection is made via the etheric identification details to create an 'energy image'.

If you fit a visualized image of yourself into the human form on the paper in front of you, for example, what you have on the paper now is your etheric body image. This image is energetic in its nature and reflects your energetic state at this moment.

When you 'place' the healee's energy image on the paper, the image reflects an energetic state of the person at the present moment. On this image of the etheric body, you can measure the energy, and determine the energetic and physical state.

You may check the energy of the image with your pendulum. If your pendulum spins clockwise over the image, it shows a good energetic shape and physical health in general. If you observe anti-clockwise movement, you may decode that an energetic imbalance or negative energy is present in the bio-energy field, and physical illnesses are present on the physical level.

If your chart or drawing does not show the force centres (chakras), you may draw them in the correct positions. When you have mastered placing the image mentally on paper with chakras, you can do the healing procedures.

On such an energetic image, you may easily assess the chakras' performance, the energetic and physical condition of yourself, your family members, or even pets. Moreover, you will be able to perform chakra healing.

You can help yourself with your own drawn etheric image and your pendulum to recognize all imbalances and disturbances in your own energy system and on the physical level, and heal yourself by opening your chakras, removing energetic blocks, and balancing your energy.

At this point we will clarify one or two points. If the healer was in the same room as the patient, he would have no problem in assessing the chakras of the patient. With the patient lying on a therapy table he would just hold the pendulum over each chakra in turn and assess it's function.

Remember that in energy healing, the right hand gives energy and the left hand receives energy - for a right handed person. Therefore, hold the pendulum in the right hand away from the patient and place the left hand on each chakra at the back of the patient. A positive spin will be anti-clockwise at the back.

Frederick Joseph Bloggs
03/08/1955   LL11 6LL
fred@home.co.uk

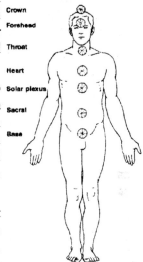

Crown
Forehead
Throat
Heart
Solar plexus
Sacral
Base

Chakras on Etheric Body Image with etheric identification details.

There will be no difference when working at a distance with our body scan or drawing. Either hold the pendulum in your right hand and point with your pointer to each chakra in turn and observe the spin or hold the pendulum directly over the chakra on the paper and observe spin.

At first, start a general chakra assessment by placing the pendulum over, or point at, the root chakra (the first chakra) and following with the next five chakras. Observe the movements of the pendulum over each chakra. Take notes about the chakras' states, listing observable symbols of pendulum movement for each chakra and your sensations for further detailed assessment.

This completes the general assessment on the front side of the chakras. If the pendulum showed clockwise movement over all chakras, indicating that all chakras are opened and functional, there is no reason to perform the chakra assessment on the back, since when a chakra is in working condition on the front, it is functional on the back also.

To assess the chakras from the back, use a rear view of the human form, or draw the person's form again and write the full name, birth date and other details as usual. Write 'back' on the top of your drawing to give command for perceiving energetic information from the back.

Repeat the chakras' assessment on the back. The natural spinning of chakras from the back is in an anti-clockwise movement. If chakras are spinning in any other way, they are not working properly or they are closed and need cleansing.

If you observe that the chakra is dysfunctional either on the front or the back, you should perform a detailed assessment of the organs or body parts that correlate with the chakra on the physical level. With a detailed chakra assessment, you may determine what organs or body parts have an energy imbalance or are weakened physically.

When an energetic imbalance in the system is discovered, it indicates physical discomfort or illness on the physical level. Each chakra influences organs, body parts, and systems located in its area.

When the chakra is healthy and working properly, it influences organs, body parts, and systems of its area in a positive way, bringing health and vitality. However, closed and dysfunctional chakras also affect the health of their correlated organs, parts, and systems, bringing in imbalances and illnesses.

A detailed assessment is performed on the organs or body parts by using lists of names or anatomy charts and asking YES/NO type questions of your pendulum.

The possible movements of the pendulum have been given before but are repeated here:

<u>Clockwise</u> Open and Functional, feelings governed by the chakras are integrated and balanced, physical system should be functioning.

<u>Counterclockwise</u> Closed, feelings governed by the chakra are not assimilated, physical systems not fully functional.

<u>Horizontal oscillation</u> Holding energy, a strong block, noticeable resistance to the feelings associated with the chakra, physical symptoms are likely to be due to repressed emotions.

<u>Vertical oscillation</u> Energies being focused from the personal towards the spiritual, some physical disturbance likely

<u>Erratic or Elliptical movement</u> Energies in chakra are unbalanced and feelings governed by the chackra are erratic.

<u>Standstill</u> No energy being circulated, will lead to physical symptoms.

Method 4 - Direct Identification from the Human Body

This method was taught to me by Gabrielle Blackburn in her Radiesthesia Course.

By holding the pendulum over the body, you can detect any energy distortion indicating an imbalance. The energy normally flows up and down the body and follows any curve, such as a bent arm.

You can detect negative conditions in the body involving an organ or a gland by inquiring about functions and systems while moving the pendulum slowly over the part and asking appropriate questions.

Remember, however, that a pain may give a negative energy distortion reading in one area, but this may be a reflex only, with the cause being in another part of the body. A headache, for instance, may be caused by a digestive problem.

You can check this method on yourself by making the following little test. If there is nothing wrong with your arm, give it a good slap; you will immediately be able to take a negative distortion reading (counter-clockwise rotation) which shows that there is an energy loss at this point.

You can see exactly how far this reaches up and down the arm, showing the extent of the little injury. As it is a very minor one, the pendulum will slow down in its rotation almost immediately and within a minute or so return to its normal neutral swing, indicating that the trouble is resolved.

Method 5 - The Hand as an Indicator

By holding the pendulum over the tips and other points of the fingers of either hand (as shown on the next page) you can determine the state of health or disease in the body.

This is very helpful in finding out quickly about the major systems, functions, and conditions of the physical body. It is not always possible to have your equipment available, such as in an emergency when you need some quick answers.

This method uses the points in the hand which reflect from the various parts of the body, and you are, of course, not measuring the hand itself. This will tell you about the acid-alkaline balance in the body and also about the condition of the heart and the blood circulation.

Furthermore, you can determine the level of physical energy in the body, as well as the etheric energy, which always gives a higher reading since it feeds the physical body.

Only in cases of shock or out-of-the-body states will the etheric energy get dangerously low, below the level of the physical energy. Just before death, the etheric energy will disappear completely - in fact, before the physical body takes its last breath.

As you can see, the above paragraphs refer to face to face diagnosing.

If you wish to use this method at a distance, just put the persons details on the chart, name D.O.B. etc. and whilst holding the pendulum in your dominant hand, hold your pointer in the other hand, point to the hand positions and ask your questions.

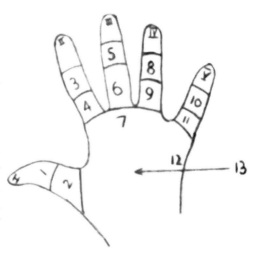

Energy Distortion Points In Hand.

Energy Distortion Points In Hand.
I   NERVOUS SYSTEM -- Brain --Physical Energy
            1 Etheric Energy
            2 Acid Alkali Balance
II   RESPIRATORY SYSTEM
            3 Bronchial
            4 Lungs
Ill   DIGESTIVE SYSTEM
            5 Liver
            6 Stomach
            7 Intestines
IV   URINARY SYSTEM
            8 Kidneys
            9 Bladder

V   REPRODUCTIVE SYSTEM
> 10 Male: Testes -- Prostate
>   Female: Uterus -- Ovaries
> 11 Genitals
> 12 Blood Condition and Circulation.
> 13 Heart Function.

Method 6 - Magnet Dowsing

It is worthy of note that in his book, Magnet Dowsing, Dr. B. Bhathacharya advocates the use of a small horseshoe magnet as a pendulum. This amplifies the sensitivity of the pendulum greatly.

To increase the sensitivity even more, he further advocates holding a second magnet in the other hand during testing.

This is similar to a method that I use myself, but my method seems to be more sensitive, less cumbersome and has further uses.

My magnetic pendulum was made as follows: I borrowed my wife's Rose Quartz Pendant which has six flat faces, pointed at one end and a metal chain attachment fixture at the other end.

The size of the pendant is approximately 6mm between any two diametrically opposed faces, 40mm long and weighs about 15g. Two small bar magnets (15mm x 3mm x 1.5mm) were attached to two opposite faces of the pendant at the length mid-point with sticky tape.

The two magnets are fixed so that they attract each other through the crystal (opposite polarity). This setup appears to excite the crystal and make the pendulum very sensitive - it can be used very successfully as an 'Etheric Weaver'.

The Etheric Weaver

I can hear most of you saying now *"What on Earth is an Etheric Weaver ?"* Read on and be amazed !

The Etheric Weaver is a Metatronic Tool used to balance and align the chakric energies; it can be used as a direct and a distance healing tool - both on oneself and others.

The Etheric Weaver consists of a perfectly clear 7 inch laboratory grown quartz crystal covered with a clear colour gel, which may be single colour or multi-coloured.

Two magnets are placed in reverse polarity on the sides of the crystal, and copper wire is wrapped around both crystal and magnets. A 24k gold plated chain with a small quartz crystal on the end is used to hold the hanging Etheric Weaver.

For healing others, start by suspending the Etheric Weaver about 3 - 4 inches above the feet of the person with whom you are working. Very slowly move the weaver up one leg, then the other leg, then up the body, from one hand to the shoulder and then the other arm, and around the head.

If the etheric weaver starts to spin (any direction), hold it over that area until the spinning stops.

The Etheric Weaver works to heal injuries (old and new), and heal blockages and rents within the etheric field. It works with the person's whole meridian system and not just the point it is suspended over.

The healing takes place in no set time but is dependent upon the state of the etheric field of the individual receiving the healing.

Self Healing & Distance Healing with the Etheric Weaver

Take a photograph of yourself (or a visualized image on a piece of paper) which includes the whole of your body - head to toe, and follow the directions outlined above over the photograph.

If you do not have a photograph available, stand with your left palm facing upwards in front of your body and suspend the Etheric Weaver holding it with your right hand, over your palm. Then imagine the whole of your body - again from toe to head, and the Etheric Weaver slowly moving up your body - just as if you were using a photograph.

The Etheric Weaver can also be used for distance healing using a full body photograph or an image in your mind of a person, animal or place - and following the same procedure.

As you can see, we have strayed ahead of ourselves and touched on Healing. You cannot mention the Etheric Weaver without mentioning healing. Not to worry, Healing starts soon !

There is another 'tool' that I use regularly which is similar in use to the 'Etheric Weaver', this is the 'Ptah Pendulum'. It is a diagnostic and healing tool.

The ptah pendulum was invented, after much research, by John Living who lives in Canada. I have found that it is just as effective as the Etheric Weaver - and costs less !

The 'Ptah Pendulum'

The pendulum's history and descriptions of it's many uses can be found on Johns web site -- www.in2it.ca/tools.htm and in the Holistic Intuition Society's 'Shop Page' at the end of this book.. It has many uses are beyond the scope of this book and I will only describe it's use in healing, both hands on and distant healing.

I will now explain how I use the Ptah pendulum in the work I do - but as explained above it has a myriad of other uses.

Signals

In all work with the 'Ptah Pendulum' a clockwise circle indicates YES and is the 'Input Mode'. An anti-clockwise circle indicates NO and is the 'Extract Mode'. When asking a question it does not matter which end of the Pendulum is held.

The 'Ptah Pendulum' will extract or input, and then swing towards the next position that it needs to go - the direction could be one of two ways, since it is swinging, and your Intuition will guide you to the correct place.

If you go in the wrong direction, I have found that the 'Ptah Pendulum' will not circle (or make a very small signal) - so reverse the direction that you are moving the Pendulum. When in the correct place it will circle to do the needed work.

Holding the 'Ptah Pendulum'

In extract mode, the hand holds the shorter of the two coils. For input mode, the longer coil is held. To avoid bending the coil that is held, hold it at its bottom - so that the strain is not transmitted to the part of the coil above your hand.

Healing Action

For distant Healing, John uses a doll for females and a teddy bear for males. This token is defined as representing the Healee. I, on the other hand, always use Human Form diagrams for distant work.

This diagram is enlarged to A3 size and is laminated in plastic. Start by passing a small magnet (clearing magnet) over the diagram to remove any residual energies from previous usage.

The etheric matrix details, name, date of birth, address etc. are written on paper with a self adhesive backing which is then attached to the laminated diagram. Hold the pendulum over the centre of the diagram (Solar Plexus area), and make an anti-clockwise circle (extract mode, shorter coil in hand) around this point, widening in a spiral to enclose most of the Healee.

Now hold the 'Ptah Pendulum' stationary at this point - it will start to circle on its own accord to extract bio-negative energies, or swing to show the direction for you to move to find a 'problem' area. The Ptah pendulum will then circle over a problem area.

When the circling finishes, the 'Ptah Pendulum' will swing, pointing to the next location of bio-negative energies; move it slowly in the direction indicated until it starts to swing again. This is repeated until it remains stationary.

Now change to input mode - the longer coil is held in hand, making clockwise circles - again on its own accord - and this procedure is repeated. Logically this should remove all bio-negative energies, and replace them all with bio-positive energies. But the metaphysical world is not logical !

To make certain that all has been cleared, keep on repeating the extraction mode and then input mode until no circling occurs.

As a final check, start again at the start point and make a spiral, then go to the start point and see if any swinging or circling occurs. If so, then repeat the whole procedure again - and keep on until there is no swinging or circling.

Chapter Seven

Chakra Assessment

Chakra assessment shows the energetic, emotional and physical conditions very precisely. During the assessment of a person's image chakra system, you will perceive the energetic, physical and emotional conditions of this person.

Chakras - their Correlations

<u>Root chakra</u>: penis, groin, testes, vagina, anus, bladder, coccyx (tailbone), bones, and the sexual and reproductive systems.

<u>Sacral chakra</u>: spleen, ovaries, adrenal glands, uterus, kidney, urinary tract, lower abdomen, large intestines, appendix, sacrum, sexual system, and energy level.

<u>Solar Plexus chakra</u>: musculature, pancreas, stomach, liver, gallbladder, small intestines, blood sugar, lower, middle, and upper spine, diaphragm, upper abdomen, solar plexus, and digestive system.

<u>Heart chakra</u>: lungs, windpipe, breast, chest, ribcage, bronchi, heart, circulatory and lymph systems, blood pressure, esophagus, shoulders and shoulder blades, mucous membranes, immune system, and thymus.

<u>Throat chakra</u>: throat, vocal cords, ears, nose, mouth, jaw, neck, shoulder clavicles, sciatic nerve, legs, feet, knees, arms, elbows, hands, thyroid and parathyroid, skin, respiratory system, colds, and sinus allergies.

<u>Brow chakra</u>: eyes, sinuses, headache, forehead, autonomous nervous system, pituitary gland, cerebrum (the part of the brain responsible for senses, visualization, and verbal/auditory), cerebellum (the part of the brain responsible for motor coordination, reality contact, balance, dizziness, and the epilepsy centre), brain stem, and the hypothalamus (the part of brain responsible for stress response).

<u>Crown chakra</u>: central nervous system, pineal gland, hair, head top, cerebral cortex (the part of the brain responsible for thinking), and mind agility.

On the back it is better to assess the whole spinal column, which corresponds to several different chakras. You may assess all other organs on the back chakras in the same way as on the front.

When you have discovered which chakras are dysfunctional or unbalanced, you need to perform a detailed assessment of organs or body parts in the areas of these chakras.

For the detailed assessment, you need charts of body parts and organs - or you can draw your interpretation of what these look like, with the etheric image for specific organs or body parts belonging to the area of the dysfunctional chakra.

Conditional Chakras

For example, with a dysfunctional sacral chakra you draw the organs which correspond with this chakra. Draw a 'conditional chakra' on each organ to insure that you receive the exact energetic information you need from this organ.

Pass your pendulum slowly over each organ image. When you perceive a positive energetic signal (clockwise spinning on the front) from a specific organ, you know that this organ is functioning well.

If a perceived signal is negative (counter-clockwise movement on the front), it means this organ has an energetic imbalance or disturbance that can cause weakness or illness. If the pendulum is still, it means that the organ is already weakened and possibly unhealthy, and needs healing.

When you have mastered visualization, you may draw just the organs under the written energetic identification, mentioning the name of the organ while corresponding the organs mentally to the person's etheric image.

Young. Mary Jane

10.02.1955   LL12 0AU

To do this, write the person's energetic information and the organ's name on the top of the drawing, and draw the chakra on the organ or body part.

By doing so, you connect the energetic field of this etheric image with the organ's energetic field.

Liver

Organ, 1 Chakra

Thus, you may perceive and interpret energetic information from this energetic part or organ and assess the energetic state, determining which organs retain an energetic imbalance and perceiving possible energetic information about negative energy of weak organs or body parts.

When you assess an energetic condition on a drawing with many physical organs, put one chakra on each organ or body part.

However, to achieve a more precise assessment, you must put at least three chakras on the organ or body part.

By doing this detailed assessment with three chakras on the organ, you may determine even which part of this organ is unbalanced or disturbed on the energetic level. You may also draw one part of an organ for a more detailed assessment (put chakras and energetic identification on it as well).

Pass your pendulum over the organ, body part, or its cut, and remember or list energetic symbols and signals for prospective healing.

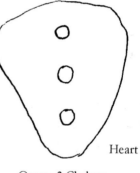

Young. Mary Jane
10.02.1955   LL12 0AU

Heart

Organ, 3 Chakras

To make a quick assessment, draw pictures of the body parts and organs you are interested in before your assessment, and write the energetic identification of the person above the drawings.

Dysfunctional Chakras and Body Malfunctions

Dysfunctional, closed, and blocked chakras can lead to and cause physical illnesses.

- terminal illnesses always indicate a depleted <u>Root Chakra</u>.
- low energy level indicates a dysfunctional <u>Sacral Chakra</u>.
- regular headaches indicate an unbalanced or dysfunctional <u>Brow Chakra.</u>
- digestive problems indicate a dysfunctional <u>Solar Plexus Chakra</u>.
- throat problems and regular colds indicate a dysfunctional <u>Throat Chakra</u>.

Besides an organ assessment, you can distinguish some illnesses on the physical level. Let us classify some illnesses and their correlation to dysfunctional chakras.

Such malfunctions as obesity, hemorrhoids, constipation, physical weakness, arthritis, prostate enlargement, bladder problems, reproductive problems, and menstrual cramps are correlated with dysfunctional Root Chakra.

Kidney illnesses, spleen problems, impotence, frigidity, uterine bladder problems, food cravings, toxins in large intestines, and gas pain are correlated with dysfunctional Sacral Chakra.

Ulcers, diabetes, hypoglycemia, digestive problems, liver problems, hiccups, and burps are correlated with dysfunctional Solar Plexus Chakra.

Asthma, high blood pressure, breathing allergies, cough, lung's illnesses, heart problems, and immune system illnesses are correlated with dysfunctional Heart Chakra.

Problems with arms, hands, legs, feet, mouth, thyroid, flu, neck ache, headache, allergies, skin problems, sore throat and sinuses, ears problems, and nausea are correlated with dysfunctional Throat Chakra.

Blindness, eye problems, headache, migraine, colds, brain-physical and brain-psychological problems, addiction and obsession, brain stem problems, and nightmares are correlated with dysfunctional Brow Chakra.

Depression, distress, alienation, confusion, mind agility, and hair problems are correlated with dysfunctional Crown Chakra.

Distress and Chakras

We mentioned that the brow chakra and the crown chakra are responsible for psychological problems, stress reaction, distress, and depression. However, it has been observed during many long years of experience by researchers that distress and depression in turn cause all other chakras' dysfunctions.

We cannot imagine our lives without stress. We encounter many stressful situations every day: traffic on the road, personal relationships, job interviews, not having enough time, communication with others, sleep disturbances, and various other extreme situations.

As people and their attitudes differ from each other, so do their reactions.

Our inherent ability to react to threat or danger with a series of biochemical changes in our organisms on the physical level (the 'fight or flight' response) helps us deal with extreme situations.

These biochemical changes, made by the sympathetic nervous system, increase heart rate, breathing rate, metabolism, muscle tension, and blood pressure, as well as decrease blood flow from the extremities (legs and arms), and digestion.

Prepared in this way, an organism becomes ready to fight or run from an external event. When the stressful situation has passed, the organism returns to its normal state.

Relaxation response occurs as the organism returns to its normal state, releasing stress, strong emotions, and tension. The relaxation response mechanism turns off the stress response in this way: the brain stops sending signals to the organism about the hazard, and in minutes metabolism, heart rate, breathing rate, muscle tension, and blood pressure return to normal levels.

If the mind and body cannot reach relaxation response and the stress response condition continues uncontrolled, it can cause secretion of corticoids by the adrenal glands, which inhibit digestion, reproduction, growth, tissue repair, and so on.

When stress becomes distress ('negative' stress) and lasts for a long time, all chakras close and become dysfunctional or blocked.

If this stressful condition is prolonged and the mind still receives signals of threat, the mind will continue to keep the physical body aroused. This causes energetic bio-negativity, energy flow imbalances, and the presence of stale or stagnant energy.

All other subtle bodies contract, because they can no longer communicate and receive vital energy through closed chakras.

Moreover, the chakras cannot function at all when people stay in prolonged stress (distress) because their chakras become congested with stale or stagnant energy, or overcharged through unexpressed strong emotions and even expressed strong emotions.

When the chakras are closed, dysfunction can occur at the physical level. A distressful physical body state affects one's whole energetic system, and in turn, the whole energetic system, when dysfunctional and low energetic-wise, influences the physical body.

On the physical level, chronic stress and a disturbed energetic state can increase the occurrence of many illnesses and weakness in the physical body. Chronic stress and energetic imbalance can cause muscle tension, fatigue, hypertension, migraines, ulcers, or chronic diarrhea.

Closed, blocked, or dysfunctional chakras and conditions of the whole human bio-system lay marks on the person's destiny, character, communication with others, and well-being. Many people live with closed or dysfunctional chakras due to consistent stress.

In such energetic conditions, they may experience anxiety, fear, depression, weakness, unhappiness, dissatisfaction, insecurity, emotion suppression, indifference, inability to express feelings, and inability to love and trust.

With closed and dysfunctional chakras, people cannot communicate with others effectively, or have success in any commencement or career as well.

Why do people have continued distress ? Distress causes the chakras to close, and then closed chakras prolong distress in turn.

In a case of distress, chakras cannot open and cleanse themselves naturally. We must cleanse and open our chakras by ourselves, help any bio-negative energy, tension and strong emotions to be released, stabilize bio-energy, and restore psychic, emotional and physical health.

Emotional and Mental Issues and Blocks

As we have stated, our emotions, thoughts (our subtle bodies) and physical well-being are closely linked and interrelated.

First we must change our attitudes about ourselves and our lives.

Energy follows our thoughts. When we feel good and positive about ourselves, we cause good and positive things to happen in our bio-energetic systems, our subtle energetic bodies, and then in our lives.

When we become more positive and affirmative, our energy changes in a positive way, and we feel good and energetic.

An effective way to decrease the possibility of distress in our lives is by integrating positive activities and optimistic moods and thoughts into everyday life.

In order to weather negative stress and to have lower frequencies of illness or weakness, people have to view difficult situations and threats of life from a positive point of view - as challenges, possibilities to prove or examine themselves, or opportunities for personal growth.

People who can cope with negative stress undertake stressful events and stressors in a positive way while getting life experience. They can neutralize distress and make positive conclusions from negative experiences. Moreover, these people can stabilize their energetic health while recovering from distress.

On the physical level, coping with stress begins from an awareness of one's own body, analyzing any states of tensions, aches, and physical sensations.

On the energetic level, coping with stress or any irregularity begins with discharging blocked, stale, stagnant, and negative energy from the bio-energy system.

The roots of human problems spring from the energy conditions of their bio-fields. Negative thoughts, strong emotions, and inappropriate physical actions are energy problems. However, energy problems can occur because of the energetic influence of others as well.

Bio-energy systems interfere with those of others and influence each other. In this way, others' bio-energy systems can bring problems to one's own system.

'Energy damage' can be introduced into one's energy system by others as well. Brought intentionally or accidentally, such an 'energy damage' conveys negative energetic information into one's bio-system, piercing subtle bodies and forcing chakras to close.

This can happen during communication with upset or angry people because of the intersection and interference of subtle bodies during a highly charged conversation.

Our negative thoughts and emotions bring negative bio-energetic states of energy, even if we have not received it from the outside world. Our own negative thoughts and attitudes can block vital energy flowing in our subtle bodies and physical bodies.

People with low self-esteem and self-confidence tend to pull energy into their systems, particularly negative energy, since low self-worth is negative. People with low or negative self-characteristics hold back energy in their chakras, creating energy blocks. They do not release negative energy, but accumulate it in the energy systems.

These energy blocks prevent people from having positive relationships and from fulfilling and enjoying their lives. With blocked chakras, people do not have full access to their vital energy, leading to negative states of mind, confusion, and depression.

How do energy blocks occur ? When children are told they are bad, dull, uninteresting or by other negative terms, they create mental, emotional, and even physical blocks for themselves which, later in their lives, causes fears, inactivity, doubtfulness about their abilities, loneliness, and numerous pains.

Any blocks show an alteration in destiny that prevents one from fulfilling one's life purpose. A block can be provoked by a physical problem, negative emotion, wrong mental belief, or unexpressed feeling - it can affect the whole human system.

Physical blocks reflect any disharmony or disturbances in the physical body such as diseases, pains, or any physical problems.

Physical blocks often prevent us from physical activity, causing mental and emotional blocks and deteriorating our feelings. These negative feelings and beliefs can, in turn, deteriorate our wellbeing.

Mental blocks are beliefs that prevent us from developing our inner selves toward peace and spirituality. Mental belief is a powerful 'mechanism' which can affect our well-being, attitudes, emotions, and actions through either positive and negative thoughts.

Mental and physical healing can be manifested through positive, affirmative thoughts, whereas, negative thoughts bring energetic imbalances, blocks, and illnesses.

The mental body, as the strongest body, has forceful impact on the physical body. We are what we think. The implications of negative or false beliefs programmed into mental patterns bring continued damage until the physical system is fully destructed.

Emotional blocks occur when people suppress strong feelings and emotions, storing them inside themselves. Such repressed feelings or emotions become destructive for energetic, physical, and psychological states.

It is not healthy to hide feelings and emotions inside us, but we often do this, afraid to express any feelings or emotions if they seem different from accepted norms.

Suppressing or hiding of any feelings or emotions or their absence at all can cause emotional blocks and prevent creative development or growth as well.

Spiritual blocks stem from a misunderstanding about our inner-selves, our spiritual connections with the universe, and our place as cosmic organisms in the universe. Spiritual blocks are the most complicated blocks.

A misunderstanding of our life purpose on the spiritual level leads to disconnection of our spiritual (cosmic) selves from the Divine Source.

When spiritually blocked, spiritual selves lose the power of uniting their bodies, minds, and souls into cosmic organisms. They are not able to maintain the health of our cosmic organisms or to carry their special mission upon this plane.

Spiritual blocks about our own 'true essence' lie within our souls. The soul records the emotional, mental, and communicational experiences and events in all our lives, and it imprints beliefs about these experiences, aspects of life and death, selves and others, and good and bad in our temporary physical bodies as well.

Releasing blocks

The main cause of many of our blocks or chronic unsatisfactory states and behaviors is the result of unhappy experiences imprinted on our subtle bodies in moments when we were highly receptive or suggestible, particularly in childhood.

These blocks may remain stable in us for a long time, for our whole lives, or even extend into future lives unless released or cleansed.

We need to choose positive thoughts, positive and confident feelings about ourselves, and meaningful relationships with our inner-selves and with others to avoid presence of constantly blocked energy in our bodies.

Our brain states and behaviors are not beyond our control. We are not powerless, and we are not victims of our beliefs, our past, our feelings or our environment.

We can change states intentionally, quickly, and at will. We can choose the healthiest way of handling feelings - releasing them or letting them go.

We can only benefit by discharging blocked or negative energy from our bodies through healing and cleansing our chakras on a regular basis.

Healthy chakras not only give us the possibility of increased self-awareness, emotional stability, mental clarity, and spiritual growth and maturity, but also the ability to heal ourselves and others.

In the next chapters, we will show how you can always be freed of negative or blocked energy in a new and innovative way so you can maintain your health and the health of your loved ones.

Chapter Eight

Etheric Body Image Healing

Only the principles directly relating to this chapter are restated below. This does not mean that the other principles do not apply here - they do.

The most important of these in order of priority are numbers 9, 5, 7, 8 and 10:

5. Principle of Contamination   Diseased energy is transmissible. It could be transmitted from a patient to another person or to a healer. The diseased energy of a subject could contaminate a person, an object, an animal, or a plant. Therefore, to avoid contamination, it is extremely important for healers to flick their hands when sweeping and after energizing, and to wash their hands and arms after cleansing and energizing. This also applies whilst healing at a distance.

7. Principle of Cleansing and Energizing   In healing, giving life force is not enough; it is also necessary to remove the diseased energy. Removing the diseased energy is called cleansing. Giving life force to a patient or an object is called energizing. The rate of healing can be accelerated by applying the principle of cleansing and energizing.

8. Principle of Radical Reaction   When energizing is done without removing the diseased energy, a crisis may take place in the form of temporary worsening of the condition. This is called radical reaction. This could be avoided or minimized by thorough cleansing.

9. Principle of Receptivity   A patient has to be receptive or at least neutral in order to receive the projected Pranic energy. Being relaxed also helps increase the degree of receptivity.

Without receptivity, the projected Pranic energy will not be absorbed, or only a minimal amount of it will be absorbed. Patients may not be receptive because: they are biased toward this type of healing, they do not like the healer personally, they do not want to get well, or they are in general not receptive about anything.

10. Principle of Stabilizing   Projected Pranic energy tends to leak out if it is not stabilized. Stabilization is done by energizing the treated part with light whitish-blue Prana, or covering the treated part with pastel blue Prana with a 'wiping' motion of the hand. Symptoms tend to recur if stabilization is not done.

Before we move on to the healing techniques, I would like you to spend five minutes on learning a further Pendulum Programme.

Hold your pendulum over a piece of white paper, mentally start the pendulum rotating in a anti-clockwise motion (Extract Mode) and tell your subconscious that this motion is removing Diseased Energy. Now start the pendulum moving clockwise (Input Mode) and instruct your subconscious that this motion is ushering In Positive Healing Energy.

Healing Technique 1 - Internet Healing Work

In the previous chapter, the first diagnostic method was given in a workshop by Joe Smith. Later in the workshop he went on to give a simple healing method which is given now in Joe's own words:

It is possible to do healing over the net with just the email address for an address. It seems the Angels have it all figured out. This is just further information to make the etheric connection.

When I get a request for 'healing' I do a body scan on the person with their permission and try to find the areas that need work. Sometimes they tell you what is the matter or suspect is the matter.

I did some work for a fellow that just knew he had prostate cancer. I could not find it and told him so. He went to several Doctors and found out that it was just enlarged and not cancer.

Now that you're at your computer and have the scan in front of you with the persons name on it, and any other history that you know, you're ready to go. If it is the prostate area as was the case of this fellow, you would ask your spirit guide or whom ever you ask or just your self to please send healing energy to this fellow to releive the problems he is having.

Hold your pendulum over the Body Scan. Your pendulum will start to spin in a clockwise motion and let it run till it is through. Now it might seem a stretch of the imagination to believe this but several on my healing list can tell you it did work for them.

Intent is the important part of all energy healing. It is similar to sending a thought form. The important thing is don't send your 'healing' to anyone unless they ask. If they are beyond asking, in a coma and a kinfolk asks you, that is fine.

On occasion you can send the help to the person and just park it next to them so they can use it if they need it. But if you sent it over the net you won't have this problem. No matter where the problem is you can figure out a way to send healing to that person.

Maybe that person is very low on self-esteem. In that case send him a basket of self worth, tell him/her that "He/she is valuable".

The problem does not have to be medical. Every body should know that some one loves them for what they are. So send them love - lots of it. To be able to help someone is a wonderful feeling.

The next time someone asks for help on the list take out your pendulum and get to work. You can say a prayer for them and that is good - but to use your pendulum to send the help multiplies that energy several times. You don't always have the subjects e-mail address, so just send it anyway. The Angels will find the right person.

I sent healing energy to Israel and it took 18 minutes one time and 24 hrs the next time. But it did get there.

'Healing' of the subject also depends on how they accept it.

One person I did a body scan on wasn't very receptive to the info I sent her. I told her that she needed to have her heart checked.

3 months later she did - and had a heart attack in the Doctors office. A 4-way by-pass was performed, so I sent my guide to help and asked him to get anybody else he could find to go along as she was going to need all the help she could get. It was nip and tuck.

A couple of days later he showed up back here at the house and I asked him how it was going. I got the feeling not to good. He went back down and she pulled through. She will never know how many Angels and guides were there pulling for her !

I did not do healing on her at that time as that was several years ago and I hadn't realized that I could do it.

Just think if we got a bunch of good Internet healers how much good we could do. If I had done healing on this lady she might not have had the close call. Maybe she needed to go through this.

Think about what I've told you, you all can do this if your heart is in the right place.   Joe

Thanks to you Joe. No doubt you have noticed that Joe did not remove any diseased energy before ushering in positive energy. If this worries you, all you need to do is hold the pendulum over the body scan and give the mental instruction to remove diseased energy. Then just wait until the anti-clockwise motion stops – it is now finished - you can now proceed.

Healing Technique 2 - Force Centre Therapy

In this method I use the interpretations of the Case Sheet/Body Scan given by David V. Tansley, and the Broadcast method given to me in a radiesthesia course by Gabrielle Blackburn.

Now we return to our case sheet from the previous chapter.

All forms of healing, irrespective of their origin, are directed towards one goal: the restoration of harmony and balance to the complexity of energies and matter that blend to form the subtle and physical anatomy of man.

The centre therapist differs from the orthodox Radionic practitioner in as much as he utilizes the subtle force systems of man as his point of departure for diagnosis and treatment.

The physical organic systems are of secondary importance, because they can only respond to and reflect the measure of harmony found in the para-physical bodies. As previously mentioned, unless the chakras are functioning in a reasonably balanced and harmonious manner, there can never be an expression of good health upon the physical level.

Recognizing this, the practitioner aims his treatment specifically at those chakras which exhibit a state of imbalance. By normalizing their action and removing blockages, he enables the energies which are seeking expression through the low-self to have free play, thus restoring health to the organism.

The prime healing agent used in centre therapy is colour, which can be supplied by several means. Colour has been found to be the most effective healing agent for this particular form of energy field healing.

Colour is related to the fourth ether whereon most disease patterns of an etheric nature are located, so perhaps for this reason it is most effective.

Case Sheet for: *Mary Whatshename*   Date: *2008 FEB 30*
Address: *211 Mangrove St, Banyan City, Coromondel*
Phone H: *(515)279-8313*   C: *(515)709-6623*   W: *n/a*
DOB: *1972 JUN 31*   Other Data: *mary@unintel.com*
Past Problems: *Sinus trouble, poor visibility, digestive disorders.*
          May have suffered abuse.
Present Conditions:
Vitality Index: *55*   Spleen Chakra: *25-O*

Chakra	+N-	Blockages	Astral	Mental
Crown	N			
Ajna	57 -	E		
Throat	40 +			
Heart	10 -			
Solar Plexus	N			
Sacral	N			
Root	N			

Miasms, Toxins, Physical Anomalies: *Syphilitic*

	ETHERIC	ASTRAL	MENTAL
Congestion			
Over Stimulation	Y		
Lack of Co-ord.			

The procedure for determining treatment is as follows, each question being posited mentally.

1. Which of these chakras exhibiting an imbalance require treatment ?
2. In what order should they be treated ?
3. Which colours are required to normalize each chakra ?

The above questions, based on our hypothetical case sheet reproduced above, would produce the following treatment programme.

Of the four dysfunctional chakras, only three require treatment in the order and with the colours indicated below.

- Violet   Spleen Chakra
- Orange   Heart Chakra
- Blue   Ajna Chakra

There is no indication that the throat chakra requires treatment, and in fact the normalization of the Ajna may directly influence this centre in the course of treatment.

The next factor to consider is the syphilitic miasm. The procedure is to ask which colour is required to disperse the miasm. Green was the indicated colour in this case.

All miasms are treated by way of the base chakra. The over-stimulation of the etheric body will also disappear with the removal of the miasm.

It can be taken as a rule that if the base chakra comes up for treatment because there is an imbalance in its action, then there is no need to select a colour to clear any miasms present.

Miasms disperse through the action of any colour placed into the base chakra. On the other hand if the base does not require treatment, then it will be necessary to find a colour to treat the miasm by way of that centre.

Every individual has a different caliber of physical and etheric body. Chakras are vibrating at different speeds, and disease patterns are of an individual nature too.

For this reason colours will vary for each patient; one may need green to clear a blockage in a chakra, whereas another patient with what appears to be an identical condition, needs violet or yellow.

Radionic Broadcasting

Let us now turn to the mysterious art and science of broadcasting in radiesthetic terms. It is not as yet possible to explain this phenomenon scientifically; however, it is possible to send a broadcast and let the results speak for themselves. How this works may not be clear, but that does not alter the beneficial results that are attained and attested to by empirical experience.

A broadcast uses actual physical properties and sends the essence of a colour to the primary witness: yourself or another person. Distance is no hindrance. The broadcast affects the etheric body and the vital energy field of the individual. It then enters the physical body in the same way that all light, colour and vital energy does.

Broadcasting is one of the most powerful and exciting means of restoring balance in the body, one that affects not only the physical but also the mental emotional levels. A broadcast can restore equilibrium in a way that few other methods are able to do.

A broadcast must be very carefully prepared so that all the components are working together. It must be sent out in perfect harmony to be effective and bring order to the recipient. Since broadcasting is a very powerful tool, approach it with the greatest respect.

When considering a broadcast, the very first thing to check is to see whether or not you should do it at all. You can send a broadcast either for a specific condition or as a general energy boost.

Use your witnesses (Body Scan with details) and keep in mind what you are doing for a condition, then simply ask your pendulum if you should send a 'Broadcast' . If you get a positive reply, you can proceed. Your Case Sheet or Body Scan Chart will be used as a primary 'Witness'.

How Long To Broadcast

Then the next factor you must determine is how long the broadcast should last. For instance, you can use a 'time chart' showing the possible treatment time, and your pendulum will point to the correct time.

This is very essential because too long a broadcast time would have the same result as over-dosing. Enter the time on your broadcast chart.

Repeating the Broadcast

The last thing you must check is whether or not to repeat the same broadcast again that same day. If not, then you can check the results and the patient's condition the following day by going over the broadcast chart of the day before. See if a broadcast should be repeated exactly, or if a change is indicated with regard to any one of the components on it.

Having a carefully made-up chart in the first place makes it so much easier to keep a check on a condition from then on. If no change is indicated, you need not go through the whole procedure again.

You can understand now how easy it is to forget a detail. It is essential for one to be a responsible pendulist, so keep a precise record for this very reason.

Some broadcasts are so highly effective the first time that the components will change to the second and third phase after just one broadcast each. Consequently only three broadcasts may be necessary to get the desired result. However, it is much more likely that each one will have to be repeated (depending on the gravity of the situation) before a change is indicated.

By checking the reading of the condition with which you are working each day, you will note the amount of change. The effects of a broadcast will take some time to enter and affect the physical body, so you cannot expect to get an accurate reading immediately after sending one out.

However, often a fever will go down, or a pain will subside or disappear altogether, during or soon after a broadcast, thus indicating that you are on the right track.

How To Send A Broadcast

You are now ready to set up an actual broadcast. First place the primary witness (suitably identified Anatomy Chart, Body Scan or Case Sheet) you have chosen on a table made of a neutral material such as wood, glass, or plastic, with the head or top of the anatomy chart to the North.

Next you will need the colour specified. I use 6-inch-square 'Cathedral Glass' plates; I have two of each colour for use in a broadcast.

Glass has a polarity which must be aligned with the North-South magnetic field of the earth. You can determine this polarity in the glass plate by placing it on the table and holding the pendulum over it.

A YES swing will show that it is properly aligned with the north-south line. If rotated it will show a negative reading, if rotated twice a positive reading, and if rotated three times a negative reading again.

By the positive swing you can easily establish which way the polarity runs from one edge to the opposite edge. This is the right way to place it on the witness.

It will be helpful to store the glass in such a manner that you need not check its polarity every time; you can do this by laying all the glass plates in the same direction, or by standing them all up the same way.

Next place an 8 oz. glass or jar containing pure water on the colour plate, and put an ordinary 6 inch square piece of plate glass on top of this container. Now put a similar size glass container almost full of distilled water on top of that. I use distilled water to avoid any excess minerals; however, if it is not available it is not absolutely imperative. Other water, as pure or well-filtered as possible, can be substituted.

Water radiates energy. Its beneficial effects are felt whenever you are near an ocean, a lake, or a river. The water will help radiate the energy from the broadcast set-up to the person on the receiving end. Now place the matching colour plate of glass on top of the water container.

The final item you need is a large horseshoe magnet. I use a 16oz. magnet which has a 50-lb. pull. A 10 or 12 oz. magnet will probably do as well.

Find the positive pole by a positive swing over one end; the other end will be a negative swing. Place the magnet with the positive end to the North on top of the second coloured glass plate. The opposite, negative end will point to the south.

Take a moment now to check to see if you have gotten everything correct by asking for a positive swing from the pendulum.

Should it show a negative swing, you may have forgotten something; perhaps you forgot to line up one of the three glass plates or to align the magnet properly in a north-south direction; if so, you will have to go back and correct this, or the broadcast will not work.

As soon as the magnet is placed on top, the broadcast starts.

<u>Testing the Broadcast Energy</u>

As soon as you have completed the entire broadcast set-up, the pendulum will show you the energy radiation being sent out from it, if you test it all around the set-up.

Now set a timer for the correct time needed for the broadcast and let it go. Remove the magnet as soon as the timer rings; this will stop the broadcast.

Your pendulum will show you some interesting things.

First, just before the right amount of time has elapsed, the pendulum will start swinging from the positive YES swing to neutral, then go negative, back again to positive, and then stop completely.

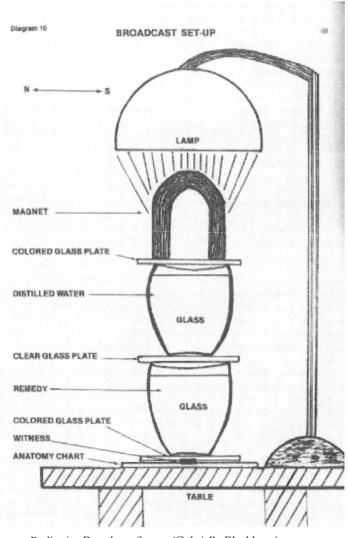

Radionics Broadcast Setup. (Gabrielle Blackburn)

The pendulum is indicating that the broadcast is completed ! Observe this if you like; you will find the way the pendulum seemingly wants to talk to you fascinating !

<u>Dismantling a Broadcast</u>

When you dismantle a broadcast set-up, you will find that the polarity in the glass plates is almost zero and you will get very little rotation from the pendulum.

This must be corrected, either by washing the plates in cold water, which is a nuisance, merely by clinking them gently together, or by scraping one over the other - the sound will restore their resonance.

Do this before you put them away so that they are ready for use the next time you need them. You need not check this out each time: after once testing this for yourself, just take it for granted, and get in the habit of restoring the resonance by clinking them.

This alone will show you that something has happened during the broadcast, since they will usually be run down like an old battery.

<u>A New Dimension</u>

I have developed some additions to the original broadcasting procedure, as a result of my own research. My dissatisfaction with certain aspects and limitations led me to do intensive psychic research to develop new methods. These additions include the use of light as a source of energy.

I have found that the strength and quality of light plays an important part in the energy pattern transmitted in the broadcast. After all, spiritual healing is always done in what is known as the 'White Light'. My investigations resulted in my adding this fine quality of light, which I was already so familiar with in my other healing work.

When I first started working with broadcasting, I found that glands were very difficult to affect. By psychic investigations of this particular problem, I worked out a method of using light on the glandular system and obtaining much better results with all types of conditions.

I found that placing a 100-watt lamp over the broadcast set-up intensified the entire broadcast, and very positive results were obtained. It must be at least a 100-watt lamp to have the proper effect. Therefore, always check by asking whether 'Light' should be added to a broadcast.

The White-Light Broadcast

In addition to the above use of light, when broadcasting to a chakra, I have found it to be a tremendous improvement to use white stained-glass plates and white light, instead of coloured plates. This has proven to be the most efficient broadcast for improving the functions of the glands and other systems in the body.

In addition, this type of 'White-Light Broadcast' is highly affective in correcting shock and emotional imbalance.

Necessity of Using the Pendulum Wisely

Let me once again stress caution and careful adherence to the detailed procedures described here. Careless, half-hearted efforts in this most subtle and vital form of healing will not only fall short of beneficial results, but could be harmful.

It is important to work always with the greatest integrity for the benefit of yourself or another.

No license is needed for this type of healing, but one should use all of this information, with its inherent potential, wisely so as to prove the value of pendulistic work and encourage its acceptance by others.

In the above method as prescribed by Gabrielle Blackburn there is one thing that makes me a little uneasy. In both David's and Gabrielle's broadcasting methods (David's not mentioned here), they use either coloured celluloid or glass plates respectively to provide the required colour to the witness during broadcasting.

I feel that the application of colour rays may be too general. There is a need to direct the colour to a specific target and only that target.

For instance, if a chakra has a need for a certain colour then that chakra alone should receive that colour. Other chakras or bodies may be adversely affected by that colour !

There is a way to be more specific with colour application: the use of Crystal Cards - or better still Touchstones - is highly recommended. Full descriptions of these and their usage are given in the next chapter.

Healing Technique 3 - Pranic Healing

I consider Pranic Healing as taught by Master Choa Kok Sui as being the most powerful and effective form of energy field healing that I know. I hold this view even though I am a Master in Reiki, Chios, Focal Touch Healing, magnified healing and have qualifications in other energy field healing modalities.

There are four basic procedures in Pranic healing which are also of importance in any form of energy healing including distant healing:

- Scanning -- covered in earlier chapters.
- Cleansing.
- Energizing.
- Stabilizing.

Cleansing is absolutely essential as the stale, dirty and negative energy must be removed first. As Master Choa Kok Sui says: *"If you had half a cup of cold stale coffee left and you wanted a top-up, you would not pour the fresh coffee on top of the stale coffee. No, you would remove the cold coffee first"*.

A second example would be: a sponge full of dirty water would be squeezed out first before attempting to take in clean water.

The Pranic healing advanced technique for localized cleansing is quite simple. The left hand (receiving hand) is held about three inches away from a dysfunctional chakra, or body part, with the palm facing the body.

The hand is rotated in an anti-clockwise motion for five revolutions whilst, at the same time, moving the hand away from the patients body. You are in fact drawing an anti-clockwise spiral away from the chakra or body part.

The fingers are then flicked to remove the diseased energy into the visualized waste disposal unit. This cleansing action is repeated at least ten times (fifty rotations) or until you 'feel' that the cleansing is done. In a majority of cases, cleansing alone can effect a cure - or at least a big improvement.

Energizing the chakra or body part with Prana (life force energy) after cleansing is a similar technique. This time, the right hand (giving hand) is used. The left arm is placed at the side and then bent at the elbow so that the forearm is parallel to the ground, with the palm of the left hand facing upward.

The right hand is placed in front of the chakra or body part with the palm facing the body. The hand is then rotated clockwise for five revolutions. This is repeated ten times (fifty rotations). The chakra or body part is now energized.

Stabilizing is achieved by using a painting motion over the chakra or body part whilst visualizing a pale blue colour. In other words, paint the chakra or body part pale blue.

The above three actions are written for 'hands on' energy healing. We are now going to use the same techniques to heal at a distance.

The human body form chart we will be using is derived from the chart shown on the following page. It is assumed that this is a unisex chart and will be used for both female and male but without the chakra names.

We know from previous chapters that it is easy to use such a chart/ drawing for diagnostic purposes, just ask YES/NO questions and get answers or hold the pendulum over each chakra and interpret its motion.

An Amazing New Technique

Is it possible, also, to use the chart/drawing as a healing tool ?

The answer to this question is a definite YES. It was used in the first healing technique of Joe Smith, and in the second technique it was part of the broadcasting method.

It will now be used in a very much more imaginative way which will make the hair stand up on the back of your neck.

For this technique we will follow the Pranic Healing protocol, viz. Scanning, Cleansing, Energizing and Stabilizing. The hypothetical Case Sheet used earlier will be used again in this section. Scanning was covered in the last chapter on diagnosis and will not be gone into further here.

You will recall that our hypothetical case has a low Vitality Index, dysfunctional Spleen chakra, Ajna chakra, Throat chakra, Heart chakra, Syphilitic miasm and an overstimulated etheric body.

The next item to prepare is our Body Scan/Drawing sheet.

The Etheric Link Identification details must be written on top of this sheet. I use an letter/A4 size sheet to help me with my eyesight deficiency but smaller is just as good.

To strengthen the etheric link, bring the person into your awareness and carefully fit them into the outline drawing on the table in front of you. Once this is done, there is no need for you to dwell on the image or visualization as the etheric information is instantly absorbed by the drawing.

This information is not dynamic. In other words it only reflects the condition of the person at the time the visualization fixing was done.

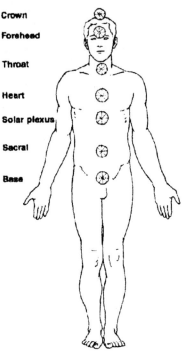

Human Body Form Chart.

Crown
Forehead
Throat
Heart
Solar plexus
Sacral
Base

<u>Cleansing</u> is the next procedure to be carried out. This is achieved by drawing out spirally the diseased, negative and stale energy. At the end of the spiral withdrawal the hand would be raised slightly and then vigorously flicked earthwards to throw off the bad energy into the visualized bio-plasmic waste disposal unit.

Cleansing Spirals

Personal Data not shown.

At a distance, the same thing is achieved by drawing, in pencil, an anti-clockwise spiral from the centre of the chakra or body part outwards.

When the spiral is outside the extremities of the drawn body, turn the drawn line upwards, then abruptly downwards for a short line, then terminate the spiral and line with an arrow pointing downward. If you wish, you may draw a 'U' shape under each arrow head to simulate the waste disposal unit.

If you recall, only three of the four dysfunctional chakras (Spleen, Heart and Ajna), needed treatment and in the order printed. The cleansing spirals are drawn as shown in the order given.

After drawing the cleansing spirals, wait for a few minutes and then try the pendulum test over each treated chakra. You will notice an improvement in the swing: you may even have normally functional chakras after just the cleansing procedure.

If there is no improvement in a chakra, hold the pendulum over the chakra and physically make it rotate clockwise (front view) for a few moments. Now try the pendulum test again.

Energizing is the next step. As in the 'hands on' method, we are going to usher in Prana in a clockwise spiral motion into each chakra or body part that needs treatment.

The same body scan/drawing sheet that we used for cleansing will be used again for energizing.

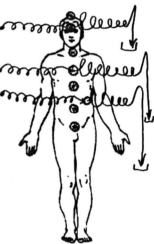

On the opposite side of the body to the drawn cleansing spiral, draw a largish dot and in the same motion, draw a clockwise spiral towards the chakra or body part to be treated.

Terminate the spiral with an arrow head in the centre of the chakra or body part. Draw spirals in the same order as for the cleansing treatment.

Note that the personal etheric information should be placed on these diagrams - and all that you use !

Fig 12 - Energizing Spirals
Personal Data not shown.

There are two items remaining untreated on the Case Sheet, viz. the syphilitic miasm and the over-stimulation of the etheric body. The over-stimulation of the etheric body will disappear when the miasm is treated successfully.

To treat the miasm we need to apply the colour Green to the Root chakra. This can be achieved with moderate success by drawing an Energizing spiral into the Root chakra using a green crayon or pencil.

The same procedure can be used to apply the appropriate colours to the Spleen, Ajna and Heart chakras. When the spirals are finished, the chakra circle, and a little outside the circle, can be filled in with the spiral colour, eg. violet in the case of the spleen chakra etc.

However, colours should not be over-used in drawings because of the possibility of over-energizing and, thus, over-stimulating. The situation should be continually monitored using the pendulum.

Returning to the hypothetical Case Sheet for a moment, you will find it extremely useful to compare the initial numerical readings for Vitality Index (55) and the percentage dysfunction numbers for the chakras, with readings taken after treatment.

This is a good way to monitor your treatment success !

Stabilizing is the final action which completes the treatment for this session. Scanning; finding problems, cleansing; removing diseased energy and energizing; ushering in life force energy (Prana), could all be to no avail without Stabilizing.

The diseased energy which was removed could find it's way back in again. The positive energy (Prana) ushered in could leak out again.

If this was a 'hands on' session, you would close by visualizing using one or both your hands to 'paint' over the treated parts with Pale Blue light. This is all that is required to stabilize the treated parts.

In distant work the same is achieved in one of two ways.

1). Take the sheet that you have been using with all it's details, spirals etc and draw an egg shape all around the drawing in a pale blue colour. You can also draw a few lines in the same colour putting a thatch like fill in of the egg shape.

2). If you have a small torch handy, you can fit a pale blue colour filter over the glass to give a pale blue light. This should then be passed over the drawing, in a painting motion, for a few minutes.

Using a Pendulum Instead of Drawing Spirals

Personally I prefer to use the pendulum in Cleansing, Energizing and Stabilizing instead of drawing Output, Input, and Painting procedures as above. The method of doing this is explained in the next section of this book.

Etheric Body Image Healing

A unique opportunity is offered to heal people effectively without their direct participation in the process of healing, and at any distance. Distance in this method has no meaning; there is no distance for energy.

This method of Etheric Body Image Chakra Healing is possible because the energetic matrix possesses an energetic connection with an individual to be healed. This matrix reflects his or her energetic information and physical state at the time of the assessment and healing.

This is how this method of energetic healing differs from others, it allows the healer to work with an individual at any distance and in an expansive aspect of the human energy field that is not possible with other methods.

With this method's help, it is possible to positively influence and maintain people's physical conditions and health on a regular basis, and even prevent any physical illness or heal already existed imbalances without touching or giving any medicine. You can easily work in all the areas of bio-energy system to bring balance.

You can work on all chakras, major and minor, on the physical body or out-of-body, and on all subtle bodies as well. You can work on any physical organs, body parts, and body systems. You can relieve negative stress, negative thinking, and depression or any emotional discomfort.

You can relieve any mental disturbance or condition, bringing peace of mind and optimal mental health.

This method of chakra healing is also safer than many other healing methods. A chakra healer in direct contact with a healee has to be physically, emotionally and energetically healthy, and his or her aura must be thoroughly cleansed of energetic negative information and in balance.

However, many healers can heal themselves very rarely, if at all. Healers themselves may be enervated, stressed, or have high blood pressure or any number of imbalances in their own energetic systems or physical bodies, which they may pass with their energy to the healee.

In the method of Etheric Body Image Chakra Healing, everyone has a possibility to heal themselves and maintain his or her energetic and physical health before helping others.

Extracting Bio-negative Energy - Cleansing

In Pranic healing, bio-negative energy is always drawn away from chakras, organs or body parts by an anti-clockwise motion of the extracting hand.

When closed, dysfunctional or blocked chakras, are discovered the primary task is to cleanse them of everything that prevents healthy functioning and let them function normally.

In Pranic, bio-energy, and chakra healing, the most important thing is removal of weak, ill, stale, congested, or blocked energy from chakras, organs, body parts and subtle bodies before energizing by bringing in new energy.

When people are less spiritually developed, they tend to bring more energy in than they give out. During illness, they may acquire energy from more energetic or spiritually developed people.

These people are called 'energetic vampires'. They accumulate vital energy with their negative energy, and still have imbalances and blocks. Vital energy, when added to negative, stale, and stagnant energy, loses its value. Prana is only of vital strength for humans when it enters clean, functional chakras and subtle bodies developed in their growth.

Healing by energy healing brings energetic health when vital energy is brought into an already cleansed and balanced bio-system.

People who are not very developed in their spiritual growth may also be open to negative forces. Negative energy or negative information comes into their chakras, causing them to feel even worse than they do or to act in even more negative ways.

Negative forces cause energy damage, imbalance, and dysfunction on the energetic level. On the physical level, bio-negativity causes chronic illnesses and permanent weakness. On the emotional level, people become unstable emotionally, unexpressive, secluded, unfortunate, or aggressive and malicious.

On the other hand, evolved and spiritually developed people have more energy flowing out of their energy fields than flowing in. They cleanse and balance their energy, and then radiate it out.

People with high energy have immensely coloured auras or even over-balanced (whitish) auras. When people feel peaceful and joyful, their energy flows out, radiating from their bodies and opening their chakras.

As long as the energy flows or spirals away from the body, people exist at a refined emotional and energetic level. If the energy spirals back into the body, it can cause a negative or stressful reaction.

When chakras are cleansed, opened and functional, they bring as much energy to the bio-energy system as it needs and filter the energy appropriately for the body's use.

Any pain or tension will indicate that something is going wrong with the energy flow somewhere in the body. These areas of energetic 'tension' or congestion will affect chakras, causing them to close, and will show an imbalance in the energetic state.

Energy in blocked areas needs to release. If negative, stale, or stagnant energy is not released, we may feel depressed and have low energy. In our stressful times, we need to perform chakra cleansing periodically. When we go with it, work with it on an everyday basis, and allow it to continue the energetic cleansing, it will not be long until we are feeling very good again.

For chakra cleansing, the method of energetic anti-clockwise spirals is used. With the spirals' help, we draw out any bio-negative energy away from the chakras, body parts and organs, cleanse them, and normalize their healthy energetic regime.

There are many ways of extracting bio-negative energy from dysfunctional chakras, organs and body parts, but in all of them an anti-clockwise motion is implied. I will only cover one here.

This is my preferred method because the cleansing and energizing are performed sequentially in the same operation. If any dysfunctional chakras, organs or body parts are found during the assessments, these can be noted in order to return to them during the healing mode, or the healing can be carried out directly after the extracting mode.

Let's say we have found a dysfunctional chakra. I would now use my pendulum in healing mode. I would have previously programmed my pendulum as follows for the healing mode:

1). I would have instructed the pendulum to rotate over the faulty chakra, organ or body part area in an anti-clockwise movement to extract the 'not good' energy and when it had finished this part, to give me a YES signal or stop.

2). On completion, the pendulum would have been instructed to rotate in a clockwise movement to put in 'good' energy into (Energies) the area. On completion, the pendulum would have been instructed to give a YES signal (or stop) to show that this area had been healed. You can then move on to the next area of the body to be assessed and healed.

Stabilizing the Projected Prana

One of the potential problems in Pranic healing is the instability of the projected Prana. The projected Prana tends to gradually leak out, causing the possible recurrence of the illness.

This potential problem can be overcome by thoroughly cleansing or sweeping the part to be treated, and by stabilizing the projected Prana.

The projected Prana can be stabilized as follows:

After energizing, 'paint' the treated part with light blue for about ten seconds. This is done by rotating the pendulum over the part or chakra; simply say mentally, *"light blue, light blue, light blue ..."* while 'painting' the treated part or chakra or by placing your awareness on your Throat chakra while 'painting' the treated part or chakra.

When I do the stabilizing technique, I hold my pendulum over the centre of the human form image, approximately over the Solar Plexus chakra.

I then rotate the pendulum clockwise in ever increasing circles until the whole body image is enclosed in the circle. This is performed whilst intending the whole body image being covered in the light blue colour.

You can perform this experiment to prove to yourself the validity of these principles and techniques:

1. Using the pendulum in 'energizing' mode, project 'white' Prana onto the top of a table for about one minute. Simultaneously visualize and form it into a ball about the size of a tennis ball, without willing it to remain. This is the first Pranic ball.

2. Project, visualize and form another Pranic ball, blue in colour, for about one minute, without willing it to remain. This is the second Pranic ball.

3. Project and form another Pranic ball, white in colour, for about one minute, and will or mentally instruct the Pranic ball to remain for an hour. This is the third Pranic ball. Make sure the locations of these balls are properly marked.

4. Scan the three Pranic balls with your pendulum, to make sure they are properly formed.

5. Wait for about 20 minutes and scan the three Pranic balls again.

You may find that the first Pranic ball has already gone, or greatly reduced in size, while the second and third Pranic balls are still quite intact - the blue colour gives stability.

Do try this experiment. It is simple and easy to do.

<u>Releasing the Projected Pranic Energy</u>

A healer will notice that it is somewhat easier to be detached when healing strangers, than when healing one's own children, relatives or close friends. This is due to the tendency of the healer to be 'over-concerned' or too anxious with the result, because of the emotional attachment to the patient - even while healing at a distance.

Clairvoyantly, this attachment is seen as an etheric or energy cord (cord of light), linking the healer to the patient. Because of this cord, there is a tendency that the projected Prana may return to the healer; therefore, the patient may get well slowly instead of rapidly.

To avoid this, the healer should visualize himself cutting the etheric cord or 'cord of light' with an imaginary pair of scissors or knife.

Also, it is better not to think about the patient immediately after the treatment, because the etheric link might be re-established.

Furthermore, if the patient is very depleted, there is a possibility for the healer to unknowingly continue energizing the patient, even long after the treatment, which, in the long run, will cause the healer to be depleted.

Should this happen, the healer must calmly visualize himself cutting the etheric cord again.

Under normal circumstances, when the healer is calm and detached (but not indifferent to the patient), the projected Pranic energy is released, and the etheric cord is automatically cut.

When you assess chakras, body parts, and organs with the pendulum after healing, and you observe that the particular chakra or part starts working but still feebly, hold the pendulum over the chakra or part and spin the pendulum in clockwise circle movements, intentionally to help the energy flow.

This will help the chakra, organ, or body part to work once it starts to be cleansed of bio-negative energy. You may use this technique after extracting (cleansing) bad energy from all chakras, organs or body parts with the pendulum.

You should not wait until you and your family do not feel well !

Do cleansing, energizing and stabilizing for yourself and your family regularly in order to keep an energetic balance, keep your chakras opened and functioning perfectly, and to fill organisms with vital energy.

When chakras are opened and functional, they let in vital energy and regulate the energy flow for optimal energetic, physical, mental and emotional health and balance.

Remember, chakras are interrelated. If the root chakra is not functioning well, cleanse it with the brow chakra together - and vice versa. The sacral chakra can be cleansed with the throat chakra, and the solar plexus chakra with the heart chakra.

Positive energetic information may be ushered with your mental affirmative help through the third eye chakra on the copy of the person's etheric image.

Energetic Chakra System Defence

This system of energetic defence will prolong the refined state of the chakras, organs and body parts and defend the cleansed system from entry of any negative information as long as possible.

Write the energetic identification on the top of your human body form sheet. Intentionally rotate your pendulum in a clockwise motion over each chakra in turn. Instruct the pendulum to rotate while you visualize colours in order of where the chakras belong.

Thus, red is used for the root chakra; orange - the sacral chakra; yellow - the solar plexus chakra; green - the heart chakra; blue - the throat chakra; indigo - the brow chakra; violet - the crown chakra.

Instruct the pendulum to stop rotating over each chakra when it has received sufficient energy, and then move on to the next chakra.

After this, you may hold the pendulum over the centre of your body form sheet as previous. This time as you rotate the pendulum clockwise in increasing diameter circles visualize each circle being a different colour, starting at Red, Orange, Yellow, Green, Blue, Indigo and Violet. You now have a rainbow around your image.

Now you have the energetic chakra defense to deflect negativity from yourself or others. Keep this image for as long as you need.

You should renew this image once a month for any accumulation of bio-negative information; this will prevent the possibility of it entering the chakra system again. You may throw the image away, or burn it and replace it with a new one.

It is recommended that you perform the chakra assessment for yourself and your relatives on an everyday basis (or at least on a weekly basis) to find out what chakras have become closed or dysfunctional due to stress, any influencing factors, or others' energetic information.

When you feel indifference in your good 'form' or appearance, a low energetic state, apathy, or become tired easily, you should assess your chakras. If you discover that your chakras may be dysfunctional, fix them first with pendulistic spirals to remove negative information, then usher in healing information if needed.

You may perform all these procedures for yourself, your children, family members, or even your pets. Soon you will find that you can start living a new, fulfilling life, and have perfect relationships and communication. You will be able to prevent illnesses, normalize them if you have them already, and always control and maintain your physical, psychic, emotional and energetic health.

Specific Uses of the Etheric Body Image Healing

Withdrawal of Bio-Negative Energy or Information

In order to maintain energetic, spiritual, emotional, and physical health you must perform the cleansing of all chakras on both the front and back etheric body images periodically.

Pains and Bruises

To relieve any pain or bruise, you need to extract (cleanse) negative signals out of chakras and places of pain. If the pendulum describes any movements other than circular, clockwise movements, the energetic signal is negative.

There are many specific uses of the Etheric Body Image Healing. For example, an ache in the knees may occur due to imbalance in the kidneys. In this case, we need to energetically check the kidneys and knees.

Place a 'conditional chakra' (an 'imaginary chakra' drawn to get enhanced information) on the kidney of the etheric body image, and assess the energetic state with the pendulum.

If you perceive any negative signal from the kidney (uneven or counter-clockwise pendulum movement), draw the negative energy from the leg, with the pendulum.

After this, assess the troubled knee. If it shows any negative signal, draw a chakra on the knee and lead out weak energy from it as usual.

If there is pain in the elbow, assess the elbow and the throat chakra as well. Assessing the elbows in the place of pain, you will perceive a negative signal. Perform the extracting of negative energy from the elbow and the throat chakra.

To heal bruises on the hands or legs, it is enough to find the place of pain with the pendulum assessment, describe this spot on the image with a conditional chakra, and use the technique of withdrawal negative energy from the drawn chakra.

High Blood Pressure

To determine high blood pressure, assess the spinal column.

Any tension and heaviness in the pendulum movement over the spinal column on the etheric body image will indicate high blood pressure. To lower high blood pressure, prepare an 'etheric body image' with the person's energetic information on it, mentioning 'on the back'.

Extract the high blood pressure, beginning from the brow chakra through all chakras to the root chakra. On the front, perform the withdrawal of negative energy from all chakras also.

Low Blood Pressure

To relieve low blood pressure, it is necessary to extract negative energy on the back of the etheric image, starting from the root chakra up to the third eye chakra. On the front image, perform the withdrawal of energy from all chakras .

Eye Tension

Assess the energetic state of the eyes by putting conditional chakras in the location of the eyes on the etheric image.

An eye which is disturbed will show energetic tension. Draw negative energy from the eyes relieving tension on the front of image. On the back, withdraw negative energy from all chakras with counter-clockwise movements of the pendulum.

Carpal Tunnel Syndrome or Overworked Hands

Withdraw weak energy from the throat chakra. Describe the hands with conditional chakras and draw the negativity from the hands as well.

Ear Problems and Colds

Withdraw congested energy from the ears on the image and from the throat chakra.

Legs

You can 'cleanse' legs in a case of painful condition and energetic disturbance along with the throat chakra.

Breast Feeding Problems

Check each breast with the pendulum. Draw the corresponding conditional chakras for the breasts, then draw the negative energy from the weakened breast out as usual.

Together with the breasts, you need to cleanse the root chakra, the sacral chakra, and the heart chakra on the front. On the back, lead the negative energy out from the same chakras.

Lower Back Pain

To relieve lower back pain, it is necessary to cleanse the lower three chakras on both the front and back etheric images.

Shoulders (Nerve Inflammation, Calcium Deposits)

Cleanse bio-negative energy out from the conditional chakras drawn on the shoulders of the etheric body image.

Withdraw bio-negative energy from the solar plexus and heart chakra on both the front and back etheric images.

Headache

To relieve headache, withdraw negative energy from the brow chakra and root chakra on the front and back images, or from all chakras if needed.

Teeth or Mouth

Describe the mouth with a conditional chakra, and withdraw energy out from the mouth chakra and the throat chakra. On the back, 'cleanse' the brow chakra.

Toothache

To relieve toothache, draw the corresponding chakra in the area of pain. Extract negative energy in the usual way. Cleanse the throat chakra and root chakra as well. Repeat the procedure for the back etheric body image.

Nose, Sinuses

Draw the corresponding chakra for the nose. Perform the extracting of negative energy away from the nose, the throat chakra, and the root chakra for the 'on the front' image and from the brow chakra, throat and root chakra for the 'on the back' image.

Throat

Cleanse the sacral chakra and the throat chakra on the etheric image.

Flu, Common Cold and Weakness

Withdraw bio-negative or weak energy from all chakras and both sides of the etheric images (front and back).

Liver or Intestines

When we observe energetic imbalance while assessing organs (liver, intestines), we place a chakra on the liver or intestines, and lead bio-negative energy out of the conditional chakra with the pendulum.

Kidneys, Bladder

In a case of energetic imbalance in the kidneys and/or bladder, draw the conditional chakras on the kidneys and the bladder. Withdraw bio-negative energy from the kidneys and bladder with the pendulum as usual.

Lungs

Draw conditional chakras on both lungs. Extract negative energy from the drawn lung's chakras with the pendulum in the usual way.

Nervous Illnesses, Insomnia

Cleanse all chakras with the pendulum for the front and back etheric body images.

Usher healing information to the brow chakra on the separately drawn etheric body images, whereas from the other side withdraw any left negative energy or information from the brow chakra that prevents healing.

Spinal column

The condition of the spinal column is very important for the whole energetic system and general physical health. All chakras and subtle bodies link to the spinal column. All chakras divide the spinal column into areas that belong to each chakra:

- the coccyx vertebral region covers the root chakra;
- the sacral vertebral region covers the sacral chakra;
- the lumbar vertebral region covers the solar plexus chakra;
- the thoracic vertebral region covers the heart chakra and the throat chakra;
- the cervical vertebral region covers the brow chakra.

Each vertebra reflects the same chakra characteristics as its particular chakra.

The interconnection between all chakras and the cosmos depends on the possibility of energy flowing freely through the spinal column. Spirit and matter are connected and interrelated with the help of the spine.

The vertebral column supports and unites the physical body and the whole energetic system as well; so perfect spinal condition promotes both energetic and physical healing.

On the physical level, there are nerves passing through each vertebra, connecting all organs. Each vertebra is responsible for a particular organ's health.

When a nerve is compressed by a vertebra, the correlated organ is affected as well. Through the vertebras, organs are 'connected' to the correlated chakras and each other.

On the emotional level, the condition of each vertebra affects an emotional state, and in turn emotional state can affect vertebras.

Working on a healee's spine with bio-energy of the hands, healers can determine which organs have energetic and physical imbalances by way of perceived energetic signals.

Every vertebra signals in a negative way if there is an imbalance in the particular organ correlated to this vertebra.

Healers can place an 'activated' energetic finger of one hand on the organ, and use a finger from the other hand to find the correlating vertebra, searching for an energetic signal of correlation between the correct vertebra and the organ. Then, both the organ and this vertebra can be healed.

In the case of etheric body image healing, nevertheless, we assess the vertebral column independently, concentrating on each vertebral area or specific chakra vertebral region in addition to chakra assessment to find out even subtle imbalances in the etheric and physical bodies.

Draw the ethereal image of the spinal column along with the person's energetic information. With the pendulum, assess each vertebra, or at least the chakric area or each vertebral region on the spinal column of the etheric image, to find the vertebras or vertebral regions which signal with negativity.

If the healee complains about a specific area of the spinal column, you will find an energetic imbalance in that area (lower, middle, or upper spine).

Cleanse the chakras on the 'back' image as usual. Work with all lower chakras on the image to withdraw weak energy, or all middle chakras or all upper chakras when pain exists in a particular area of the spine.

Moreover, as with lower chakric dimensions, often spiritual dimensions are involved. If there is imbalance in the lower chakra, chakric area, or vertebral area, you need to check and heal its upper counterpart (chakra, chakric area, or vertebral area) on the top of the spinal column as well in order to achieve the balance in the energetic system.

In addition to chakra cleansing, if you find imbalance on any vertebra or vertebral region imbalance on the 'back' etheric image, draw a conditional chakra in that place and withdraw blocked energy from this troubled area.

This procedure will be especially helpful in freeing physical and emotional blocks which easily pull us out of energetic equilibrium, or have already affected the spine on the physical level.

Techniques from Sahaja Yoga

The Ice Pack

A quick tip for those who may be finding difficulty in maintaining a period of thoughtlessness in their meditations. Very often unbidden thoughts are the result of an overactive liver (a 'hot' liver in Sahaja terms).

This is easily remedied by placing an ice pack or other cold pack on the liver on the right side of your body during the meditation. You will find this amazingly effective.

Raising Kundalini

It is our Kundalini energy rising up the spine which takes our attention higher into the state of thoughtless awareness. This exercise helps to strengthen, steady and establish the attention in the highest energy centre, the Sahasrara Chakra.

Figure A

Figure B

Figure C

Figure D

Raising the **Kundalini**

At the beginning and end of meditation it is helpful to raise your own Kundalini. Begin with the left hand at the front at the level of the abdomen; palm facing towards the body. While rotating the right hand around the left hand, move the left hand up the front of the body and over the head.

Use this movement three times, and on the third time tie three knots over the top of your head.

Placing a Bandhan

A simple exercise for protecting your subtle body and for preserving the state of meditation is to put on a bandhan. This exercise can be done before and after meditation.

Place the left hand at your side at the level of the waist with the fingers pointing towards the photograph of Sri Mataji (see Appx 4).

Using the right hand, describe an arc, starting at the level of the left hip, going over the head, down to the right hip and back again.

This movement should be done seven times.

This exercise should be done after raising the Kundalini at the start and end of meditation.

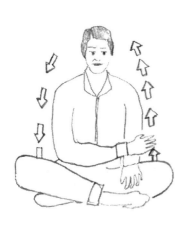

Figure A

Figure B

Putting on a Bandhan

Working on yourself to clear a chakra

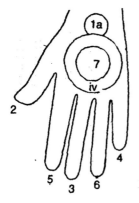

Chakra Points
On Hands.

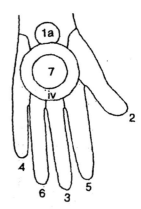

It is possible to clear any obstruction in one's own chakras as evidenced by a tingling or heat in a corresponding finger. This is done by moving the hand in a clockwise motion (clockwise from the viewpoint of someone looking at you) over the relevant chakra.

For instance, if you feel a tingling in the left little finger you will know that the left heart Chakra is not completely cleared. So you can take the right hand (most Sahaja techniques use the right hand as the actor as it represents the hand of action, whilst the left hand represents the hand of desire) and describe a clockwise motion over the heart area on the left hand side of your body (as if stirring a cup of tea vertically with your four fingers).

You can do this for seven or twenty one rotations, or until you feel some benefit. Most people will feel the results of the vibrations on the actual chakra with practice, but don't worry if not - you may rest assured that it is doing the job in any case !

Clearing an Obstruction in ones
own Chakra

Whilst rotating the hand we can also say the relevant 'affirmation' to help re-establish the pure quality of the chakra. If you cannot remember the correct affirmation, then simply say *"Mother, please clear this centre"*, addressing the mothering energy of Kundalini within.

Working on Others

You raise your Kundalini and put on a Bandan as you would in your own meditation.

To help others, you stand or sit behind the person you are working on (so they have their back to you).

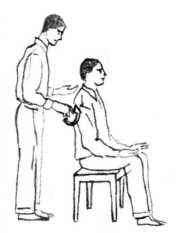

Then, from behind, raise the Kundalini of the person you are going to work on and give them a Bandhan. If you have developed enough sensitivity in your hands or fingers to feel the 'catches' or obstructions in the other persons' chakras (by tingling or warmth in your fingers which correspond to his/her chakras), then you can work at the back of the person with your left hand out towards the photograph of Sai Mataji - see p.233, in Appx. 4.

Clearing A Chakra

If you have not got a picture then keep your 'attention' (or concentration) on your Sahasrara chakra at the top of your head.

Rotate your right hand in an anti-clockwise direction seven or twenty-one times (the chakras always spin in the same direction, so you are in effect doing the same as if rotating the chakra clockwise from in front of the person).

Repeat this action until you feel your finger or hand go cool. Again you can use the appropriate affirmation for the affected chakra.

If you are unable to feel the 'catches', then ask the person you are working on if they feel any tingling or heat in their fingers. If they do, then work on the appropriate chakras.

If neither of you feel any sensations, then you can play it safe by simply working up the central channel, starting from the Muladhara centre and working up each Chakra in turn.

When you have finished working on the person raise their Kundalini and Bandhan them. Then raise your own Kundalini and Bandhan in the same way that you would finish your own meditation.

Chapter Nine

Colour Healing

Finding out the defective chakra and then correcting it with the appropriate cosmic ray (Colour) will be the key to the cure of such terrible diseases like TB, cancer, insanity and epilepsy which are the despair of the doctor.

Magnet Dowsing, Dr. B. Bhattacharya

As we look around us, we notice that everything we can see has colour. Although we may be aware that we react to these colours in different ways, most of us probably do not realize that colours not only directly affect how we feel, physically and emotionally, but even how we behave.

Thinking about it for a moment, you would probably agree that most people seem to feel better and are more cheerful on a bright, sunny day than on a gloomy, dull one. Similarly, you might have felt unhappy or depressed at some time, and then been cheered by the sight of a brightly coloured object.

Light and colours, which are the different wavelengths of light, are perceived by the eyes and absorbed by the body through the skin and the optic nerves.

They penetrate into the brain, where they are processed and utilized by the hypothalamus, the region of the brain that links the central nervous system to the hormonal system, and the light that penetrates to it at various wavelengths triggers a complex biochemical transfer within the body.

When hormones and enzymes are exposed to coloured light, they themselves undergo changes in colour and begin to have different effects on the body. This is why people who are subjected to prolonged periods of darkness, during which their body cannot absorb any light, suffer from vitamin deficiencies, hormonal disorders, disturbances of the normal body cycles, particularly sleep and metabolic functions, and depression.

However, we are not totally dependent on our eyes to perceive light and colour. The ability to see without the use of one's eyes is known as eidetic ability. This means that 'looking' and 'seeing' take place exclusively in the brain, which creates strong mental images without the assistance of the optic nerves.

Visions and the 'seeing' of the shamans are the result of this process. That colour and light can be 'seen' internally to a great extent without the aid of the retina is shown by the descriptions written by the Spanish Saint Teresa of Avila in the sixteenth century, and by those of Eskimo shamans documented by the Danish explorer and ethnologist Knud Rasmussen in the early years of the 20th century.

The literature of mysticism, religion and anthropology contains many accounts of individuals' striking experiences of indescribable light, brilliant colours and the sense of multidimensional space, which remain invisible to onlookers.

Such inner visions are often considered to be more impressive than mere optical sight, and seem to be experiences of such intensity that they remain vividly in the individual's mind for decades, and are rarely forgotten.

Inner sight is not a sign of psychological abnormality, as was believed for a long time, but rather the sign of healthy stability and flexibility. The healthier an organism is, the more flexibly it responds to internal and external influences and stimuli.

Experiments conducted in the former Soviet Union even investigated the possibility of perceiving colour solely with the sense of touch. What seemed impossible was actually achieved: several of the people tested were able to feel and 'see', to correctly identify colours through their fingertips - and were even able to read letters !

That the human body is equipped with two 'safety systems', eidetic sight and the sense of touch, to help it perceive light and colour without eyesight shows how important these elements are to our physical and emotional life.

There is no dividing line between physical and emotional factors. Emotions are energies that can have direct effect on the body, its metabolism and its overall health.

It is important to use colours to aid the healing of chakras. Colours are waves of different wavelengths or vibratory frequency. Any living organism radiates it's own colour as auras or chakras do.

White Prana from the universe influences our well-being, and it refracts into the seven colours of the spectrum in our organisms, as light refracts and disperses into seven visible colours when it passes through a prism.

Each colour represents a particular portion of the universal light, has its own vibration, and comes to us through the chakra system in varying frequencies by the way of the psychic (force) centres on the bodies.

These seven colours are seen radiating from our physical and subtle bodies and passing through each chakra.

Vibrational energy of all colours influences our bodies positively, supports healing, and removes blocks within the energy fields and chakras.

In terms of vibration, chakras are zones of highly concentrated energy which are connected to various locations and areas in the bodies.

We are susceptible to both positive and negative vibrational or colour effects of bio-energy in our lives. Differences in vibrations affect well-being, mood and emotional condition.

All organisms and cells exist as energy, and each form has its own frequency or vibration. Energy vibrations bring either a sedating or stimulating effect on the stream of energy through an organ, causing a natural biochemical reaction.

The various organs of the body also possess functions of sedation, stimulation, or neutralization through their characteristic frequencies.

When the different parts or organs vary from these expected normal vibrations, the physical body becomes either diseased or does not function properly.

When the energetic/element balance within the body is distorted, physical diseases occur in the body. All illnesses originate on the etheric plane in the forms of energetic imbalance, and these imbalances then affect body organs and systems on the physical plane.

Energy bodies can be healed by the energy properties of colours. As the colour rays accelerate in frequency, their wavelengths are shortened and they influence humans in different ways.

For example, the colour red has the longest wavelength and the lowest vibratory rate of the visible spectrum, whereas violet has the shortest wavelength and the highest vibratory rate. Thus, red is the 'densest' of all colours and is always closer to the dense physical body. Violet is the most subtle.

The Aura

Modern biophysics has confirmed that human beings are composed not only of bone, muscle and tissue (mere physical matter), but also of a body of energy. Consisting of quanta of light, which are produced by every cell in the physical body, this body of energy thus corresponds to the etheric bodies identified by esoteric healers through the ages.

One could say that every person is a rainbow, since everyone radiates his or her own colour vibrations, which form an aura, a sort of cocoon of etheric bodies enveloping the physical body. Located above the physical body's surface, this body of energy also ranks above it in terms of importance, since it directs and regulates everything that affects us.

All substances, environmental factors, and living beings emit certain frequencies of energy. Those in our immediate environment are absorbed through our aura, the medium for the interaction of human and other energies, and directly affect us physically, emotionally, and mentally.

Sensitive individuals may even feel uncomfortable or unwell merely in the presence of people or other factors that emit a lower frequency - their own higher-frequency vibrations are drawn out and absorbed by the weaker source, leaving them drained and weak.

It is also believed that all illness first appears in the etheric bodies and then slowly advances into the physical realm. For as long as an illness remains invisibly in the etheric bodies, it can be reached and removed only through vibrations. Therefore, whether or not we feel well, are healthy or ill, depends to a large extent on the health of our aura.

In order to become less susceptible to the ever-present external influences and to treat illnesses in the etheric bodies it is tremendously important to strengthen the aura.

The chakras are energy centres. Each of the seven major chakras is associated with an area or organ of our physical body, and vibrates at a specific colour wavelength. This energy penetrates our physical form and emanates from there into infinity.

Thus the chakras are the way in which spiritual information and life energy can reach the human body. At one time the chakras were considered to be merely a theoretical aspect of Indian medicine.

Today, however, it is possible to make the energy of the chakras, which radiates into the aura, visible by means of Kirlian photography. To trained therapists, pictures produced by this special high-voltage photographic technique clearly indicate any problems in our state of health.

Colour Therapy

All of us have and need colour in our life. If you could see a person's aura with the naked eye, you would see how layer upon layer of energy envelops the body in the colours of the rainbow.

There are an infinite number of colour vibrations in the world, but all of them are based on the seven main colours that vibrate in closest harmony with the body's organ centres, and so are associated with the chakras.

Since living things consist of colour, they can absorb colours purposefully and specifically. Just as the balance of the chakras can be disturbed by altering their natural vibrations, stimulating the chakras by means of corresponding colours markedly improves and balances their condition.

By adjusting vibrations, colours can thus alleviate certain physical ailments and have a beneficial effect on our health.

Each chakra absorbs energy from the colour corresponding to it. When the colour is placed on the chakra, the wavelength of the colour harmonizes with it and causes it to expand. Chakras must be correctly stimulated and balanced: too much energy circulating through a chakra is just as undesirable as too little.

Harmonizing the Chakras and Subtle Bodies

The following guide to the effects of certain colours on the chakras, subtle bodies, and miasms is included to provide the practitioner with some general information on the subject. It must be remembered that there are no hard and fast rules, colours for certain chakras or conditions will vary at times; those set out here are the ones that seem to occur most frequently in practice.

The crown chakra is stimulated by orange, green, blue and indigo. It is calmed by red, yellow and violet. Indigo and violet are the best colours for removing blockages from this centre.

The ajna chakra is stimulated by red, orange, blue and violet, and calmed by yellow, green and indigo. The colour best suited to removing blockages is green.

The throat chakra is stimulated by red, and calmed by orange, yellow, green, blue, indigo and violet. The best colours for removing blockages are blue and violet.

The heart chakra is stimulated by red, orange, indigo and violet. Calming effects can be obtained from yellow, green and blue. Red and indigo remove blockages from this chakra.

The solar plexus chakra is stimulated by red, orange, yellow, green and violet. Calmed by blue and indigo. Orange, yellow and blue remove blockages of the solar plexus chakra.

The sacral chakra is stimulated by red. Orange, yellow, green, blue, indigo and violet have a calming effect. For removal of blockages use blue or violet.

The base chakra is stimulated by green, indigo and violet. Red, orange, yellow and blue have a calming effect. Green is the supreme colour for removing blockages of this chakra.

The spleen chakra, supplier of Pranic energies to all of the other chakras, is stimulated by red, orange, yellow, green and violet. Blue and indigo have a calming effect. Yellow, indigo and violet remove blockages of the spleen centre.

Other Healings with Colour

The practitioner will frequently detect miasms in the etheric body, normally located on the level of the fourth ether. As colour functions on this ether, miasms readily disperse when subjected to colour frequencies broadcast to the base chakra. The following colours are suitable for clearing the three basic miasms:

The syphilitic miasm clears through the use of yellow, green, blue or indigo.

The tubercular miasm should be treated with yellow or green.

The cancer miasm responds to red, green, blue, indigo and violet.

Conditions of the etheric body may require specific colours to normalize them, so for congestion use green, blue, indigo and violet. For over stimulation use green to obtain a calming effect.

For lack of co-ordination between the physical and etheric vehicles, as occurs in petit-mal and other similar conditions, green is the colour of choice.

Astral problems are often found so it is as well to know the best colours for these factors on the astral level. For astral congestion use blue. Over stimulation calls for green or blue, and lack of co-ordination between the astral and etheric bodies is best treated with green.

Inflammation of the brain, certain brain tumours and some forms of insanity are treated via the crown chakra. The calming colours are selected in such cases in order to quieten the action of the crown centre which is usually overactive in these conditions.

Any problems related to the pituitary body are treated via the ajna chakra. Neuritis, migraine headaches, regular headaches, eye and hearing problems as well as hay fever, sinus, and catarrh trouble all respond to treatment of the ajna.

Many disturbances of the nervous system may be treated via this centre as it governs the lower brain stem. Migraines are usually caused by a lack of balance between the force fields of the pineal and pituitary glands, so look to both of the head chakras when tackling this condition.

Heart trouble, certain diseases related to the autonomic nervous system and the vagus nerve, and circulatory trouble should all be treated via the heart chakra.

Diseases related to thyroid imbalance are treated by way of the throat chakra. Respiratory diseases such as asthma and tuberculosis, bronchitis and emphysema are all treated via the throat chakra.

Energetic Properties of Colours

There are of course certain broad generalities that may be applied to colours. For instance blue and green have a calming effect, and are found to be very useful in the treatment of acute conditions.

Blue is usually excellent for low back pain, if placed by way of the base chakra to the spine. Blue seems to have an affinity for the throat centre and is very useful for treating conditions of the lungs such as asthma, or for sore throats and bronchial troubles.

Green will have a calming effect for headaches if applied to the ajna chakra and nervous system. Green is a colour very frequently used to treat the ajna centre, and in India emerald gem medicines are used to treat conditions allied to the brow chakra.

Reds and oranges on the other hand are stimulating and may be used to increase vitality and tone up the circulatory system by way of the heart chakra. Varicosities may be treated in this manner.

Yellow too is an excellent stimulant, especially for toning up the nervous system.

Violet is often used in infectious conditions as it tones up the etheric body, and helps it to throw off the vibratory force of the invading bacteria or virus.

Each of the factors in the case which need treatment are taken in turn, and a card may be prepared showing which chakras and systems are to be treated.

Problems Relating To Colour Therapy & Distant Healing

Energy Field Healing is the healing technique of the future. It addresses the disease and illnesses at their root and does not just treat symptoms. Illness and disease is treated by ushering vibrational energy into the recipient's etheric force field.

Colour is the most powerful source of vibratory energy that the centre therapist has available.

For the 'hands on' centre therapist, the use of colour presents no difficulties at all. On the other hand, the centre therapist working at a distance seems to have insurmountable difficulties.

The method described earlier where colour was applied generally to the whole human form drawing does not appear to be specific, but treats the whole drawn form and all it's chakras with the same colour.

The second method illustrated, where spirals of the appropriate colour were drawn leading into the chakra is a marked improvement. The writer feels though, that a more intense and specific method must be available.

I pondered this problem on and off for weeks - no, months !

And there it was, the answer to my prayers !

I was sifting through my e-mails for the day when I notice an e-mail in my bulk inbox from someone I didn't know. The contents of my bulk box are usually deleted, as they are always adverts. Something made me open this mail and it read something like this:

"Hi Bill, Found your name on the web and I feel we have some common interests. If you go to this web site you will find an e-book that you can download for free".

The book was downloaded and I sat up most of the night reading it over and over again. The writer was talking about things called Crystal Cards, which I had never heard about. Apparently there were two sizes; one like a credit card, and the other was an equilateral triangle with one inch sides and a small hole in one corner. A small portion of the book is reproduced below:

Crystal Cards

These make use of the healing power of colour with the special properties of crystals, are a 'waste' by-product of American space research.

When exposed to mechanical pressure, crystals emit electrons; they can store information and their special structure makes them well suited to programming. In space research they were generally used to store information.

American astronauts had noticed both physical and psychological disorientation when leaving the Earth's gravitational field. In an attempt to take remedial action, the idea of using the properties of crystals was put forward.

The astronauts were given small containers with pyramid-shaped crystals to take with them on their space flights. The crystals were charged with the Earth's mechanical vibration, which is 7.83 hertz. The result was that the astronauts were able to spend time outside the Earth's magnetic field without suffering from their previous disorders.

While attending a conference at the NASA Space centre, a science teacher from Michigan had an interesting conversation with astronaut John Glen.

During a break between meetings, the science teacher was adjusting a gold Crystal Card that he was carrying in his shoe to balance his polarities.

Mr. Glen, standing nearby, noticed the Gold Crystal Card and immediately approached the science teacher.

The former astronaut pulled from his pocket a pack of 7 Crystal Cards ! During the ensuing conversation Mr. Glenn stated *"all the astronauts carry the Crystal Cards."*

Crystal cards are made of aluminium because it is a lightweight, soft metal that lends itself to the special, costly process of etching in the crystals. Thousands of microscopic, pyramid-shaped aluminium oxide crystals (corundum crystals) are etched into the cards by a complex electrochemical process.

By using naturally occurring tiny, live mineral crystals, the cards become carriers of cosmic energy, which is enhanced by the pyramid shape. You can distinctly feel this energy through the skin and nervous system, through the chakras or other energy centres.

After being etched, the cards are coated with specific shades of non-toxic colours. The storage capabilities of the crystals are combined with the wavelengths of the colour vibrations, and the amplification of the effects of the colour through the crystalline pyramids is what gives the cards their amazing power. The energy field of the cards also emits negative ions, which are vital for our well-being.

The cards are available in twenty colours, and are accompanied by information for their use in treating a range of physical and psychological ailments. Most crystal cards are the size and shape of a credit card, but some are equilateral triangles.

Both types have the same effects on the body and are referred to as 'cards' in this book. They can be applied to specific parts of the body, carried in a wallet or pocket, or used to energize food or drink.

The Pendulum Test

Each card has a positive and a negative side. To identify the sides use a pendulum. If the pendulum circles clockwise above the card, the side facing up is positive; if it circles anti-clockwise, the side facing up is negative.

Positive and negative are not associated with good and bad in this context, but describe a physical process or property: the vibrations of the positive side create input, while the negative side extracts vibrations

If you continue to hold the pendulum above the card, you will notice that after a while it will stop circling in the initial direction and begin moving the other way. The process reverses again after another few minutes.

This proves that there really are pyramid-shaped crystals etched into the card, as radiesthetic tests have detected alternating reversing circular vibrations above pyramids in general. Use only the direction of the first swing to mark the crystal card. It is a good idea to mark the negative side, which should face towards the body in most cases and for most purposes.

Scientific Tests

Further tests on the crystal cards were made in Austria, where Werner H. Duschnig performed a radiesthetic test.

He, too, found that the edges of the cards, which are only one millimeter thick, draw in energy from their surroundings, and that this energy is then released through the active (positive) flat side, or face, of the cards. If you were to be too close to the edge of a card, or the side of a stack of cards, for too long, it could reduce your own energy levels.

However, you could use the energy that is released again through the active card face to help build up the body's energy fields and structures.

Test report

Test object: Crystal cards, chakra set

Test conditions: The tests were conducted at a location approximating neutral geopathic conditions. Any potentially disruptive fields generated by electrical cables and instruments or appliances were eliminated as far as possible.

Each test object was measured in two positions:

1) horizontally, lying flat on the table, and

2) vertically, fitted into a holding device that permits the object to be aligned with the various points of the compass. In particular, the stability of emission frequency relative to compass alignment was measured in this position.

Radiation intensity (R) and the corresponding frequency (F) were measured in both positions.

Definitions:

The concept of radiation (emission) is borrowed from physics, as this phenomenon has similar properties. Frequency is another familiar concept, which is used to describe the second aspect of the energetic phenomenon being measured.

Every living thing - plants, animals and humans - has its species-specific 'radiation', which falls within a characteristic range of frequencies.

In this report the range of such frequencies, or frequency band, is termed the range of life energy, and extends from 7.25 to 11.47 Hz. The emissions of the individual chakras and their specific frequencies fall within this band.

At 9.15 Hz, the radiation of the human body falls in about the middle of the frequency band of life energy, and in this report is called 'human energy'.

All test objects exhibit the typical characteristics of one neutral side and two active areas:

1) Energy is drawn into the object.

2) This factor is irrelevant to the purpose and use of crystals cards.

3) The energy drawn in laterally is emitted in intensified form by the active axial side, opposite the neutral side.

The frequencies of the individual chakras are matched with astonishing precision, especially in the horizontal position. The corresponding radiation emission seems to be strong enough so that when the crystal cards are applied directly to the body they can achieve a harmonizing effect on the various chakras. However, it seems that this influence becomes possible only when the active side is facing the chakras.

Therefore, for effective use of this product, it is absolutely necessary that the cards be appropriately marked or labelled, and that detailed instructions accompany them.

Determining the active side by means of pendulum dowsing by the user, as suggested in the instructions, is absolutely recommended.

In the set of test objects provided for this examination the colours of the heart chakra and the brow chakra were clearly mixed up.

Product Description:

• Red: horizontally, red radiates in the frequency of the base chakra; vertically, this frequency is attained when the active side faces northwest.

• Orange: horizontally, orange radiates in the frequency of the sacral chakra; vertically, this frequency is attained when the active side faces north.

• Yellow: horizontally, yellow radiates in the frequency of the solar plexus chakra; vertically- this frequency is attained when the active side faces southwest or southeast.

• Green: horizontally, green radiates in the frequency of the brow chakra; vertically, this frequency is attained when the active side faces west or southwest.

• Blue: horizontally, blue radiates in the frequency of the throat chakra; vertically, this frequency is attained when the active side faces southwest or north.

• Indigo: horizontally, indigo radiates in the frequency of the heart chakra; vertically, this frequency is attained when the active side faces west or east.

• Violet: horizontally, violet radiates in the frequency of the crown chakra; vertically, this frequency is attained when the active side faces southwest.

Conclusions:

As already mentioned, the accuracy of frequency matching is especially remarkable when the test objects are horizontal.

Labelling the active side of each card, and the provision of detailed instructions for use are desirable. The switch in the colours for the heart and brow chackras, possibly an error that occurred during manufacturing, must be corrected.

Werner H. Duschnig

Vienna, 29 August 1992

Duschnig performed these tests with great precision; they show impressively just how accurately the crystal cards correspond to the vibrations of the individual human chakras.

It is important to clarify the discrepancies that Duschnig appeared to find.

The green card, which bears the colour of the heart chakra, was measured as radiating at the same frequency as the brow chakra, whose colour is indigo. Similarly, the indigo card exhibited the frequency of the heart chakra.

Duschnig assumed that a mistake had been made in the manufacture of the cards he tested.

I believe that there may be another explanation. Our feelings are often superceded and stifled by our thoughts - our heart and common sense often tell us very different things, and many of us have suffered from being torn between, for example, our heart saying YES and our mind saying NO.

So it might be that the frequencies of the heart and brow are responsible for balancing and aligning these two conflicting centres in order to decrease the gap between emotion and intellect.

The positive and negative sides of the cards may be determined by dowsing with a pendulum - experience shows that even people doing this for the first time are successful. I have asked a considerable number of people to try the pendulum test and, to the great surprise of every one of them, the pendulum moved in more or less well defined circles. The size of the circles is unimportant, and reflects only the person's dowsing ability. You to can use this easy test to identify the active side of crystal cards and triangles.

You can probably see now why I became excited about crystal cards. Unfortunately, on contacting the makers of the cards, I was informed that they were no longer in production !

I decided to give the Internet one more try. Using my favourite search engine, I put a search out for 'micro-crystal cards'. Eureka ! One site - prosperity.com - came up but the only stock showing in the chakra colour range was red, orange, yellow, and green - and only in the triangle shape size.

An e-mail was hurriedly sent to prosperity to enquire about any possibility of further stock. A reply from a lady called Holly was quick in coming - sorry no more stock available. One of each card of the colours mentioned was ordered by credit card.

Another e-mail from Holly was quickly received to which I had to reply, as it was a receipt for my purchase. In my reply I mentioned how I became interested in the cards and what I intended using them for.

Holly responded by asking if I was aware of "TouchStones" and in case I wasn't, she enclosed a blue one with my order - free of charge !

TouchStones

These were news to me, so back to prosperity.com for knowledge. The information there indicated that they had the same properties as the cards with one slight drawback, as far as my use of them is concerned - they appear in the illustrations to be cylindrical.

They are not; when mine arrived in the post, I was delighted to find that, apart from being pretty, they have a flat back and a slightly convex front. The back cover has illustrations of four TouchStones.

TouchStones are created by hand with layers of coloured glass and a variety of dichroic glasses fused together. The size of each one is approximately one and a half inches long, three quarters of an inch wide, and a quarters of an inch thick - making them easy to carry, wear as jewelry, hold during meditations, or enhance your colour readings or therapy sessions.

The main characteristic of dichroic glass is that it has a transmitted colour and a completely different reflective colour - and the colours shift depending on angle of view. With the play of light together with colour, dichroic glass lent itself perfectly with our purpose.

The Chakra Set of TouchStones - red, orange, yellow, green, blue, and indigo - are fused with a very light silver beam-splitter dichroic coating so the colours vibrate. The violet one has been fused with a much heavier Violet dichroic glass. Silver dichroic coating was chosen as a protection of your energy to ward off any negativity in your environment while carrying them

There are also Silver, Copper, Gold, Blue Violet, Magenta, Rainbow black TouchStones and rippled varieties including Amber, Aqua, Emerald, Lavender, Sky Blue and Turquoise. All are reasonably durable and strong but they are glass and they will break if tested by dropping or throwing on hard surfaces.

For more information, visit www.askforprosperity.com

Email: info@askforprosperity.com

Telephone: vox (502) 454-4967, fax (502) 458-5623

Description of Chakra TouchStones

Red - The Power TouchStone

Red is used to balance the Root Chakra and denotes the essence of self. Use it to tap into your self energy. During meditations you may receive a projection of all things you are or can be, and feel your vitality and blood being healed. It is great for sexual encounters, big business deals, and self-introspection when a greater inward vision of 'why You are' is desired. Carry it when you need an energy boost.

Orange - The Action TouchStone

Orange is used to balance the Spleen Chakra. When you are feeling sad, depressed or unworthy, carry it to revitalize your emotions and sex drive. You can find greater self-confidence, release your inner fears, rejuvenate extra enthusiasm and juice, while meditating with it. Carry it when you want to focus on being worthy of all great things that are abundant in the Universe and be ready to receive the miracles you deserve.

Yellow - The Achievement TouchStone

Yellow is used to balance the Solar Plexus Chakra, and help you 'get off your butt' and do something. Any time you feel an excuse coming on, use it to move past the 'but' in your thought process. Carry it when seeking success and setting goals. During meditation, it can help you focus on life, health, business and love decisions.

Green - The Unconditional Love TouchStone

Green is used to balance the Heart Chakra; it relates to all matters concerning healing, love, growth and balance. Emotional and physical healing have been associated with it. Place one on the soil of a plant to energize and help the plant grow ! During meditation, it can help you touch in with your loving self.

Blue - The Expression TouchStone

Blue is used to balance the Throat Chakra and is associated with self expression, communication and peace. Use it in communication so that your ideas are clear and your words are easily understood by others. When in a possible confrontation, carry it to assist in resolving issues peacefully. Meditation with it can help you say what you mean and mean what you say; use it to focus on what you want to say - and feel the Blue ray of healing being sent to you.

Indigo - The Visionary TouchStone

Indigo is used to balance the Brow Chakra, sometimes referred to as the Third Eye; it is used when releasing old habits, or tapping into your wisdom, your vision, and your intuitive self. Problem-solving can be so easy when we use all of the attributes we already have available to us, especially intuition.

Meditate with it to open your Third Eye, look into your future, and release old patterns of 'shoulda, coulda, woulda' and the like. It can assist in reflection of situations and provide you with insightful answers.

Violet - The Spiritual Connection TouchStone

Known for its royalty origin, Violet is the colour used to balance the Crown Chakra; vision, love, spirit, and calmness are qualities that can be enhanced. Use it for guidance, spirituality and to see things more clearly during meditation and feel the Violet ray of healing. By centering yourself and carrying a Violet TouchStone, you may find love will come to you - and most probably from the place you least likely thought was possible.

White - The Cleansing TouchStone

The White stone is a culmination of all colours, just as is the case in the spectrum of colour. Use it when all things seem to be out of place. When all colours are not in their correct perspective, White cannot be attained. The White TouchStone is associated with purity; cleansing the mind, body and soul are good. Be sure to wash it often to insure a clear meaning of purity.

Black - The Absorbing TouchStone

This is the only TouchStone that does not have a dichroic element fused in. If it were to have dichroic glass in it, the absorption rate would be much lower. Use it to absorb negative energy and disperse that energy away from you. Place one on top of electronic devices, especially computers, to absorb the electronic smog they produce. Carry one for protection when confrontation is eminent.

Rainbow - The Energizing TouchStone

Carry it when you cannot decide which colour is best suited for you. Many people wear one as a pendant and carry a separate one with them for specific energies. Use it to balance and increase your energy levels. This TouchStone could help revitalize, you so use it when are feeling sluggish or tired.

Testing the TouchStones

Now that I had in my possession five small crystal card triangles and one TouchStone, I needed to carry out some tests. Out came my light weight pendulum which I use for this type of fine work. Each card was placed on a table one at a time. The pendulum was suspended over each face and the swings noted.

Each card displayed a clockwise (positive) rotation on one face and a counter-clockwise (negative) rotation on the opposite face.

Now for the TouchStone. I must admit that I was not expecting much here - "Ye of Little Faith" ! The pendulum swung beautifully in a clockwise motion over the front face and in a counter-clockwise motion over the back face. Not only did the pendulum swing, the degree of swing was greater than that over the cards.

At this time my wife was out walking and had not seen the cards or the Touchstone. On her return, I asked her to do the pendulum test on each card and the Touchstone. She had no idea why she was being asked to do this, but her results were identical to mine.

At that time my wife was suffering from a frozen shoulder which was extremely painful and had about 80% lack of mobility.

She went to see a Physiotherapist for about four weekly treatments. This proved to be very painful with little improvement. Next came acupuncture for about six weekly treatments.

This proved to be more successful, lack of mobility reduced to about 65% and the pain also eased a little.

During this period I was giving short sessions of Pranic healing which took the pain away instantly, only to return when my wife forgot her ailment and tried to reach up for something out of normal reach.

I prepared a chakra profile for my wife and found that all her chakras were functioning normally, except one. The throat chakra was dysfunctional by 19%, under-active, and had a blockage in the exit of the chakra.

Inquiry as explained in earlier chapters resulted in treatment for this chakra being required, the colour to be used was blue, and the length of treatment by the magnetic broadcasting method was to be seven minutes.

The body scan sheet for my wife was on paper and all her etheric link details had been added, the negative withdrawal spiral from the throat chakra drawn in, and the scan sheet was then placed over a black sheet of card with the head facing North.

The blue TouchStone was washed in cold water, dried and placed over the throat chakra on the body scan sheet with it's face pointing upward.   An 8oz. Straight sided clear glass tumbler was placed upside down over the TouchStone.

As it was daylight, no extra lighting was added to the setup.   No doubt, a 100 watt daylight lamp would have added to the efficacy of the broadcast. The timer, set at seven minutes, was started and the large magnet put into position on the inverted tumbler.

During the broadcast, the radiation was checked with the pendulum and found to be positive in all directions.   At about six minutes, the pendulum was suspended on the North side of the setup about 12 inches away. It was rotating clockwise as expected, then went into a neutral swing, then counter-clockwise, then back to neutral, then clockwise for a couple of spins and finally stopping, indicating the end of the broadcast.

Following the Pranic Healing protocol, the session was completed by stabilizing.   This was achieved by stroking the area treated with the blue TouchStone. I am not sure at this time if the placement of the TouchStone, negative face against the chakra, was correct as this position would signify withdrawal of negative energy from the chakra.

Two hours later, the throat chakra was checked again. The chakra was still dysfunctional but there was an improvement, this dropping from 19% to 16% dysfunctional. The degree of dysfunction of the chakra was checked again after twenty four hours. It had now dropped down to 10% dysfunction, showing an overall improvement of about 50%. There is now no pain in the shoulder under normal usage and the mobility has improved slightly.

When used as above, the TouchStones have a distinct advantage over the Crystal Cards. Being transparent, the light passes through the stone, 'picks' up the colour, and places it directly into the chakra or body part. The cards have to rely on the positive or negative radiation from their faces, but the Touchstones radiate in a similar fashion as well.

Throughout the book, I have said that all the techniques herein can be used on your pets and yourself.

To do a session on yourself, prepare a case sheet and body form drawing by asking questions of the pendulum and proceed as if you were working on another person. Don't forget to add all the etheric link details of yourself to the sheets.

To do a healing session on an animal such as a cat, dog or horse just proceed in exactly the same way.

If you are not much use at drawing you will need an animal body form chart with chakra positions indicated. There are numerous sites on the Internet showing these.

Extracts from emails on using TouchStones

The first set are from Patricia, a lady from New Mexico.

"My name is Patricia, and I am the lucky owner of an entire set of Holly's touchstones.

I happened upon Holly's website ... I saw the TouchStones, and got really excited. I could feel the energy off the website. I immediately purchased the set ... was extremely excited at the energy that radiates off them when you actually touch them. I had been looking for additional tools to help myself heal, in addition to a little dog ... I have been working for a while with animals and healing. I have a small female Chihuahua who came to me that was very, very frightened of people. She had not been socialized - she did not like people at all. I began working with her slowly and realized she needed additional help.

I also saw on her website some charms that were crystal. I purchased those too in hopes of helping my little dog. The energy from the crystals is much less powerful. It is a good constant slow dose for a dog, but not the higher pitch that the TouchStones are at.

I have had the TouchStones for a little over a month, and the results have been quite remarkable for myself and my animals. Peppita will now come to me on her own, when before she ran away. I also discovered that she sees. I sat with her for quite some time and we addressed the issues that were scaring her.

I rubbed her with the green Touchstone for healing after I had rubbed her with the black one for about 30 minutes. She was still terribly frightened. So, I kept working with her.

After reflecting on things, I decided that what she needed was balance, so enter in the Rainbow TouchStone. I began having her sleep with me. I placed the rainbow, green and violet Touchstones under the pillow.

At first she moved away from the energy. In a combination like that, I found that I had a hard time sleeping myself, so I moved them a little farther under the pillows so they weren't quite as strong.

A few weeks ago my other dog became physically ill, and we had to rush her to the emergency vet clinic. After a scare and some immediate rescue, she found the rainbow TouchStone under the pillow and placed it right along side herself !

I watched her in amazement as she rubbed herself on the stone ... she was so much better by morning. ... they have been a huge blessing for myself and my dogs."

"Hello again Bill ... I have begun the process each night of laying out all 21 TouchStones in a long row across the foot of the bed. I have 3 dogs and they each decide which colour they want to sleep with each night ! Sometimes it's different from the night before, sometimes it is the same.

I carry with me each day the black TouchStone because of where I work. I discovered that placing it on top of my computer made me sick, so I then tried my right pocket, the same thing ... when I placed it in the left pocket the energy changed and I began to feel better. At work it needs to be cleared on average of three to four times a day.

Each night we sleep with the stones because in my estimation most of the real healing is done while one sleeps. I could be wrong, but so far, I have found in my own case that it works."

Yet more input arrived, this time from Europe. A lady called Doris emailed me from Switzerland:

"Hello Bill ... I'm writing from Switzerland and I have been working for many years with Dr. Tal Schaller on holistic healing - including physical, emotional, mental and spiritual bodies.

I have been using TouchStones on many different people (older, younger) for body pains, mental pains, emotional pains and of course spiritual blocks. My results were always good.

My first experience was working with them a lot on myself and I can guarantee you that they works perfectly.

For example, if I have a tummy ache (second chakra or navel chakra) and if I stay with the TouchStones and balancing the energy on all colours, all chakras (persisting with the orange) you can be sure that when finishing the work, my pain has gone.

Of course I can feel where there is less colour on each chakra; with the Stones and my feeling and energy, I put some more colour on the chakra as needed. When you control all chakras colours, you can balance them. Sometimes I have to work more - particularly on one colour most, of course. I also must say that they works when a person is completely blocked.

In Love and Light   Doris"

We all think that TouchStones work well in different healing modalities. So, all you would be researchers out there: buy, beg or borrow a set of the TouchStones and get to work !

Using the Pendulum to Assess a Chakra's Colour

The average diameter of pendulum swing over a chakra on a body image is about 1 inch. A smaller diameter indicates a lack of colour in that chakra - and hence low energy.

A diameter in excess of 1 inch over a chakra indicates an over abundance of colour and possibly an overactive chakra.

Remember that such diameters are also dependant upon the sensitivity of the user - so check by asking for guidance as to the indication as shown to you, especially until you have confidence in the meaning of various diameters of swing.

If you get variations in swings, you can always play '20 Questions' to find out the meaning of such signals !

Perform assessment of all chakras using the characteristics of colours, and correct their work with needed colours.

Chapter Ten

Bio-Scalar Energy

The human body (organism) needs to take in air, food and water to sustain life. It needs, above all else, to take in 'Life Force Energy', Prana, to heal itself and allow life to continue.

This life force energy has many names in different cultures such as Chi, Ki, and Mana but in these notes we will use the name Prana.

Prana is readily available to all life forms as it pervades the Universe in never ending supply. Pranic energy is an electro-magnetic wave energy just like the electricity in your home, it has frequencies and moves in a wave form.

In it's natural state it is white and when it enters the physical body through the etheric body and chakra system it is refracted into it's component colours, just like light going through a prism, and then used by the chakras and associated endocrine glands to sustain the body.

Whereas Prana has been known about for thousands of years we now have a newly identified energy called Scalar Wave energy - probably more important than Prana in sustaining life - which was first talked about at the end of the nineteenth century.

It is only in recent years since the human populace has made deeper studies of Quantum Physics that we have become aware of this energy.

Like Prana, this energy pervades the Universe but because this energy is synthesized from Prana in a precise and distinct way, it is probably less abundant.

Standing Waves

The literature states that the scalar energy is created when two common electro-magnetic waves (such as Prana) come together from two opposite converging vectors (opposite directions).

When the energy vectors meet, the equal frequencies cancel each other leaving a standing or stationary energy.

The space the scalar occupies is not a vacuum but alive with checked and balanced energies.

The literature describes that it can be created naturally when similar frequency electro-magnetic waves in the environment, such as Prana, meet from two different vectors. Therefore, small random scalar energies are always present in the environment.

The term scalar was first used at the end of the nineteenth century by the eminent physicist Nikola Tesla where he referred to it as standing energy or cosmic waves. Einstein gave reference to the scalar energies in the 1920s. Yet even today modern physics textbooks and scholarly publications rarely mention scalar energies.

This is understandable. The electro-magnetism that we know so much about has frequencies, wave action and motion that we can measure.

Scalar energy is described to have zero frequencies, to be static, a stationary energy that therefore cannot be evaluated by our current frequency instruments. We do know how to create this energy - but only its effects tell us that it exists in space and has power.

Bio-scalar Energy

As seen above, scalar energy has been known about for over one hundred years and there is an abundance of literature about it on the internet.

Nevertheless, no one had thought of it as being present in living organisms let alone what it does in such organisms.

Dr. Valerie Hunt has spent a number of years working in this area - she has coined the word 'Bio-Scalar' to refer to scalar energy in living systems.

Electro-magnetic energy is the most plentiful constant energy of our universe. It is a part of all structures living and dead, and the atmosphere. We create electro-magnetic energies in the atoms of our living cells, which we enhance by the reaction with the atmospheric energy field.

We know this expanded energy field as the human aura. Without this bio-field life would not exist and there would be only an inner bio-chemical mix.

To summarize, the bio-energy field is composed of electrical and mechanical energy (frequencies). It comes from the body, passes through the body as waves of energy (frequencies). In its free form it is high in frequencies because its source is atoms.

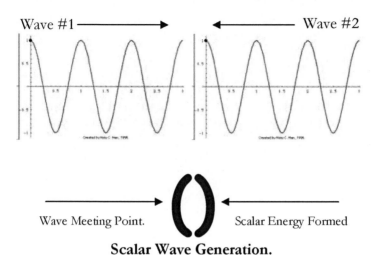

Wave Meeting Point.   Scalar Energy Formed

Scalar Wave Generation.

The neurological system is also electro-magnetic but the source is neurons, not atoms, giving a much lower frequency spectrum.

Whereas the nerve electro-magnetism activates muscles, brain, heart and breathing with frequencies from 0 to 25 Hz (cycles per second), the human energy field from atoms is measured at about 500 Hz to the frequency of light.

Recently another form of electro-magnetism that is organized into a different pattern has been discovered. It is no longer a wave, but is changed to a standing or stationary energy. In physics this is called a scalar wave. When it exists inside the body it is called a bio-scalar wave.

This scalar energy does not flow like waves but it does occupy space and increases in spatial mass. When the space it occupies is sufficient (this varies with people), the energy expands outward in circles of energy, like ripples in a pond.

This energy expanding in circles directly influences the body's fluid systems - blood and lymphatic. Lab tests have indicated that red and white cells tend to stick together when there is illness, injury or poor health.

According to the famous Max Planck Institute in Germany the scalar energy un-sticks the cells. Circulation is remarkably improved in lymphatic and blood systems to flow smoothly. Good flow of bodily fluid systems hastens healing.

It is believed the creation of the bio-scalar wave is the essential electro-magnetic healing phenomena of all healing procedures.

Accessing the Immune System by Scalar Energy

Health is the ideal state of a constantly self-healing organism. Before disease or dysfunction settle into tissue the immune system, the body's first line of defense, with its protective hormones, enzymes and cells has become weakened.

Yet regardless of the state of the immune system, if the transportation of these vital substances to the tissue cells is blocked or inefficient the local tissue becomes sick.

Sluggish, lymphatic circulation occurs when the body is unable to handle normal metabolic substances and particularly the tissue protein from viral, bacterial and cancer destruction.

We sense such circulatory disturbances with local tightness and pain; we learn to place heat or cold on the areas to make them feel better.

Our hands gravitate to the tender spots to rub softly or dig deeply into the tightness. We know that massage, manipulation, rhythmic exercises, and body work assist our rapid healing.

Our doctor may tell us that our immune system is not handling the problem, and that we need drugs or injections to stimulate the weak system, or extensive lab tests to find out the cause. Almost never do doctors try to evaluate the state of the lymphatic circulation as a primary or equal source of our body's poor immune response.

The exquisite specificity of the chemical aspects of the immune system seem to have helped doctors to forget that the important transportation of immunity may be lagging.

We reiterate our earlier statement that before disease or dysfunction takes place the immune systems guards have been overcome. The flexible plasticity of a healthy body is lost, due to disease or aging.

Dr Valerie Hunt's Experience

During extensive research of hands-on-healers and psychic surgeons who effect deep tissue and open the body surfaces I pondered many questions.

How was it possible to part skin, nerves, blood vessels and connective tissue to open deeper tissues without trauma ?

And how is it possible to re-suture such a spontaneous incision without a scar, pain or break in tissue integrity ?

I intuitively sensed that somehow the energy used by psychic surgeons was different from that generated by average good hands-on-healers. As a researcher of energy fields I was less interested in the psychic surgeons cure rates than in how they opened the body.

Their explanation fell upon my deaf psychic ears - that there was no electro-magnetic wave action, that somehow opening the body was accomplished in a more passive state. Serendipitously I recalled the static scalar, standing wave, a concept in physics still in its infancy.

The energy that we experience in our bodies is electro-magnetic waves radiating from the atoms of all our tissue cells. When this energy radiates away from the originating atoms it has a life of its own as an organized electro-magnetic field, now available to interact with other atoms and fields.

If such electro-magnetic waves meet head on at 180 degrees with another wave of the same frequency a scalar wave is created.

This means that the energy from the two like waves does not take another direction or even a different frequency.

Instead it becomes an enfolded, thicker glob of the same energy or a standing scalar field. At first this scalar energy was believed to be a vacuum. Now it is understood that it is a dynamic pile of non-directional energy.

It is known that all fields have surface bonds which keep fields relatively intact and not dissipating. Yet when the surface bond is weakened the field expands in all directions, smoothly.

With this information in mind we experimented with creating the scalar wave inside the body. We discovered that when we released the surface tension by thought the scalar expanded rapidly in all directions. The scalar energy became less dense and the cellular tissue followed the same path as it became less compressed.

The lymphatic circulation was then under less pressure and flowed more freely. As a result the cellular protoplasm also de-densified, making the tissue less turgid. People experienced that the painful tight areas of the body became lighter, thinner and less engorged.

In such a softer state the body accelerated its healing by removing the tissue 'garbage' and bathing the cells with the immune system 'guards'.

I believe, if you learn scalar exercises you will activate your self healing of all illnesses, for yourself and others, faster than any other single exercise. Before you practice any specific meditation suggested to heal your disabilities you should first activate your scalar field.

Chapter Twelve

Healing With Scalar Energy

To strengthen our understanding of scalar energy, let us repeat:

- The literature states that the scalar is created when two common electromagnetic waves come together from two opposite converging vectors or angles; where the energy vectors meet the equal frequencies cancel each other leaving a standing or stationary energy.

- The space the scalar occupies is not a vacuum but alive with checked and balanced energies. The literature describes that it can be created by electro-magnetic generators or naturally when similar frequency waves in the environment meet from two different and opposite vectors. Therefore, small random scalar energies are always present in the environment.

Probably when human thought and intent make major changes in bodily tissue it occurs by creating and informing the scalar energy at the most microscopic level, the nucleus of the atom.

It has been discovered by Prof. Valerie Hunt that when the Mind-Field is consciously focused, intent can direct electro-magnetic frequencies to enter the body at opposite ends of a straight angle or line, i.e. front to back, up to down, right to left - placing scalar energy in the trunk, head and legs.

It is believed that the bio-scalar is the sustained energy for healing that all successful healers create and direct. In the same way each of us can create the powerful resting bio-scalar energy and by thought we can direct it to bodily areas and give it instruction to: eliminate pain, heal traumatized tissue, destroy disease and eliminate tumour growths.

Certainly this is not a new thought to the healing arts, however the mechanism by which the mind creates and directs this energy is new and scientifically verifiable.

After the energy starts pooling at the centre of your body, this is where your intent takes over. The energy is now consciously directed to a location with information as to what it is to accomplish, such as: remove pain, clear trauma, destroy disease, rebuild degenerated tissue, and absorb growths.

Depending on the severity of the health problem this procedure should be continued for 10 minutes to several hours.

<u>Generation and Storage of Bio-Scalar Energy</u>

To bring scalar energy into our own bodies we should focus on its coming in on the inhaled breath.

It is further emphasized the importance of pulling the energy into the body from more than one direction, and having it meet at the centre. The energy builds in that centre and can be felt there.

Then the procedure is to consciously direct the energy to a specific location along with information as to what condition we wish it to create there.

This energy, when used in this way, is totally benign. It does not accumulate. Undirected, it will simply dissipate and flow out.

The discovery of Bio-Scalar energy helps us realize the magnificence of the human mind to direct our destiny, to use our consciousness to create this powerful energy for healing self and others. It strengthens our security with independence from drugs. Its only side effects are the improvement of health.

Many excellent healers create this bio-scalar energy automatically without awareness or realization that they have manipulated the structure of electro-magnetic waves.

The scalar energy will increase in size up to a certain point if you continue creating it. When the internal pressure increases, the surface tension will lessen, and the energy will expand in bodily tissue. Your intent can also start the expansion, which continues until the energy is dissipated and returned to electro-magnetism.

You cannot store scalar energy indefinitely. If you need it you must re-create it. During the expansion phase the energy spreads out over molecules, cells, organs and systems. This is when healing takes place.

Remember that the scalar energy is force by expansion. The human mind instructs it in its direction and its focus.

Bio-Scalar Energy Meditation for Healing - #1

This meditation, briefly described below, is based upon the fact that scalar energy is created along a straight line where two separate-but-equal energies meet.

Although standard measurements seem to say that these two energies have zeroed each other out, what is happening at the meeting point is quite far from 'nothing' !

Here are the highlights of the meditation to mobilize scalar energies:

1. This exercise can be learned best when sitting. After acquiring the skill it can be repeated while standing or lying down.

2 Prepare your field by breathing through and spinning the chakras.

3. Visualize straight lines bisecting the body from head to toe, back to front, and right to left, with the end points at equal distances from the body, and all meeting in the centre.

4. Focusing attention on the two ends of each of these lines; 'see' or 'imagine' a frequency or a colour that is common to both - white light, a combination of all colours, works well for a start.

5. Breathing slowly and completely, and without effort, bring the frequencies in along the straight lines to where they all meet in the centre of the body.

6. Continue until you experience 'fullness'. This represents a dynamic pile of non-directed energy, scalar energy going nowhere. Remember that the scalar energy is force by expansion. The human mind instructs it in its direction and its focus 'what to treat'.

7. Now is when the quantity of energy begins expanding outward through all your cells toward the body surface. This is like an inflated balloon becoming larger, or like a big glob of moist substance on a paper towel the energy is expanding outward on the surface beyond its original space.

Allow this to continue until the centre scalar energy has been dissipated outward loosening tight muscles and connective tissue and expanding the space between cells.

8. Create the scalar field again but this time try to breathe from all directions into the centre of the body simultaneously - as though you are a radiating sun that is now reversing its energy inward on each inhalation to centralize the energy.

9. When your scalar field is full you will start to experience its spontaneous even expansion toward the body surfaces. You focus your attention upon allowing this slow spreading apart of all cells, giving them 'breathing room'. The body area will seem larger and more resilient.

10. At this point, you may consciously program the energy with what you want it to accomplish and then direct it to wherever it is needed.

It is recommended that the procedure should last at least 10 minutes, or even several hours, depending upon the severity of the health problem.

The procedure for healing others is more or less the same as healing oneself.

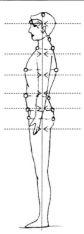

When healing another person it is best to increase and stabilize your own electro-magnetic field first, followed by visualizing or hands-on treatment using the same procedure as creating a scalar in yourself. It is better to create the scalar for another person while exhaling.

Electro-magnetic energy being drawn in from front and back to form Scalar Energy pool in the centre of the body.

How Does the Bio-Scalar Energy Heal ?

Improving circulation.

Research in 1950 at the Max Planck Institute in Germany found that when a mechanically created scalar wave was introduced into a petrie dish containing living cells, the cells separated, lost their clumping and became more active within the fluid medium.

This is a significant finding. All disease, injury or degeneration is accompanied by swelling and stasis in blood and lymphatic circulation. The body's healing substances are then immobilized.

Apparently the expansion aspect of the scalar energy improves circulation by removing the pressures.

It has been found that the scalar energy remarkably reduces swelling.

Improving chemistry.

Puharich found improvement in the immune and endocrine systems from in vitro study of scalars. Rein did extensive biological studies using the Tesla watch. Lymphocytes exposed to the Tesla watch scalars increased proliferation by 75% compared to the same watch without a scalar coil.

Using other scalar generators he discovered a modulation of basic biochemical communication between nerve cells.

Byrd also showed scalar energy increased the strength of low-level EEG frequencies. Rein found individual differences in biological responses to both electromagnetic fields and scalar energy.

Research has shown that the individual's signature pattern of the electro-magnetic field, probably the coherency of the individual's field, predicts the responsiveness to both energies. Furthermore, Rein questioned how much effect on bio-tissue could be uniquely attributed to the scalar wave since it exists in a larger electro-magnetic field.

Clinical Evidence of Bio-Scalar Healing

Healing with Bio-Scalar Energy started only in the 21st century.

No illness, injury or surgery that the scalar energy did not help has been encountered. The speed and completeness of recovery is outstanding.

Injury

Traumatic injuries, fractures, dislocations, subluxations, and bone spurs have been completely healed in approximately one quarter of the average time. With one person pulverized fractures, where bone setting was impossible, re-grew down normal pathways in five months.

Acute pain ordinarily only relieved by codeine or morphine became tolerable with across-the-counter analgesics.

Medical Conditions.

The anticipated time for surgery was considerably shortened.

Bleeding was minimized with low haemoglobin patients. Recovery seemed to be much faster and more complete.

Healing of hyperactive nervous disturbances like skin rashes or shingles were cured or shortened to days not weeks.

More serious hyperactive diseases like scleroderma were greatly improved. The debility and course of action of viruses and bacteria was shortened.

During congestive pneumonia there was rapid improvement of breathing without the introduction of oxygen.

Cancer patients reported improved tolerance to chemotherapy.

A degenerative liver condition following hepatitis C was greatly improved.

Cellular degeneration was eliminated with one patient, another improved through standing and walking.

A patient with a massive stroke with poor prognosis continues to improve.

Scalar energy was particularly effective with ill domestic animals.

<u>Releasing Emotion.</u>

Healers report more incidences of release of tissue held emotions when they activate the bio-scalar.

Two patients who learned to create their own scalar energy reported breaking a long drug addiction without withdrawal symptoms.

<u>Conclusions.</u>

Clinical results from treating some common medical problems show that a combination of ordinary electro-magnetic fields with Bio-Scalar energy causes the fastest and most complete healing.

The Bio-Scalar energy adds the unique qualities of strength and sustaining power for enduring changes.

The discovery of the Bio-Scalar energy has many other pluses. It lets us know again the magnificence of the human mind to direct our destiny, to use our consciousness to create this powerful energy for healing self and others.

It strengthens our security with independence from drugs. Its only side effects are the improvement of health.

Bio-Scalar Energy Meditation for Healing - #2

This exercise can be learned best when sitting. After acquiring the skill it can be repeated while standing or lying down.

Prepare your field by breathing through and spinning the chakras.

Visualize your entire body as a container where you will draw in electro-magnetic energy with each inhalation, bringing it into the centre of the body. Do not move it out or up or down, just in.

Start by breathing energy in through the front of your body, head to toe.

Then focus your attention upon breathing energy through the back of your body, also head to toe, into the centre so it meets the 'front energy' and folds upon itself, going nowhere.

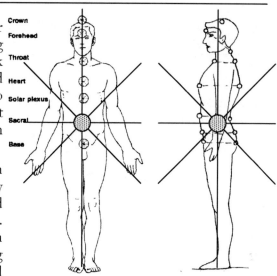

Next breathe through both sides of your body simultaneously, right and left, from head to toes. Let the energy again meet the same opposing energy building up and enfolding into a scalar standing field in the centre of the body.

Electromagnetic energy being drawn in from all directions to form Scalar Energy Pool in centre of body.

Now concentrate upon the top of your head and the bottom of your feet to breathe in energy until it meets in the middle of the body to enfold upon itself.

The centre of your body is now filled with a powerful quiet pool of energy. Now is when the pool of energy expands outwards, through all your cells towards the body surface, like a balloon inflating. Allow this to continue until the centre scalar energy has dissipated outward loosening tight muscles and connective tissue, and expanding the space between cells.

Create the scalar field again but this time try to breathe from all directions into the centre of the body simultaneously - as though you are a radiating sun that is now reversing its energy inward on each inhalation to centralize the energy.

If you have difficulty comprehending all sides at once go back to meditation #1 with isolated directions.

When your scalar field is full you will start to experience its spontaneous even expansion toward the body surfaces. You focus your attention upon allowing this slow spreading apart of all cells, giving them 'breathing room'. The body area will seem larger and more resilient.

We now have the Scalar Wave pooled at the centre of the body so what do we do next ? There are three possibilities.

(1). If left to it's own devices the surface tension of the Scalar Wave will deteriorate and break. This allows the scalar energy to expand slowly and smoothly throughout the body where it does all of it's healing work.

This expansion takes only several minutes.

(2). We can participate in this healing work. All that is necessary for us to do is consciously instruct the Scalar Wave to expand and it will do so. The result will be exactly the same as in option (1).

(3). In this option, we again take control of the Scalar Wave.

The energy is consciously instructed to go to any part of the body eg. a tumour in the lungs and do it's work. This healing is obviously more intense.

With option (3) you can only tackle one problem at a time. If there is more than one problem in different parts of the body you will have to create a Scalar Wave for each problem.

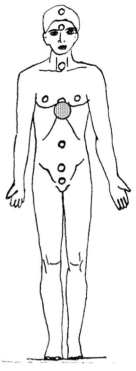

'Etheric Body' Image' showing the Scalar Wave pooled at it's centre.

Distant Healing with Bio-Scalar Energy

We have seen that you can create a Scalar wave for 'self-healing' and for healing others. Can it be possible that we can heal at a distance using the 'etheric image' ?

I have found this to be possible for healing, at a distance, yourself, others and pets also.

In this section we will use the 'etheric body' image as previous.

For the type of work we are about to do, we will use a copy of the human form on letter/A4 size paper. If you have an artistic bent you may wish to draw the images yourself with pencil.

Some people think that this approach is more effective in the healing. The drawing does not have to be artistically correct, a drawing similar to the one shown would be fine.

Firstly make sure you are as relaxed as possible. Take your copy of the body image and, add the 'etheric matrix' information as before, name, date of birth, post code etc. Then by intent place your visualized image into the drawn image.

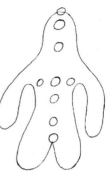

Hand Drawn Body Image

Next draw eight (four pairs) of diametrically opposed (opposite direction) arrows pointing to the approximate centre of the human form.

These arrows are to be used by you as a guide for the visualized waves of electromagnetic energy (Prana). The waves of energy must be drawn in pairs, one coming from one direction and the other from the exact opposite direction.

When these waves meet head on at the centre of the body image the Scalar Wave will start to form and pool in the centre of the body.

Each electromagnetic wave starts at the cosmic doorway (dot) and ends in the Arrow Head.

Fred Bloggs   03/08/1955

CH1 6AG

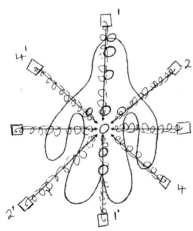

Hand Drawn Body Image complete with arrows and spirals which simulate e-m waves and create the Scalar Wave.

The key to success with this method is INTENT. You intend that waves of Prana follow the lines into the centre of the body image.

When sufficient waves are drawn the scalar wave is complete.

Hold your pendulum over the 'centre' and program it to rotate clockwise whilst the electromagnetic waves are entering the body image.

Program the pendulum to stop when the process is complete. This may take up to ten minutes.

Now the scalar is pooled in the centre of the body. You may now will the scalar to expand throughout the body to do it's work, using the pendulum as before to do this.

If left to it's own devices, the pool of scalar energy slowly and smoothly expands throughout the body as explained earlier.

You may of course direct the energy to anywhere in the body as explained.

To direct the energy we will use clockwise spirals.

Fred Bloggs
03/08/1955
CH1 6AG

In the example shown the problem is in the head area, for example, brain tumour.

If you are treating a specific part of the body, you need to direct the scalar to that part.

Use the pendulum as before to achieve this.

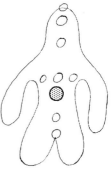

Pool of Scalar Energy in 'Centre' of Body

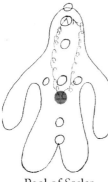

Pool of Scalar Energy being directed to the head area to treat a tumour.

My students and I have used this distant healing procedure for some time now with great success.

There are probably many ways of 'broadcasting' this healing but I have not heard of any others.

Chapter Thirteen

Focal Touch Healing

If you choose to practice the techniques outlined in this book, you will explore a practice that breathes fresh air into ancient healing teachings. As you progress in this work, you will find yourself changing in many positive ways.

You will discover a new understanding of the outer world and your inner-self, and the ability to control it 'consciously and energetically'. You will develop powerful inner strength and high self-esteem, empathy for others, and extraordinary perception and intuition.

You may feel as if you are a newly born person with sixth sense - the bio-energy ability. You will be able to perceive the energy fields of all living things and assess the energetic health information of anyone.

You may relieve any personal distress easily on an everyday basis, and negative moods like depression will become a thing of the past due to your new, positive outlook and ability to control your thoughts. Your mind will be clear and alert. Your thoughts are healing, and your powerful healing energy will follow your thoughts.

Just bear in mind that you were born with healing ability. You have not lost this ability, you only need to be shown how to use it and have your energy channels open again.

When you embark on the path of Focal Touch healing, you will find yourself using words like 'cure' in place of 'healing' more often than not. You may also find it frightening at first to be given the ability to channel such powerful energy as that available from the Healing Flame. Please don't worry, you cannot harm anyone or yourself with this energy - it will only flow if the intention is pure.

Once you have begun Focal Touch Healing work, your goal is to continue your work and healer's development, always exploring and strengthening your abilities. May you open your own door to the Future of Good Health.

An Amazing Introduction

This is an extraordinary story that started in October 2003. Bill Ellis, is a Master/Teacher in several modalities of Energy Field Healing.

This seemed to be the trigger that started the sequence of events which followed.

The local Spiritualist Church which Bill and Sue, his wife, attend was the focal point. A healing circle is held there every Wednesday evening which they attend to give healing. Through the Church he naturally came into contact with mediums and clairvoyants.

Bill, himself, had no tendency in this area, or so he thought, until recent events changed his mind completely.

One night about 3.00 a.m. Bill awoke feeling quite refreshed and with no desire to sleep. He lay on his back and stared at the ceiling that was clearly seen in the dim night light from the corridor outside the room. He did not see visions but the message he received was like a thought form that said: *"So you have written a book. Well, don't think that's the end of it. You still have a lot of work to do."*

Not understanding what this meant he found himself asking, *"What are you talking about ? What work do I have to do ?"*

The answer that came was astounding: *"There is a new healing method that we want you to get involved in; it will require you to be attuned during an initiation ceremony."*

For days he wrestled with these thoughts trying to fathom their meaning. Then he received a telephone call from a medium, Gary, who he had met in the spiritualist church. Gary told him that Spirit had a lot more knowledge to impart, and that Gary himself would also be involved. This was given some thought for a few days, then he had an urge to ring Jean whom he knew quite well and was a very good medium. Jean has the ability to tune into him, even over the phone. He asked if she was aware of the affects. The answer she gave was as follows: *"Yes, there is a new healing. It was lost to humanity thousands of years ago but is now to be offered again. It is not like Energy Field Healing but is far more powerful and intense. The energy emits as a very intense and focussed beam from the thumb, index finger and middle finger of either or both hands, as if holding a pen for writing."*

Over the next two days he received messages that told him he would need only one attunement that would be performed by Members of the Healing Council, using three mediums and one observer - his wife Sue. All five of them are Master/Teachers in Chios, Reiki or both.

Because Bill felt he lacked the confidence to gather this sort of information, he decided to call a meeting of all five concerned.

They met at Jean's house with no preconceived ideas and no idea what they were going to talk about. None of them were prepared for what followed. A Being was channelled through Jean, who had slipped into trance. This was the first of many meetings with Xanthia.

This was their first introduction. *"My name is Xanthia. I am Arcan of the Healing Council and Warden of the Healing Flame."*

Xanthia went on to say that if Bill agreed to be attuned, the initiation would be carried out by all members of the Healing Council, using the chosen mediums to channel the energy. Bill agreed to be attuned and a date for the attunement was set.

On the specified date the attunement was carried out. As a continuance of the attunement, all five participants had to carry out certain tasks for the next seven days. A candle was lit each day at the same time by each person for seven days. During this period whilst the energy was growing in Bill, it was noticed that the remaining four became aware that some healing powers were also manifesting within them.

It transpired that the 'Four' had received a first attunement also during the main attunement. After the seven days had lapsed Xanthia and the Healing Council assisted Bill to attune 'The Four' to Master Level.

After these attunements, they had further meetings where more knowledge was imparted to them from Xanthia for the various healing procedures.

Attunement

The details of Focal Touch Healing are given here, and it is hoped that these will enable you to have success in its use.

However, you may find that you need an attunement by a 'Master of Focal Touch Healing' to make this healing modality fully operational. Such a Master (such as Bill Ellis) may well charge for the attunement - to cover the time and effort that is committed.

This initiation procedure is not the same as an attunement for other modalities of energy healing and having one will not enable you to perform in the other.

Originally it was believed that such an attunement had to be given 'person to person' - but it has now been determined that it can be given 'mind to mind', providing that the initiate has obtained a full understanding of the methodology involved, as presented here.

In exceptional circumstances you may find that the 'Healing Touch Council' gives it directly to you.

I trust that you will treasure this knowledge and use it wisely, especially to help others.

The Basis of Focal Touch Healing

This is a very ancient form of healing which has been given before and was used millennia ago. However, it was last used about 5,000 years ago when it was lost due to disbelief, human's need for novelty, and persecution of the healers. Now it is being sent again for the greater good of the earth, man and life.

There are two major differences between this Healing and other forms of Energy Field Healing:

1). The healing is performed on the disease itself and not its energy counterpart in the Etheric body. For example, if you are called upon to give healing for a tumour, you would treat the tumour where it resides in the body and not the chakra associated with that part of the body where the tumour resides.

2). In other forms of Energy Field Healing, the diseased, stale and negative energy is removed from the Etheric Body before energizing with Universal Life Force Energy (Prana, Ki or Chi etc.).

Focal Touch Healing does not use Universal Life Force Energy as we know it. The energy used is much more powerful and until July 2005 we were not told what this energy is, what it is called, or how it is channeled through the healer. We now know it as Zero-Point energy.

This Zero-Point energy is condensed by the Healing Flame down to Tachyon energy, channeled through the Healer and then transferred to the diseased part of the Healee as a high intensity narrow beam of energy.

The beam is then detached from the Healer, where it stays protruding from the Healee's body ! Other beams of the energy are placed into the Healee, but at different angles. The healer knows how many beams to use.

When the last beam is placed, they will gradually retract into the diseased part of the Healee. This energy is then sealed in by the Healer where it mingles with the diseased energy and transforms (transmutes) it into positive life giving energy. The time this procedure takes depends on the degree of disease.

There is one more very important difference between Focal Touch Healing and forms of Energy Field Healing. In most forms of energy field healing there is no way for self-healing - and if there is, as in Reiki, even Masters find that the energy flow is nowhere as intense as when healing others.

Focal Touch self-healing, on the other hand, is just as intense for yourself as when healing others !

There are two levels of Focal Touch Healing:

1). Practitioner. At this level you will be attuned to the 'Energy' by a Master/Teacher of Focal Touch Healing. You will also receive all the required information to enable you to heal in all aspects, including Physical Healing, Emotional Healing, General Maintenance Healing, Mental Healing, and Spiritual Healing.

2). Master/Teacher. A further attunement is given. This attunement will not only open your channels to healing to a higher degree but will open you to a level that enables you to attune others.

More on Attunements

Being attuned to become a Practitioner or Master is a beautiful and life-changing experience. No-one can really describe exactly how or why it works, but it does. In effect it is a miracle.

This is a special, extraordinary benefit. The process permanently clears and balances the most important energy paths within the body which channel and transfer the healing energy.

It also automatically releases some negative karma from the receiver. This is the universe's way of rewarding the person for consciously choosing the path of healing.

As a Master, it is perfectly in order to practice giving multiple attunements to the same person repeatedly, as there is no danger of overloading them ! It will also provide a different type of healing for them at the same time, and it isn't necessary that they become healers themselves.

When you are completely comfortable with the attunement process and have ample practical experience in all types of healing sessions, you will be ready to start teaching if you wish.

As with every other part of Focal Touch Healing, giving attunements is a very simple process. It involves performing a series of movements in a correct sequence, with no effort or conscious control of energy from you. The complete attunement sequence will be provided.

Brief Notes of Channelling with Xanthia

People will seek you all out and guidance given to the delight of all.

Let the healing energy be free to follow its own will and it will be successful. You must remember that Spirit will choose the person to be attuned and they will be put forward accordingly. What feels right is the correct answer. Likewise the people to be healed will be pushed forward to your attention, some will be believers, some are not. However the results will speak for themselves.

To improve your energy and skill just use it ! This is a simple straight forward skill. No fancy things. Keep it simple and direct. When people change our words and add to it, it becomes complex.

This healing is non religious, there are no religious rites, prayer, or ceremony, and it can be used by anyone attuned to it. It is the intent that is important.

There is no novelty, as novelty and whims will cause it to be lost. Ground work must be correct. Simplicity is the key.

On the surface some may seem to be healed; however a lot of diseases are deep rooted. You may heal the physical symptoms.

However, the patient may need emotional healing. A feeling of weakening of the power flowing through the healer indicates that the energy within the body is coming into harmony.

A separate procedure will be shown to you for maintenance, such as general upliftment. This healing procedure will be short but will touch each level of healing, ie. mental, physical and emotional.

Your awareness will grow with practice, as this healing is intuitive, and, if necessary, hand positions will be shown.

Blessings - may you all go forward in Love and Light !

Focal Touch Healing Procedures

Before we can discuss the 'Distance Healing' aspects of this healing modality, it is necessary for you to grasp the 'Hands On' fundamentals first. You who are reading this book in 2008 and trying out the distance techniques are 'Pioneers'.

I will give brief details of the methods I have used which have been successful. But feel free to use your favourite methods - the worst that can happen is that they may not work one hundred percent. If this is the case, try mine !

The procedures which follow are as given by Xanthia, but the wording in some cases has been changed to bring their meaning into the twentieth century. These procedures are very simple !

Chakras

It is neither necessary nor desirable to enter into an in-depth study of subtle anatomy or force centres (chakras) to become an expert at Focal Touch Healing. However, a chart showing chakra names and positions is given to help you place the hands accurately in some of the procedures.

General Notes

All of the techniques in Focal Touch Healing are very simple. These techniques must never be altered to suit the whims of egotistical healers.

Whilst reading these notes you will come across references to various hand positions such as 'Position No. 1' etc.

These positions do not refer to positions of the hands on the body of the Healee, but to the positions of the fingers and thumbs of the Healer.

To make this clear, there follows a series of illustrations to demonstrate these positions using both hands. Either hand can be used during healing. Sometimes both hands are used together.

The Working Symbol

Start from the cross over in the centre and draw the left side first in a clockwise direction, back to the cross over. Continue the right side in an anticlockwise direction, finishing at the cross over point.

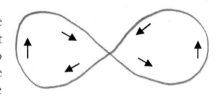

The symbol is always drawn using the dominant hand with fingers/thumb in Position No.1. It invokes intense energy, light and colour and focuses it for healing depending on the healing level intention: Physical, Emotional, Mental or Spiritual Healing.

In science, this symbol is used to represent Infinity and in Focal Touch Healing the same applies; it has no beginning or no end and implies energy moving in several directions at the same time.

Questioned about the significance of the symbol: *"The symbol has a power of its own. It intensifies and helps focus the energy. It is a symbol that has no beginning and no end. A symbol which flows. A circle is a symbol that has no beginning and no end but it flows in a certain direction. But this symbol flows across and around.*

The energy is moving in several directions at the one time and yet in the same direction, never ending, never beginning, never stopping. The energy is tuned and is truly focused. In the middle this is where the energy path's cross in the middle of the figure of eight.

At the beginning, when you feel it you may become aware of the vibration of this energy as you use it to heal, when you draw the symbol upon the head of the one to be healed.

The vibration, the movement of this energy, the never ending flow, be aware of the pain at which level you are healing; be it at the physical level, emotional level, mental level or spiritual level.

The healing fire has many flames. They are focused to a different level of healing and to the different needs of the person to be healed."

Pre–Healing Procedures

When a healer is approached by a client for help, the client usually has an idea what ails them and gives this information to the healer. This information is very useful - but may be lacking in detail.

The healer should ask questions of the client to fill in any gaps and get permission to conduct a body scan to further ascertain any other problem areas.

Position #1 - Left Hand

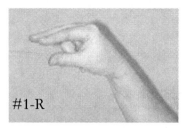

Position #1 - Right Hand

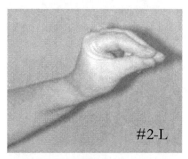

Position #2 - Left Hand

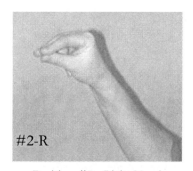

Position #2 - Right Hand

Position #3 - Left Hand

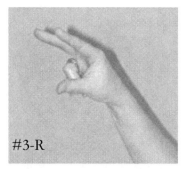

Position #3 - Right Hand

Scanning

In this procedure, you will use either or both hands with fingers/thumbs in Position No. 3.

The attunement process not only opens the chakras and energy channels so that healing energy can flow, it also increases intuition and heightens sensitivity to psychic energy. Using the chakras in the finger tips and palms of your hands, it is possible to sense where the client needs healing.

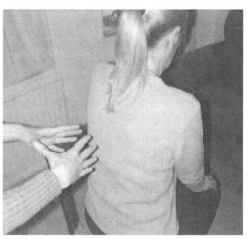

Position #4 - From Back

Ask to be shown the places that need healing, then with either hand one to four inches over the body and with finger tips pointing at the body, start at the head and slowly move down the body.

Be aware of how the energy on the finger tips and palm of your hand feels. If you feel a coolness, or sense a distortion or irregularity in the energy field, you have detected a place that needs healing. You may also feel this as tingling, pressure, little electric shocks, pulsations or a pulling on your hand.

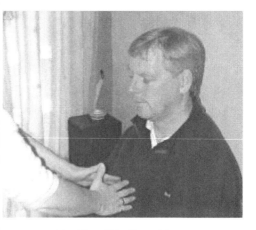

Position #4 - From Front

It is IMPORTANT to use ONLY open fingers, Position No.1, when treating Children, Animals, Frail People and the Infirm.

Your hand may also simply be guided to the right spot, and you will often know where the distortion is before your hand gets there. You may also find you are developing the ability to see the energy field.

These sensations and impressions may be so slight at first that you may think it is your imagination. However, trust your experience. As you practice, your ability to scan the aura will improve. Remember that you can always use your pendulum to amplify such sensations and signal their meaning.

When you find a distortion, move your hand up and down the body over the area until you find the place where you feel the most distortion. This is the area where you will apply healing.

As soon as you are attuned to this energy by a Focal Touch Healing Master, your ability to sense a persons energy field will become more powerful. Picking up the distortions in this field, the indications of problem areas, will become second nature to you.

In all of the Focal Touch Healing procedures the touch pressure is as a 'Butterfly Landing on A Flower'. The healing procedures that follow are not presented in the order that you will use them. The order of use will depend on the outcome of the scanning procedure and your prior knowledge of the Healee's condition.

In the majority of cases you would start with Emotional / Mental healing as any of these procedures relax the Healee - and in most cases alter their state of consciousness, which makes them more receptive to the healing.

Procedure for Physical Healing

It was mentioned earlier that Physical Healing is not necessarily the first healing that you will do on your patient - but it is placed first in the order of learning the procedures. It is placed here because it is the simplest procedure to learn and carry out.

Results with simple ailments can be miraculous and will give you confidence for later work. Results with simple aches, pains, stiffness and the like will more than likely be instantaneous and confidence building.

But be aware that even though you may know the problem, your scanning may indicate treatment in a completely different area: trust the scanning (done only with Position #3 !) for the area to treat.

It is important to use only open fingers, Position No.1, when treating Children, Animals, Frail People and the Infirm.

Stand behind the person. Start with the intention to heal, bring the symbol into mind, and fashion it above the person's head at the Crown Chakra from behind with the fingers and thumb in Position No.1. The thumb, first finger and middle finger are held slightly apart (Position No.1) and positioned over the place of healing about 1 to 2 inches away from the body.

They are held there until it feels right to bring the fingers together (Position No.2) - only if thought necessary to intensify the healing power - and NOT for children, animals, frail people and the infirm.

Light will move from your fingers into the body of the person and out on the opposite side.

Now slide the fingers along the visualized beam of light to make contact with the persons body, hold this position for a few seconds, and then slowly retrace the path of your fingers back to previous position (about 1 to 2 inches from body), pulling out the visualized light beam with your fingers.

Detach your fingers from the visualized light beam and leave it there protruding from the persons body about 2 inches back and front. If the fingers are held apart the energy will be gentle and the beam of light thick. When the fingers are brought together the beam will be very thin and intense.

You will find that with practice you will know how long to allow the gentle beams to work before making them (if necessary) more intense.

Once the beam of light is established through the body and out the other side, then another beam of light can be put in from a different angle.

As you gain experience then you will notice the intensity of the light may differ, the colour of the light will become associated with the disease, and the number of beams of light may vary. You will find that you will feel how many beams are necessary. The worse the disease the more beams of light will be needed.

In cases where you are treating arms, legs, hands, and feet, etc., the energy beam will more than likely go right through and come out the other side as stated above. On the other hand, if you are treating organs such as the liver, heart or lungs etc., then the energy beam may enter the organ, stay there, and only protrude from the body at the point of entry. This is normal - and when it retracts it will stay in the organ to do its healing work.

Endocrine Gland Colour Coding

There are seven endocrine glands in the human body which govern the immune system and control certain bodily functions.

These glands are Pineal, Pituitary, Thyroid, Thymus, Pancreas, Adrenal, and Reproductive organs.

Xanthia explained that it might be helpful for individual healers to give their own colour code references to each gland. I have found that the best way to formulate this code is as follows:

Sit in a comfortable position, close your eyes and relax. Using the list of glands and diagram provided, bring each gland in turn into your awareness - and as you do this, request a colour for this gland remembering the gland and associated colour. For instance, the uppermost gland is the Pineal and when I thought about this gland and it's position, the colour Sky Blue came to mind - and this is the colour I always use for this gland.

If you are scanning a patient with a disease which attacks the immune system, a colour will enter your mind. If the colour is pink and you have coded the pancreas as pink then you would treat the pancreas for diabetes. The chart which follows may be helpful. It shows the glands in descending order with colours used by the writer - but you will make your own colour code.

If no colour comes to mind whilst scanning, this means that there are probably no problems with the immune system and endocrine glands.

Here is a diagram showing the position of each gland in the human body. The diagram covers both male (left) and female (right).

When the treatment is complete the beams of light will withdraw into the body.

The light/energy beam will withdraw under it's own volition.

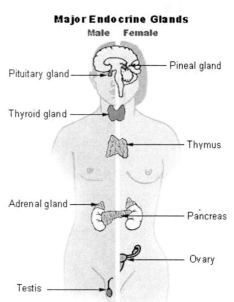

Major Endocrine Glands

Male   Female

Pituitary gland

Thyroid gland

Pineal gland

Thymus

Adrenal gland

Pancreas

Ovary

Testis

Chakra	Diseases	Gland	Physiology
#7 Crown Blue	Nervous & mental disorders	Pineal	Central Nervous system
#6 Ajna Yellow	Eye disorders	Pitury	Autonomic nervous system
#5 Throat Orange	Thyroid & Laryngeal diseases	Thyroid	Respiratory
#4 Heart Pink	Heart disease & hypertension	Thymus	Circulation
#3 Solar Plexus Red	Stomach, pancreas & liver disorders	Pancreas	Digestion
#2 Sacral Purple	Lung & kidney disorders	Reproductive organs	Genitals, urinary
#1 Root / Base Green	Blood disorders, anaemia	Adrenal	Reproductive

This may take a few moments, <u>do not attempt to force the light in with your hands.</u>

Then it is necessary to seal the treatment with the symbol. Use fingers in Position 2 to do this.

A patient may have several physical disorders, and in this case it is necessary to treat them all separately by sealing each treatment before going on to the next ailment.

All disorders may be treated in one session but must be separated by a sealing in of the energy. At the close of the healing, again draw the symbol on the Crown of the person's head and give thanks for the healing.

Procedure for Emotional Healing

Treatment of illness and disease that has already manifested itself in the physical body has been covered in Physical Healing. Most emotional problems, stress, trauma etc. eventually manifest themselves as a disorder in the physical body.

This section deals with the treatment of emotional problems whether they have manifested as a disorder or not.

The energy beams used in this type of healing are quite defuse and are much milder than the energy used in Physical Healing. Both hands are used simultaneously in Position No.1 (fingers and thumb slightly apart) to channel the energy.

1). The Healee should be seated in a straight backed chair with feet slightly apart and firmly on the ground. From behind, the Healer should place the hands on the Healee's shoulders to gain rapport.

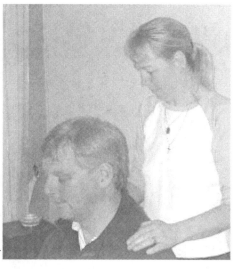

In these brief moments you should focus yourself and bring into your awareness the Intention to heal.

With Healing Intent, the Healer should now fashion the symbol over the crown of the Healee with the dominant hand and the fingers and thumb in Position No.1.

2). From the front, the Healer now places the tips of the fingers of both hands (Position No.1) lightly on the closed eyes of the Healee. The energy leaves the Healer's heart, down the arms and into the head of the Healee through the fingers and thumb.

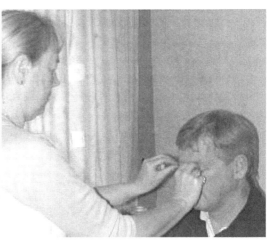

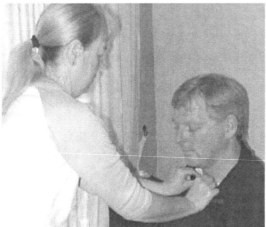

3). The energy makes its way to the Throat Chakra of the Healee where it is held by placing the hands on the Throat Chakra in Position No.1.

4). When complete, the energy will move down to the Heart Chakra and the Healer moves his hands (Position No.1) to the Heart Chakra and holds the energy there. The energy, which now is Divine Love, may be seen as a ball of fire or flame. What you are seeing is not a chakra but Divine Love generated from the Healing Flame. The energy ball now decreases in size, getting smaller and smaller, but increasing in intensity.

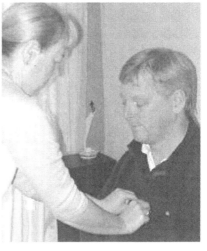

5). When it is ready, the energy ball will move down to the Solar Plexus Chakra. The Healer now moves his hands to this chakra with fingers and thumbs in Position No.2 and holds them there until it is felt that the energy is ready. When it is ready, the energy ball will expand and diffuse to fill the area with golden yellow light. The healing is now complete.

6). The Healer will now seal the front Solar Plexus with the symbol. The back of the Solar Plexus is sealed similarly followed by the Crown Chakra.

7). The Healer now places his hands on the shoulders of the Healee and both give thanks for the healing.

The one who has been healed may experience emotions welling up - no worry. Maybe complete emotional numbness - again no worry. The Healee is now instructed to continue sitting quietly for a few moments in prayer or meditation.

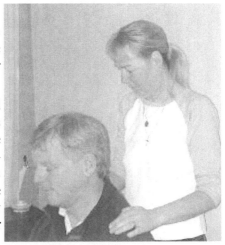

Procedure for General Maintenance Healing

You will no doubt come across people who come to you for healing but on investigation, you may find that they have no physical disease and there is no evidence of emotional problems.

Nevertheless, they will tell you that they are listless, run down, have little energy, can't concentrate and have low vitality etc.

In such cases, you need a procedure that can uplift, give an energy boost and make people, animals, and yourself feel generally uplifted. The technique which follows in this section does all these things.

The Healee may be seated, standing or lying down. Ask them to remove their shoes and to relax.

During this procedure the fingers are always used in Position No. 1

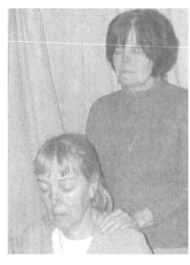

1). From behind, place your hands on the shoulders of the Healee to gain an energetic rapport with the Healee and focus yourself.

What follows next may be carried out from behind or in front, whichever is the most comfortable for both participants.

Draw the symbol on the Crown Chakra of the Healee whilst visualizing a shower like rain or mist emanating from the symbol and cascading downward over the whole body of the Healee from head to feet.

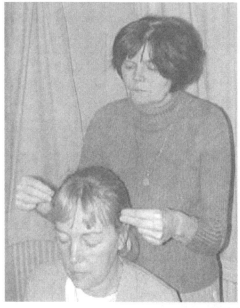

2). Place both hands, with fingers in Position No.1, on both temples of the Healee. A wide beam of mellow, soothing energy will now fill the area between the Healers hands, inside the Healee's head.

Hold this position for a short time until you feel that the energy is established. Now withdraw the fingers away from the temples, about 1 inch, and detach from beam.

3). Move your hands to the outer extremities of the Healee's shoulders so that the fingers of each hand are pointing at each other through the body of the Healee. Now establish a wide beam of the same mellow, soothing energy from shoulder to shoulder inside the Healee's upper torso. You will notice that as this beam establishes itself, the beam previously placed between the temples expands downwards to fuse with this latest beam. The two beams merge so filling the Healee's head, neck and body between the shoulders with soothing, healing energy.

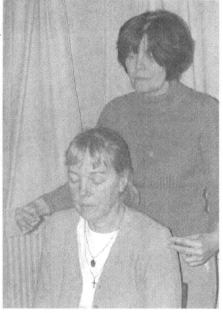

Again, withdraw and detach fingers.

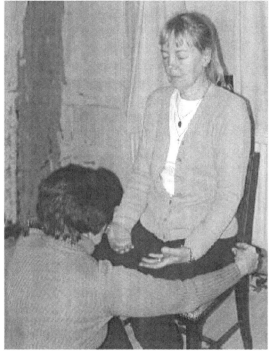

4). Now move the hands down to the Healee's hips with both sets of fingers pointing at each other through the Healee's body.

A new beam will now establish itself across this area inside the body. As this beam establishes, the energy in the head, neck and upper torso will expand downwards to merge with the latest beam. The head, neck and torso of the Healee will now be filled with healing energy.

Detach from beam as before.

5). Move one set of fingers to the nape of the neck and place the fingers of the other hand on the base of the spine.

Allow a beam of energy to establish itself along the full length of the spine.

This energy will augment the energy already present in the upper body.

Detach as usual.

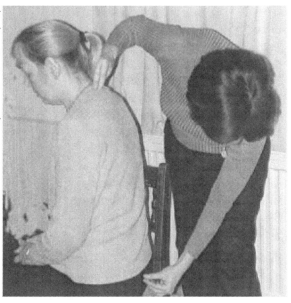

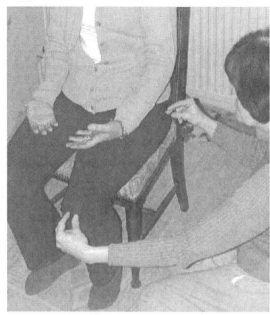

6). Place the fingers of one hand on the hip and the fingers of the other hand on the knee of the same leg.

Establish a wide beam of energy through the thigh.

When the beam is established, do the same for the other leg, detaching from beams in usual way.

7). With the fingers of one hand on the knee and the fingers of the other hand on the ankle establish a wide beam of energy through the lower leg.

When the beam is established, do the same to the other leg and detach from beams as usual.

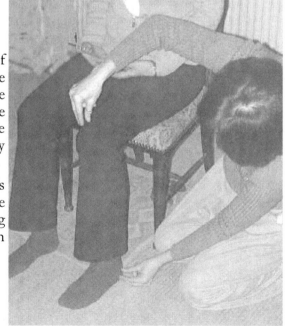

8). Now treat each foot between heel and toe.

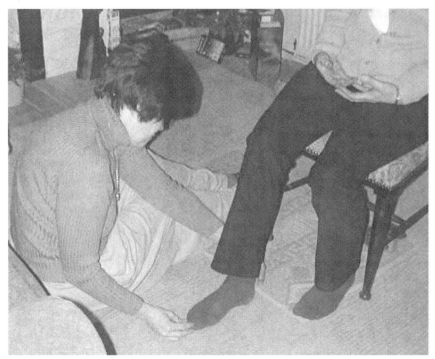

9). Move the hands back to the temples and hold this position until the light/energy surrounding the body, withdraws back into the body.

With this withdrawal of energy back into the body, the treatment is complete.

10). Draw the symbol on the Crown Chakra and then give thanks for the healing.

This is a very mild but invigorating healing and can be used several times a day on yourself, family and pets.

If you have difficulty in bending down to treat your lower legs or feet, don't worry. Place the fingers of both hands on one knee and 'will' the beam to go downwards through the lower leg into the foot, right down to the tips of the toes. Treat the other leg in the same way.

Procedure for Mental Healing

This healing is intended to alleviate mental stress, to help with mental illness, to help those who study or work under pressure, to give them clarity of mind, clear reasoning, and perception from many different angles on the same problem or task. It can be used as an aid to learning and problem solving.

When used as an aid to learning or problem solving, the procedure is short and of low intensity. The procedure is longer and more intense when used for mental stress and mental illness. Nevertheless, the procedure is the same in both cases.

There may be a great amount of confusion in the mind which may be caused by emotional trauma. In such a case, clarification of the mind by this treatment will probably remove the emotional trauma at the same time.

If you are drawn to do so, you may give an Emotional treatment followed by a Mental treatment or vice versa, this is satisfactory as you cannot 'over heal' someone, and giving one type of treatment may remove the need for the other type of treatment.

The Mental Healing procedure is particularly useful in treating phobias. Just be aware that many phobias are deep rooted and may require several treatments to eradicate them completely.

Please remember also that what may appear to you as being a trivial matter, such as a fear of feathers, is very real to the sufferer and must be treated as such.

Problems such as drug abuse, alcohol abuse, and any minor habits respond well to this procedure. Please keep in mind that animals also have similar problems and benefit from this treatment.

As with all other Focal Touch Healing techniques, you can treat yourself and obtain excellent results.

During the Mental Healing procedure, the fingers/thumbs are always held in Position No. 2. We will be using high intensity energy beams.

There will be four beams of high intensity energy passing through the head at the level of the Brow Chakra, two high intensity energy beams passing through the neck at the level of the Throat Chakra, and one high intensity energy beam passing vertically through the centre of the head down to the centre of the neck at the level of the Throat Chakra.

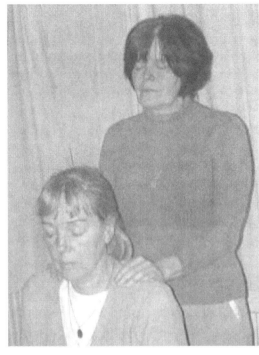

Whilst the treatment is being carried out, it will be more comfortable for both participants if the Healee is seated and the Healer remains standing.

1).As previously the Healer will start from behind the Healee.

Place both hands on the shoulders of the Healee to gain an energetic rapport with the Healee.

Subconsciously, state your intention to heal whilst focussing yourself.

2). Draw the symbol on the Crown Chakra of the Healee with the dominant hand with fingers/thumbs in Position No. 1.

As you do this, visualize an intense, brilliant light inside the head of the Healee as emanating from a crystal or flame in the centre of the Healee's head.

As the light fills the head, you will become aware of the intensity of the light at the Healee's Brow Chakra and lower at the Throat Chakra.

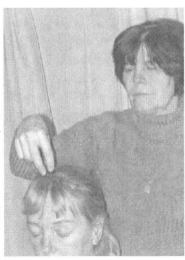

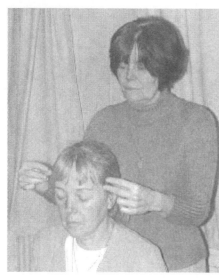

3). When the light has manifested itself fully, place the fingers/thumb of the hands on each side of the head of the Healee.

The fingers/thumb of each hand should be placed level with the top of the ears and slightly in front of each ear.

Insert the first high intensity beam from left to right of the Healee's head.

4). With the side to side beam established, place the fingers/thumb of one hand on the Brow Chakra and the fingers/thumb of the other hand on the back of the head exactly opposite the other hand - back of the Brow Chakra.

Send a high intensity beam through the head from front to back.

This beam will cut right through the centre of the side to side beam in the centre of the Healee's brain.

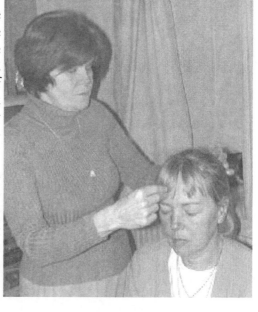

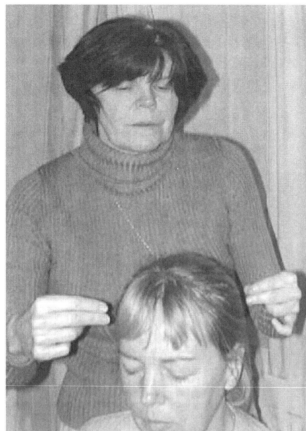

5). The next beam to be inserted goes from the front right of the forehead to the back left of the head.

It is placed in such a way as to travel through the same point in the brain where the two previous beams crossed.

6). With the three beams now established, all we have to do now is to position the final head beam.

This beam is inserted from front left to back right of the Healee's head.

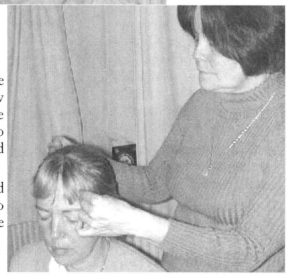

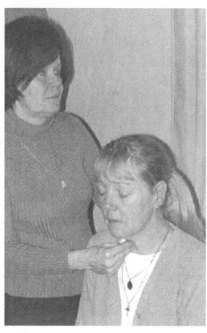

7). Mental activity is very much connected with communication; it is therefore necessary to perform healing on the Throat Chakra

A high intensity energy beam is now placed in the throat from front to back as above.

Place the fingers/thumb of one hand on the front Throat Chakra and the fingers/thumb of the other hand on the back.

Establish a high energy beam between each hand.

8). When the beam is established, place your fingers/thumbs on each side of the neck and insert a further beam of energy from one side to the other, crossing the back to front beam in the centre of the neck.

The healing is now complete and all beams will withdraw into the light of Pure Clarity in the Healee's head.

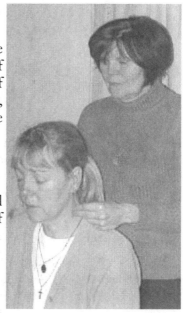

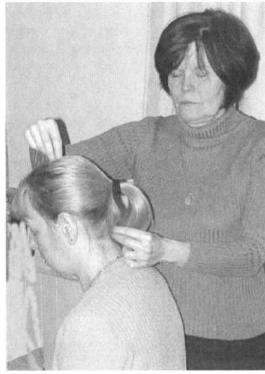

9). Finally, insert a last beam through the Crown, through the centre of the brain where the head beams meet and into the neck where the neck beams meet.

This is achieved by placing the fingers/thumb of one hand on the Crown and the fingers/thumb of the other hand on the front or back Throat Chakra

The picture shows the back position.

The Light Of Pure Clarity now withdraws into this final beam which also withdraws into the Healee's head.

When ALL of the beams have withdrawn into the head/neck, close by drawing the symbol over the Crown and give thanks for the healing.

In the case of Mental Healing it is most important that the Healee is not allowed to undertake any normal activities too soon after the treatment.

The person may be disorientated or more confused right after the treatment. This is very temporary and should be no cause for concern. Sitting quietly for a few minutes is all that is require for these symptoms to pass.

Understanding Spiritual Healing

This Healing is completely different from the previous four levels given earlier. Even though it has the same name as the Energy Field type of healing, it's purpose and methodology are completely different.

This was given some months later to the 'Five' during a group meeting with channelling from the Healing Council.

This level of healing requires a Soul to Soul melding between the Healer and the Healee. During this process, there is a complete mingling of both person's energy and the energy used in the process is unlike any energy used hitherto.

The 'Five' were entrusted with this healing but were asked not to use it on Third Parties until given a clear message to do so by the Healing Council.

The procedure was given together with the words of Xanthia which follow:

"I do not wish this healing to be used until you have exercised in the skills of the other levels. The spiritual level has a much more sensitive approach and delicacy of technique.

In this healing because it is on a spiritual level there is more a mingling of the spiritual energies between the Healer and Healee. The mental, emotional, and physical healings are irrelevant as far as spiritual healing is concerned because it is purely on a spiritual level.

It is concerned not only with the Healing Flame but Divine Love. It is approached through intuition and perception and is very delicate tuning to the vibration and colour. It will take a while before you are aware of the changes in the vibrations.

With this healing there needs to be cleansing of the healer and healee as in the attunement procedure."

Question. What is the purpose of spiritual healing ?

Xanthia: "You are healing traces, things that have been carried from past lives, into this life that affect this person. You are helping their soul to bring a close harmony between the spirit of that person, their soul and the Divine Love of Source.

Bringing together the soul's path, the soul as a whole, bringing it closer into harmony and joy and stillness and peace and tranquility.

There is always with physical entities the striving of the soul to return home. The soul gets lost or fragmented on the way. It cannot find the connection that the person needs and it affects them. This healing is to help the soul.

Help to bring forth greater perception of the soul's purpose, to bring it back individually and closer into harmony with the collective soul and each other. It is a yearning that our soul's return home, that we find our life's purpose.

We see more clearly the lessons we have to learn. We see more clearly how we are to achieve our life's purpose. This healing will help."

Question. Is this Spiritual Healing good for when someone is about to pass over and will it help them to pass more easily ?

"This would be perfect, yes. They will be resigned to the fact that they are passing over. This will allow them to put aside pain and sorrow of leaving behind the earthly body and the loved ones. They will see more clearly the way ahead to perfect peace and joy and love.

Transition from the physical to the spiritual can be difficult for some. This healing will help them to overcome that difficulty. It will help them to move away obstacles. It will help them with faith and belief in Divine Love.

There should be love. ... This is specially sent, to stay in tranquility and the connection with unconditional love. May you go in this notion to decide. This is why there is the need for clarity before beginning.

The healing you wish to do and the light within the person to be healed must be clear. Visualize this light or which ever way you visualize Source, the Divine Love of God. The essence of it is peace, love, stillness, and experience of a sense of awe and wonder.

It would help to keep this on a soul or an abstract level rather than on a personal, physical, emotional or mental level and not to be carried away to thinking of the wonder of it - but to be within that wonder and be a part of that awe and love and peace. It is to experience it with detachment. It sounds a contradiction to experience something and be fully detached. It's a paradox. But as you experience this, in time and feeling you will understand."

Procedure for Spiritual Healing

"The working symbol is drawn over the Healee's head - and above the head of the Healer.

Then visualize them coming together to make one symbol and visualize this above the head of the one to be given the healing.

The fingers are then held as if for scanning, held away from the body. Then the Healer holds the hands at the Healee's temples and moves around the one to be healed holding the hands.

When the Healer has moved all the way round, the hands are moved to above the head (crown chakra). They are held there for the rest of the healing.

As you hold them there you will become aware of vibrations and colours. You need to use the energy to bring the colours to perfect clarity, the vibrations to perfect pitch. The hands are held there till this is done. When this is done the vibrations and the light are seen clear.

The vibrations and light are drawn into the crown chakra. The light from the Healing Flame is visualized also going into the crown chakra of the Healee. Once the light of the Healing Flame ceases to flow down above the head of the person to be healed the Healer now returns the hands to the previous position.

Then visualize the light from the Healing Flame entering now their crown chakra. When that light ceases to flow the symbol is drawn above the head of the Healer and then the person to be healed.

The healing is complete.

When moving around the person to be healed to start with you will be standing behind them. As you move round that person you will return until you are again standing behind them. Then continue with the rest of the healing from behind.

You may, before you start this healing, ask the person to be spiritually healed. If there is any affirmation, prayer or something they wish to ask spiritually, ask them to say this while you do the healing. But they do not have to do that if they have nothing they wish to say or ask.

Again I caution you with the use of this healing. Wait until a high level of healing competence has acquired, so as to be able to sense the very subtleness of this healing. It is delicate. It must be used with a lot more care, delicacy and responsibility than the other healings. This will only come with the use of focal touch healing and experience.

I would describe it as the difference between seeing something here in front of you and something that is seen as if through a fog. It is harder to reach because it looks more subtle. As you use it, this subtle healing becomes much more fine with practice."

Meeting With Xanthia

One year and one month had passed since our attunements.

The energy in all of us was very strong and our knowledge of all the focal touch healing levels, except Spiritual Healing, were extensive.

At this time none of us had been given permission to use Spiritual Healing even though its methodology had been known by us for about a year.

It was November 8th. 2004 and a meeting with Xanthia and the Healing Council had been called as the answers to some questions were needed.

We had our usual cup of tea and the tape recorder was switched on. We settled down in our usual positions with Bill sitting next to Jean so that he could pose the questions to Xanthia. Bill asked most of the questions and Xanthia answered on behalf of the Healing Council through Jean who was in trance.

In about a minute Xanthia greeted us and scolded us for leaving such a long time since the last meeting. The text that follows is a direct transcription of the audio tape - but some personal items have been omitted.

Bill: Xanthia, you have taught us many things, but how can we learn to treat a specific illness or disease ?

Xanthia: "As you gain experience with using Focal Touch you will become much more sensitive with your scanning and be able to pin point where you put focal touch.

Do you mean a specific illness or one that is specific to a certain part of the body or do you mean a general one throughout the whole body ?"

Bill: I mean a specific illness. You could say AIDS for instance. How would I treat AIDS ?

Xanthia: "Again as you scan you will become sensitive to which particular gland or part of that immune system where the AIDS is most strong - and that would be what you would treat first.

Then you would move to different glands; moving around through the different parts of the immune system. While you put in rods of light energy to heal you can then do a general maintenance healing so that you cover the whole of the body.

As you use your scanning you will become much, much more sensitive and you will know exactly where to send it. Does that answer your question ?"

Bill: Yes it does.

Xanthia: "You may be aware of the illness that person has. But as you scan where you feel you ought to put the focal touch may not appear at first relevant.

You may think that I wouldn't have thought that would be the place to put it but the sensitivity of the scanning will be correct."

Bill: Thank you for that. You mention glands. You mean the endocrine glands of which there are seven major ones throughout the body, are those the ones ?

Xanthia: "Yes, the ones that control the immune system. As you work through it you will find that you are drawn to a descending order of glands and this will come to you in colours.

You will notice as you home in your awareness to a particular gland it will have its own signature colour."

Bill: I understand that.

Xanthia: "And as you treat that, you will find that the clarity of that colour changes. You may find because of any immune system disorder that a particular gland or glands will appear murky, or dark, or the colour will appear dull and lifeless and as you home in on that and you start the healing you will notice a change in the clarity."

Bill: I understand that.

Xanthia: "And as you become experienced with this you will associate that colour with that particular gland so that when you are scanning if that colour comes into your mind; then you home in on that. You will be able to colour code the glands."

Bill: Could I say that in our language we assume that a chakra is associated with a particular gland and we know that a chakra has a particular colour. Are these the colours that you mention ?

Xanthia: "No. No. These are not.   This has nothing to do with chakra energy. You are homing in on the Healing Flame energy.

You are homing in on your own higher awareness for Focal Touch and this is separate from chakra energy or chakra healing or cleansing. Do you understand ?"

Bill: Yes. Could you tell us what colours are associated with all our seven glands ?

Xanthia: "I could but I won't ! I'm not going to; I am doing this specifically as part of your advancement in your skills.   You will become aware of them. This will be given to you as you heal. This is part of your journey, part of your learning.   You will not be misguided. I leave you to explore."

[Some personal questions were then asked and answers given.]

Bill: Yes, thank you, very well. If I may I've got another question.

I have studied over the last few months the work of Doctor Valerie Hunt and would like to know if her work has anything to do with Focal Touch healing and if not, does this study stand in the way of the healing ?

Xanthia: "It has nothing to do with Focal Touch healing. Nevertheless to study anything to do with healing is never a waste of time.

Sometimes you can spread yourself too far. If you concentrate your mind on Focal Touch your healing will be greatly enhanced. If you start dispersing your energy amongst a lot of different types of healing then your energy may be spread too far. Curiosity can be a gift. It can also be a handicap. Curiosity can be curiosity for curiosity's sake. Look at these things with interest but do not try to connect them to Focal Touch. Do you have any other questions ?"

Bill: When I've been healing, both Focal Touch and other healing, I have two doctors working through me, a Doctor Peterson and a Doctor Mbosa.

Is this a normal procedure during Focal Touch healing ?

Could you tell me why they are there as certain sensitive patients see them working ?

Xanthia: "This is different. These are guides of yours. They are not working with Focal Touch because that does not need a being.

It comes direct from the Healing Flame through you or through the healer. But they can come and lend their energy. They come sometimes to observe as well. They come sometimes to assist but they are not connected directly with Focal Touch."

Bill: Thank you. That is all. Thank you again for your help.

Xanthia: "Once again I emphasize write (and do all your work) from the heart, not the mind; because when you use your mind, you analyze. You bring in the scientist side of you. Put that to one side. I know it is hard for you.

But you need to put the scientist to one side. You need to trust in your guides, trust in spirit; come from the heart. You do not need to prove anything. You don't need to know how it works. You don't need to analyze it or pull it to pieces or compare it. You know it works and it doesn't matter how. You know how strong this healing energy is.

Write about it from the heart and the love of that energy and the soul of the energy not from the cold, clear, clinical, analytical scientist side of it. That, for you, will be quite difficult. Take your mind off the railway tracks and start wandering around on the grass on the banks. You might be surprised how you enjoy it !

Seriously now, that is how you feel - from the heart. That is where I can come through being love, being open, trusting and aware - and if necessary suspending disbelief and just accepting what is, is.

Don't try to explain it, to prove it or compare it. Just say *"Ok, I'm here floating on the ceiling naked, so ok !"* You don't have to analyze it. Even if something that appears ridiculous or absurd or even impossible - just accept it."

Bill: Thank you for your help. No more questions.

Xanthia: "I thank you. Again it is good to communicate with you. We send our love. Goodbye for now."

Focal Touch Healing At A Distance

Ethics

Many people have many views on healing at a distance. My view is quite simple: if someone is sick they require help. You don't have to get permission to pray for someone who is sick and prayer is a form of healing.

I usually attach an affirmation to my distant healing: *"Please send this healing to the 'higher self' of [name] for their highest good and for the highest good of everyone else involved. If they don't want to receive the healing, just park it near to them for the use of anyone who needs it."*

When broadcasting Focal Touch distant healing, <u>intent is the key</u>. Throughout the healing keep your intention in mind.

The other key factor to keep in mind is which Hand Position are you intending to use - this is essential, you don't want to be sending 'high intensity beams' to someone such as children, the infirm and those who are frail. Remember this is powerful stuff that you are handling.

<u>Procedure</u>

a). Scan your patient using any of the methods given earlier in this book to determine the nature of the complaint. You may have been given some information when the request for healing was made.

Nevertheless, I would still advise you to scan - you may have been given only the symptoms and not the cause.

b). I try to keep good notes on my patients with such detail as shown on the chakra profile chart shown earlier in the book. The first test I like to do is the Vitality Index – a good healthy number is 75. This number is also useful because if it is low, say about 55, you can monitor your treatments on a daily basis and hopefully see the number increase.

c). Remember during the scanning to be aware of any colours that may come to mind. You did program your endocrine gland colours as shown earlier in this chapter - didn't you ? You must do this and log them as they will be with you for life. If you don't do this programming, you will not be able to tackle any problems associated with the immune system.

<u>Healing Method</u>

For some this method will be easy. If you can visualize or imagine you are in the game. If not, read the notes on visualization - it's easy to learn.

Sit in a comfortable chair, close your eyes, relax your body and relax your mind. If you don't have the ability to reach the Alpha state of mind (meditative state) quickly, don't worry - return to look at Bagha Yoga (Vizualize/Meditate Section, p. 20)

Start the session by asking 'Upstairs' for the 'energy to heal' and follow the procedure exactly as if you were performing hands on healing. Now close your eyes, relax as much as you can - use the Bagha.

Visualize your patient sitting on a chair or stool. You are the spectator and you watch yourself doing the healing on this person.

Do the healing in detail just as you would in a Hands-On situation. When the healing is complete close in the correct manner.

If you are not familiar with the appearance of your patient just visualize any person of the same sex on your chair or stool. But in this case hold your information sheet with their 'energetic matrix', full name, date of birth, age, post code etc. on it for the duration of the healing.

There are many methods for doing this healing at a distance and I have covered a few in previous chapters. But I am sure that you will find even more.

If you have any unique ones, please let me know !

Editors Note:

These beams that are inserted may be similar to the beam associated with the Assemblage Point, as described at p.53.

Bill Ellis
- Author and Master Healer

The author passed his "sell by" date as regards meaningful employment, according to the State rules, some years ago.

Bill is a chemist by profession and since 1969 ran, together with his wife, his own business.

The business activities involved the contract development and manufacture of cosmetics and toiletries for the large cosmetic companies.

He became interested in Spiritualism and mainly healing at about the same time, reading all related material he could lay his hands on.

Since then he has become a Chios Healing Master & Teacher, a Reiki Master & Teacher, a Magnified Healing Master & Teacher, a Radiesthesia Teacher, and a Pranic Healing Practitioner.

He still says that even now after teaching dozens of students, most of whom to Master level, that there is no adrenalin rush to compare to 'passing an attunement'.

Appendix 1

Principles Of Pranic Healing

Certain basic concepts are easier to understand and remember if they are labeled.

1 Principle of Life Force. For physical life to exist, it must have life force or vital energy. Life force is essential to physical life. It is also necessary for the existence of more subtle life forms.

This life force has been called by various names Prana, Ruah, Chi, Manna, and many other names. Rapid healing is brought about by increasing the life force or Pranic energy level of the affected part or the whole body

2. Principle of Pervasiveness. Life force or vital energy is all around us. It is pervasive; we are actually in an ocean of life force.

Based on this principle, a healer can draw in Pranic energy or life force from the surroundings, and give it to the patient without exhausting himself or herself

3. Principle of Diseased Energy. Disease not only exists in physical form but also in energy form. Disease in energy form is called diseased energy or diseased bio-plasmic matter. Clairvoyantly, diseased energy is seen as grayish or dark.

4. Principle of Transmittability. Life force or vital energy can be transmitted from one person to another person or object, or from one object to another object or a person.

5. Principle of Contamination. Diseased energy is transmissible. It could be transmitted from a patient to another person or to a healer.

The diseased energy of a subject could contaminate a person, an object, an animal, or a plant. Therefore, to avoid contamination, it is extremely important for healers to flick their hands when sweeping and after energizing, and to wash their hands and arms after cleansing and energizing.

6. Principle of Controllability. Life force and diseased energy can be controlled and directed through the will or through 'mind intent'.

7. Principle of Cleansing and Energizing. In healing, giving life force is not enough; it is also necessary to remove the diseased energy. Removing the diseased energy is called cleansing. Giving life force to a patient or an object is called energizing.

The rate of healing can be accelerated by applying the principle of cleansing and energizing.

8. Principle of Radical Reaction. When energizing is done without removing the diseased energy, a crisis may take place in the form of temporary worsening of the condition. This is called radical reaction. This could be avoided or minimized by thorough cleansing.

9. Principle of Receptivity. A patient has to be receptive or at least neutral in order to receive the projected Pranic energy. Being relaxed also helps increase the degree of receptivity.

Without receptivity, the projected Pranic energy will not be absorbed, or only a minimal amount of it will be absorbed.

Patients may not be receptive because: they are biased toward this type of healing, they do not like the healer personally, they do not want to get well, or they are in general not receptive about anything.

10. Principle of Stabilizing. Projected Pranic energy tends to leak out if it is not stabilized. Stabilization is done by energizing the treated part with light whitish-blue Prana, or covering the treated part with pastel blue Prana with a 'wiping' motion of the hand. Symptoms tend to recur if stabilization is not done.

11. Principle of Releasing. For healing to take place, it is necessary for the projected Pranic energy to be released. Otherwise, a substantial portion of it will return to the healer.

Releasing is done by being detached and by cutting the etheric link. The healer can be warm and caring but at the same time detached. Here, being detached does not mean being 'cold'.

12. Principle of Correspondence. What affects the energy body or the etheric body will tend to affect the physical body. And what affects the physical body will tend to affect the energy body. When the energy body is healed, the physical body will also be healed.

13. Principle of Interconnectedness. The body of the patient and the body of the healer are interconnected with each other since they are part of the Earth's energy body. On a more subtle level, it means that we are part of the solar system, and are interconnected with the whole cosmos.

14. Principle of Directability. Life force can be directed. It follows where your attention is focused; it follows thought. Distant Pranic healing is based on the principle of directability and the principle of interconnectedness.

Some Basic Principles of Healing

- The ability to assist in healing is natural to all people.

- The person sitting or lying in front of the 'Practitioner' is the 'HEALER' - the Body Heals Itself ! The practitioner only supplies the tools for healing to take place.

- Healing is a skill that can be taught and that grows stronger with practice. Practitioners become stronger at running the energy and in their healing ability over time.

- Energy follows thought. The practitioner uses intention and various meditations to create a high-energy field and uses that field to surround the area to be healed.

- Resonance and entrainment cause the area being healed to change its vibration to match that of the practitioner. The practitioner simply raises and holds the new resonance.

- No one can really heal anyone else. The person in need of healing is the healer. The practitioner simply holds a resonance to allow their body to heal itself.

- Trusting the process is essential. The work may cause temporary pain or other distressing symptoms that are all part of the healing. The life-force and the healing process work with complexity and wisdom that are beyond our conception and comprehension.

- The energy follows the natural intelligence of the body to do the necessary healing. The practitioner pays attention to 'body intelligence' and 'chases the pain'.

- The practitioner is also receiving a healing by doing the work.

- Breathing amplifies the life-force.

- Combining breathing and meditation techniques together causes the energy to line up, which increases its power many times, like a laser.

- Healing can be accomplished from a distance and can be highly effective.

- The ability to connect with one's spirituality, in whatever form it is perceived to be, and asking for help adds another dimension of power to this work.

Appendix 3

Vibrational Energy Healing

Vibrational healing accesses the limitless energy which surrounds us, penetrates us, and composes all energy and matter in existence.

This limitless energy is sometimes called Chi, Prana, or 'the force'. It has also been called the Quantum Particle Flux, or Zero Point energy. Whatever it is called, accessing it is what all living things do in every moment of their existence, else they would be dead.

Sickness and disease comes about from blocking the flow of this energy. Vibrational healing is a way to get the energy flowing again.

A healer is someone who has learned to access and direct a portion of this energy at will. But many healers have a confusion how the process of healing works.

Many healers who do vibrational healing work have the idea that they are 'flowing energy' to the client, and that the client's receipt of the healer's energy is what is causing the client to get better.

But this is not happening at all. The healer is often acting somewhat like a placebo or a conduit. The healer's presence makes it OK for the client to allow their source energy to flow through them. This is why energy which is flowed by the same healer feels different to every person.

Healers sometimes explain this by saying that the same energy feels different to each client because each client has a different energetic structure, and is blocked in different ways, so the energy will flow to different places and do different things. Or, that each client needs different energy from the healer.

But really, it is the client who is directing the flow of energy to himself, and it feels different because the client is creating or attracting different energy streams depending upon the clients needs.

The client is only uncomfortable because they are disallowing the flow of energy from their energy field which surrounds their body.

The client is pushing against the natural flow of balanced energy, blocking it.

The healer feels the energy coming through his body and hands, so the healer thinks that this energy which is flowing through him is the same energy which is flowing to the client.

But while the healer may be directing energy to the client, it is the client who is attracting or inviting his own energy stream via his change of vibration, which the healer, by their presence, has enabled the client to allow.

The client is completely in charge of the healing process, no matter what the healer is doing ! The amazing thing is that the client, through his own change in vibration brought about by the presence of the healer, may be attracting energy completely different from the energy the healer is directing ! Healers should understand this, because it is often the reason for 'failed' healings.

For example, a very effective healer may get a client who does not respond to the healer's treatment. This causes a healer to sometimes feel disappointment, or in extreme cases, even doubt of the healer's own ability.

But what is happening is that the client is not willing to accept the change in vibration that is being allowed by the presence of the healer. The healer is doing their job, it is the client who is not allowing the vibrational change necessary to unblock their energy stream. This is no fault of the healer - or the client.

It's important for both healer and client to understand the mechanics behind the healing process, so that both can remain empowered throughout the healing cycle.

No one can create in the experience of another, because each being is sovereign, creating his own world from within himself.

Although energy may flow to a client from a healer, only the client can allow it. Of course if the client shows up for a healing session, the client has already given permission to accept energy from the healer. And equally true, the energy of both healer and client are inter-mingling.

But the nuts and bolts of how energy is transmitted from healer and received by client, is all about how the client allows energy to flow into the client's energy field and body. The client will improve to the degree that the client gives permission for it, regardless what the healer does.

If the client has the idea that the healer's energy is responsible for his improvement, it can lead to dependency and disempowerment.

It is important to explain to the client that they alone determine the nature of the healing process.

The client can invite/allow the natural energy transfer that is necessary for health from his own energy field, without the necessity for the healer's presence at all. This is something that should be made absolutely clear to each client a healer works with.

Of course, almost all clients will probably elect to receive treatment even with this knowledge, but treatment will be more effective if the client feels empowered. And if treatment is more effective, the healer will draw more clients !

Sometimes when a healer thinks he or she is 'flowing energy' to the client, and that the healer's energy is responsible for a client's improved condition, egos can get bigger. *"My energy is more powerful than yours."* or *"My clients say they like my energy best."* etc.

A healer and client both should be clear what he or she is doing: the healer provides an opportunity for the client, fully empowered, to allow their own betterment.

Sahaja Yoga

This topic had such a great impact on my thinking and studies that it would be remiss of me not to include it here.

Sahaja Yoga is different from the other familiar yogic methods because it begins with Self Realization instead of this being the unobtainable dream of a distant goal. Her Holiness Mataji Shri Nirmala Devi makes this possible for being born Self-Realized. She is able to pass on Her gift of Divine Revelation to others, She derives infinite wisdom, love and power by being connected to the main power supply of the Life Source itself whilst most other people must rely upon the pitifully inadequate potential contained in their own personal batteries.

Spontaneous realization of the Divine mysteries is the first of three fundamental differences between Sahaja Yoga and other Yoga paths.

Self-Realization is the key which unlocks the invisible barrier which blocks the life force of Kundalini and this makes the 'kriya' techniques of purification and the 'asanas' of Hatha Yoga quite unnecessary, as this work is already accomplished.

Because the Divine Grace shines on the seeker from the very beginning, the ego does not develop - and this major obstacle in our ascent never emerges. This destroys all sense of separation as the enlightened ones merge together in a sea of love.

Finally, the Mother Mataji, unlike other gurus, opens up Her heart to all who seek Her Grace and turns away no one, whatever their transgressions and shortcomings may be.

This forms the simple working basis of Sahaja Yoga and although some of the teachings may appear unorthodox by ordinary yoga standards, in practice these will be found to work very well indeed.

May the Self-Realization of Mataji descend upon us all.

From a small, small seed a big tree grows. In spring, there is blossom and in summer, the flowers become fruit. Our own spiritual rebirth is as simple and natural a process.

Within us all there is a seed, a residual knowledge of Self, called Kundalini.

When the breath of divine love gives life to this seed, we find ourselves reborn into the dimension of Spirit, we discover the tree of life that exists within us, we feel the divine breath as an all-pervading vibration. Like flowers, we feel our own fragrance. We mature like fruits, into wholeness.

We have evolved from our origins in primeval matter, to the stage where we can formulate complex theories on the nature of evolution and existence. But, beyond our analysis, do we realize that evolution is still a living process, quietly and continually working towards our eventual fulfillment ?

Or do we, in our arrogance, see ourselves now at the pinnacle of human development, with Providence our hireling, and nothing better to become ?

Journey implies arrival. If so, where are we today ? Is this 'the new Jerusalem' ? How can it be ? If it is God's plan to establish His Kingdom on this earth and in our hearts, then it looks as though we still have some way to go !

We live in a world of suffering and confusion, slaves to matter and expedience, our moral sense shattered. For centuries, we have struggled for a solution through every external agency, enough to realize perhaps that the answer must lie within, with the transformation of the individual.

Many today are experiencing this transformation, evolving into the conscious awareness of Spirit, seeing within themselves that vital spark which connects them to the Absolute, watching the fear and confusion of the relative world fall away, like the old cocoon of the bright new butterfly.

In the past, there have been many great men and women who have tried to raise man's consciousness to the level at which man might know himself, but men have used their teaching to engender faction and hypocrisy. The simplicity of the original tune was too simple for their ear to carry.

Today, Holy Mother is spreading the universal message of divine love, integrating the music of past singers in a dynamic new harmony. Her audience has a more sympathetic ear. They participate as instruments in Her song. Through the realization that She manifests, they are experiencing knowledge of Self for the first time, and they are seeing the Self in others.

Her Holiness Mataji Shri Nirmala Devi has opened the door to collective consciousness, the ultimate evolutionary jump, where man finds union with himself and with his source.

Yoga means union; union with something beyond ourselves, with something essentially divine. 'Sahaja' means spontaneous, and it means 'born with you'. So by Sahaja Yoga, we mean that the means to spontaneous union with the divine is born within us all.

To achieve this union all we do is ask Her Holiness Shri Mataji and let it happen. We cannot achieve it by our effort; it is spontaneous, it just happens. It is given as a gift.

Before realization, Kundalini' exists within us in the dormant state, coiled inside the triangular bone at the base of the spine.

When awakened, it rises through the subtle channel in the spine, eventually piercing the fontanelle bone (Brahmarandhra) and passing through it. Here at the top most chakra, the Sahasrara, with the thousand petal lotus, is the point of Yoga, where the individual consciousness is united to the all-pervading power of collective unconscious. At the same time, the Kundalini awakens the Spirit which resides in the heart, where it begins to pulsate.

Thought ceases as the Kundalini passes through the Ajna centre in the brain. The Spirit, which is now awakened within us manifests itself as a flow of cool vibrations, moving across the hands and over the crown and temples like a cool breeze.

We begin to feel different sensations in the fingers, as here the Kundalini signals to us the condition of the various centres (Chakras) within. This state we call 'vibratory awareness' in which we actually feel the Self as it manifests itself through the vibrations, on the central nervous system. Since the Self, which is the Spirit, the essence of our being, now enters our conscious awareness, this is also called Self-Realization.

The whole process begins when Her Holiness Shri Mataji awakens the Kundalini. It rises automatically when touched by the vibrations that radiate from Her Being, and fills you with a sense of peace and bliss as it is guided upward under Her care and expertise. As She says so often with Her characteristic humour *"Kundalini is my job. If I know the job, why should you be upset ? You know other jobs, I know this one !"*

Shri Mataji has been teaching Sahaja Yoga and sharing the experience of Self-Realization since 1970. She was born on 21st March 1923, in Chindawara, a small hill station near Nagpur in the heart of India. Today she is the wife of a U.N. Diplomat with two daughters and four grand children. Although born in a Christian family, she has embraced the truth of all religions in Her universal teaching.

In spite of Her undoubted powers and profound depth of spiritual knowledge, Shri Mataji remains a woman of extraordinary humility, a fount of wisdom and common sense, and a constant source of laughter and delight. A personality with as many facets as a brilliant crystal, She is yet, at the core, one with the spirit of Her teaching; the pure light of love that glows in the heart of that crystal.

On 5th May, 1970, She witnessed the Sahasrara Chakra of the Virata open. The Virata is the Universal Being, God's manifested aspect in whose image we are made. Each chakra's opening in His spiritual instrument heralds a new stage in our evolution, as it creates the same potential in our own.

The last chakra to open before this time was the Ajna, which opened with Christ's resurrection. With the opening of the Sahasrara, Her Holiness Shri Mataji knew that it was time for man to rise into this desired station, into the glory of God's kingdom.

The Experience

The first thing to realize is that in Sahaha Yoga, 'something' actually happens. The experience of Self is real, not random or undetermined, but consistent and verifiable.

Enlightenment in the form of thoughtless awareness (nirvichar samadhi) takes place when Kundalini reaches the Sahasrara. When She pierces through, the cool vibrations start to follow. Surprisingly, vibrations from the photograph of Her Holiness Shri Mataji awaken Kundalini in the same way as from Her person.

By following this procedure with an open mind, you may experience Self-Realization, gaining complete relaxation and the elevation into the witness state of collective consciousness. Again, this experience is actual. It is neither the invention of an exalted imagination nor the projection of an external power, but your own realization, taking place within you.

Be comfortable at all times. First remove shoes and loosen tight clothing. Place the photograph of Her Holiness Shri Mataji so that you may sit before it in the most relaxed way. It is best to sit on the floor to have greater contact with the Mother earth, but you may use a chair if this proves too difficult. Try to sit with a reasonably straight spine - and in a respectful frame of mind.

Kundalini has Her dignity, which must always be respected, as must the attendant protocol of the Divine.

Her Holiness Shri Mataji

With your eyes on the picture, hold your hands towards it, palms upward. You may rest your hands on your lap. Close your eyes and let the mind be quite still.

If there is any flickering of the eyelids or you begin to see any lights, colours or visions, then it means there is a problem in the Ajna chakra and you should keep your eyes open and on the picture of Shri Mataji.

Attention should be loose, not fixed at any point. If there are still thoughts, try to detach yourself by watching them until they fade. Forgive anyone who has ever harmed you or made you unhappy. Ask yourself, *"What am I thinking ?"*

If you have led a reasonably normal life so far, you may not feel any physical sensation, only a gradual relaxation of the inner being. You may feel Kundalini moving up the spine to the crown of the head.

When it reaches the Ajna chakra in the centre of the brain, thoughts cease spontaneously, without effort.

Thoughtless awareness does not mean you cannot think, but that you see yourself outside the flow of thought in a state of pure awareness.

Try to remain as a witness to all that is happening, watching without thinking. There is no danger, nothing to fear - the nature of Kundalini is protective and maternal. As your mother, she only does what is best for you - her only child.

As Kundalini enters the Sahasrara chakra and passes through the fontanelle area of the skull to merge with the universal unconscious, you may begin to feel cool vibrations like a breeze on your hands.

This is the divine breeze that is mentioned in so many scriptures; as the wind of the Holy Ghost in the Bible, as the Hebrew 'ruach', as the 'chaitanya lahari' described by Adi Shakaracharya.

We discover many more references in our literature, as for instance in Wordsworth's

> 'mild, creative breeze,
> A vital breeze which traveled gently on
> O'er things which it had made,

or in Blake's:

> Still the breath Divine does move,
> And the breath Divine is love

If the breeze flows evenly in both hands, you can be sure that your instrument is in good shape and that Kundalini is rising all the way through.

Now just enjoy your realization in meditation, 'because you cannot meditate but have to be in meditation, through a happening'.

Although this sounds a lengthy process, for those who have spent their lives in the paths of righteousness, realization takes just a split second. For some of us it takes a little longer.

Sometimes you may feel cool in one hand only. If it is on the right you may place it on the heart (left side) while keeping the left towards the picture. This gives support to the weaker left side.

Alternately, you can hold the right hand away from the picture (by placing it on mother earth), as a channel for problems in your system to escape.

If the cool breeze is on your left hand only you can place it on your liver (just below the rib-cage on the right hand side) and keep the right hand towards the picture. Or you can hold the left away, palm facing you, and fingers pointing towards the sky.

Continue until the two sides are brought into balance and the flow is even in both hands.

You may feel heat, tingling, heaviness or numbness in the hands, or may be nothing at all. This means there is an obstruction in your instrument. We call these obstructions catches' or 'hadha'.

When Kundalini is working in an obstructed chakra, the subsequent friction gives rise to the heat which you may feel. You can use the elements to disperse these obstructions.

To use the fire element (Tej Mahabhuta) light a candle before the picture. Then dissolve some salt in a bowl of warm water and sit as before with your feet in the bowl (this is known as foot soaking). Obstructions will be burnt in the flame and absorbed in the salt (earth element) and water.

After fifteen to twenty minutes, dry your feet, flush away the water in the bowl, wash your hands and again check your vibrations.

There are many clearing techniques apart from foot-soaking, including the use of appropriate mantras and bandhans, and Mohammed's methods using flowers and lemons and even your own shoes.

All this knowledge is received after realization and must be put into practice if it is to be sustained. For once Kundalini has risen, She soon descends in difficult cases, to those chakras that need Her attention. While the realization is effortless, to sustain it demands a certain degree of self-cleansing and self-understanding.

With this understanding, we sustain ourselves that we may manifest the powers of our Spirit, discovering in Sahaja Yoga, our own beauty and how to enjoy that beauty in ourselves and in others.

Her Holiness Shri Mataji says *"How much you meditate is how much you love. Try to meditate daily, early in the morning and in the evening after work. First clear yourself as thoroughly as possible using the appropriate methods, then try to just sit in thoughtless awareness, which is where meditation should begin.*

Regularity is more important than length of meditation at first, the effect is cumulative It should never become ritualistic or formalized, but always be from the heart."

The most powerful meditation is usually experienced collectively with other realized souls.

With such loving and dynamic people, the vibrations are proportionately stronger and you too develop the same qualities. Meetings with other Sahaja Yogis also give you the opportunity to work on others - which is the quickest way to accelerate your own ascent. As you clear them, you clear yourself.

The Instrument

The instrument of our enlightenment is framed on a structure of three main channels or nadis (shown in figure by Roman numerals). These subtle channels are placed within the spine and find their expression in the autonomic nervous system - which comprises the left and right sympathetic nervous systems and the central parasympathetic nervous system.

The central nervous system represents the consciousness we have achieved in our evolution up to human awareness. Sahaja Yoga now enlightens the central nervous system with the awareness of our Spirit. Thus through this system we can actually feel our Spirit manifesting itself to us as vibrations.

The three subtle channels (or Nadis) called Ida (I), Pingala (II) and Sushumna (III), are placed in series creating energy centres known as chakras (I - 7). These chakras govern all aspects of our being and supply energy to all our needs and functions.

Each has a presiding deity, a particular aspect of the one Almighty God which governs that centre, placed in the original instrument of the Virata and reflected in our own. We are truly made, as the Bible says, in God's image.

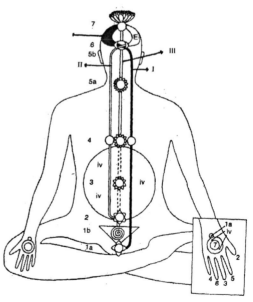

The Instrument (Physical Body)

So for instance, we find Lord Krishna in the Vishuddhi (5a) and Lord Buddha in the ego centre (F). We can awaken these deities within us through the science of Sahaja Yoga, which teaches us how to open and establish a rapport with them through mantra, which, when used by realized souls, is enlightened communication.

In this way all faiths, all truths, are integrated within the auspices of modern Sahaja Yoga, this Mahayoga.

Kundalini resides at the base of the instrument in three-and-a-half coils ('kundala' means 'coils') in the Mooladhara, which is inside the triangular bone at the base of the spine. When awakened, the Kundalini can be seen pulsating inside this bone, the sacrum, and also as it moves up the spinal chord.

This divine energy is the motive force of our enlightenment, carrying our attention to the highest level of realization. Then like our own in-built archive, She records and stores every detail of our previous existence.

She has Her own supreme intelligence, and works for you in the best possible way, with extreme loving care.

Kundalini awakening is often said to be very dangerous, accompanied by tremendous heat and pain. Such is the discovery of those who have experimented in a recklessly naive or unauthorized manner, and particularly when they have tried to associate Her awakening with sex.

In such cases, the deity who guards the innocence of Kundalini, Shri Ganesha, expresses his anger in waves of heat. The confused pioneer may also experience fits and seizures where he loses control of body and mind he may jump and howl for no apparent reason.

He may experience hallucinations. In the bliss of his ignorance, he associates the warning signals with Kundalini awakening itself, and believes himself to have undergone a profound experience of enlightenment.

The face of such a person shows all the anguish he is going through. After genuine Self-Realization, the face becomes radiant. You look much younger, the body becomes more active and well-proportioned. The whole personality becomes beautiful and magnetic. As priorities change, you assume a dignified and glorious attitude to life.

Kundalini is absolutely pure. She knows us inside and outside and will only rise in one whose desire is fixed in bathing in that same purity. It is true that Her first awakening can be very dramatic; people have felt the crowns of their heads melting like ice, and wave after wave of cool vibrations cascading over their being, their hearts flooded with joy; but where the instrument is very clear, as in children, little is actually felt - they just become that bliss and purity.

Where there are obstructions, Kundalini is gentle and soothing. You may feel some heat or tingling, but only enough to indicate the problem. As Her Holiness Shri Mataji says, *"She is your loving mother. You are Her only child. Will She ever hurt you or burn you ? She just indicates"*.

Kundalini is a healing power. As a by-product of our realization (yoga), we receive our well-being (kshema) and are able, with Her help, to establish the same in others. Most illnesses are the result of damage to the chakras. Kundalini repairs them naturally, from inside.

And so, although the fruits of Her silent industry are quite miraculous, there is no suggestion of miracle cures in Sahaja Yoga.

Unfamiliar to many She may be, Kundalini is a natural force, and it is Her nature to repair what is broken and re-unite it to the whole.

Disease occurs when the subtle qualities of the chakras are neglected or denied. The relevant chakra then becomes defective through recession of Divine energy. They may also be drained in the event of an emergency in a particular chakra, a shock for instance, when the sympathetic nervous system puts great demands on the chakras.

When such over-activity drains a chakra completely, the deity of that centre is no longer active or reflected, and that part of the body which falls within its sphere is no longer connected with the central path which caters to the whole.

The cells in that area are now on their own. In the absence of the supreme control of the organizing agent, the cells' growth becomes malignant and they recreate themselves at random, without proportion to the whole.

Now we can understand why cancer develops and why cancer can be cured through Sahaja Yoga.

By awakening the ruling deity of the damaged chakra, through the healing power of Kundalini, the chakra can be restored to health and the rampant cells again brought under control.

First we find the damaged chakra through vibratory awareness - we can feel all the chakras on our fingers. Then we take the necessary steps, directing Kundalini to the relevant centres, awakening the deities at those centres, supplying vibrations to the affected area and so on. With the help of Kundalini, by awakening, directing and balancing the energy, most diseases can be cured, once and for all.

She (the Kundalini) is the power that bestows all of these blessings upon you, and Her power in you is in direct proportion to your pure desire for Her. Her Holiness Shri Mataji says:

"Kundalini is the desire of God. It is not the desire for God, it is the desire of God Himself within you. So it can only be awakened by that desire itself. It is the desire of God within you that is being placed, and the desire of God is the Shakti. And the desire of God is that He loves you.

So do not condemn or destroy yourself or others. Keep in the centre (moderation) and respect your sustenance (dharma). The desire of God is to bestow the Kingdom of God upon you. He will have to do the job if He has to give meaning to His creation. Only thing you do is not to ruin your being by extreme behaviour".

"Sahaja Yoga is not meant for a few individuals. The whole world has to be awakened".

See www.sahajayoga.org for more details about sahaja yoga

Healing Techniques of Sahaja Yoga

<u>Working on yourself to clear a chakra</u>

It is possible to clear any obstruction in one's own chakras as evidenced by a tingling or heat in a corresponding finger. This is done by moving the hand in a clockwise motion (clockwise from the viewpoint of someone looking at you) over the relevant chakra.

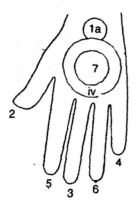
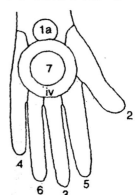

Chakra Points
On Hands.

For instance, if you feel a tingling in the left little finger you will know that the left heart Chakra is not completely cleared. So you can take the right hand (most Sahaja techniques use the right hand as the actor as it represents the hand of action, whilst the left hand represents the hand of desire) and describe a clockwise motion over the heart area on the left hand side of your body (as if stirring a cup of tea vertically with your four fingers).

You can do this for seven or twenty one rotations, or until you feel some benefit. Most people will feel the results of the vibrations on the actual chakra with practice, but don't worry if not — you may rest assured that it is doing the job in any case !

Clearing an Obstruction in ones
own Chakra

Whilst rotating the hand we can also say the relevant 'affirmation' to help reestablish the pure quality of the chakra. If you cannot remember the correct affirmation, then simply say *"Mother, please clear this centre"*, addressing the mothering energy of Kundalini within.

Working on others to help them

To help others, you stand or sit behind the person you are working on (they have their back to you, see fig.).

You raise your Kundalini and put on a Bandan as you would in your own meditation.

Then, from behind, raise the Kundalini of the person you are going to work on and give them a Bandhan. If you have developed enough sensitivity in your hands or fingers to feel the 'catches' or obstructions in the other persons' chakras (by tingling or warmth in your fingers which correspond to his/her chakras), then you can work at the back of the person with your left hand out towards the candle and photograph.

If you have not got a picture then keep your 'attention' (or concentration) on your Sahasrara chakra at the top of your head.

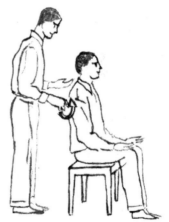

Rotate your right hand in an anti-clockwise direction seven or twenty-one times (the chakras always spin in the same direction, so you are in effect doing the same as if rotating the chakra clockwise from in front of the person).

Repeat this action until you feel your finger or hand go cool. Again you can use the appropriate affirmation for the affected chakra.

Clearing a Chakra
on Another Person.

If you are unable to feel the 'catches', then ask the person you are working on if they feel any tingling or heat in their fingers. If they do, then work on the appropriate chakras.

If neither of you feel any sensations, then you can play it safe by simply working up the central channel, starting from the Muladhara centre and working up each Chakra in turn.

When you have finished working on the person raise their Kundalini and Bandhan them. Then raise your own Kundalini and Bandhan in the same way that you would finish your own meditation.

Figure A

Figure B

Figure C

Figure D

Raising the **Kundalini**

The Ice Pack

A quick tip for those who may be finding difficulty in maintaining a period of thoughtlessness in their meditations. Very often unbidden thoughts are the result of an overactive liver (a 'hot' liver in Sahaja terms). This is easily remedied by placing an ice pack or other cold pack on the liver on the right side of your body during the meditation. You will find this amazingly effective.

It is our Kundalini energy rising up the spine which takes our attention higher into the state of thoughtless awareness. This exercise helps to strengthen, steady and establish the attention in the highest energy centre, the Sahasrara Chakra.

At the beginning and end of meditation it is helpful to raise your own Kundalini. Begin with the left hand at the front at the level of the abdomen; palm facing towards the body. While rotating the right hand around the left hand, move the left hand up the front of the body and over the head.

Use this movement three times, and on the third time tie three knots over the top of your head.

Placing a Bandhan

A simple exercise for protecting your subtle body and for preserving the state of meditation is to put on a bandhan. This exercise can be done before and after meditation.

Place the left hand at your side at the level of the waist with the fingers pointing towards the photograph of Sri Mataji.

Using the right hand, describe an arc, starting at the level of the left hip, going over the head, down to the right hip and back again.

This movement should be done seven times.

This exercise should be done after raising the Kundalini at the start and end of meditation.

Placing a Bandhan

Zero-Point and Tachyon Energy

This appendix is not obligatory, but for those of you who will not sleep at night unless you have tried to learn how the healing works, grit your teeth and work on. The rest of you may move on.

This chapter is analogous to driving a car: you do not need to know what goes on in the engine compartment to become an excellent driver.

Most of the information in this chapter is not due to my own research or experimentation. Where I have used other peoples research and writings, I have given them credit within the text.

The Amazing Promises Of The Zero Point Field

Extract from an article by Tijn Touber

Shireen Strooker is standing motionless in the middle of a large field, surrounded by 600 people. The gorgeous landscape under the mist of powerful Mount Rainier in the upper northwest of the United States is invisible to her. Shireen is blindfolded, as are all the others in the field.

That morning they all made a drawing. The hundreds of drawings are now hanging on the fence along the edge of the field. The assignment: find your own drawing blindfolded.

Shireen does a meditation exercise, pictures her drawing and thinks: *"I am the creator of the drawing and the spectator, I only have to become one with the drawing and it will automatically pull me towards it."*

Then, without bumping into anyone, she walks straight across the field and picks out her drawing straightaway from among the 600.

Coincidence ? Pure luck ? You'd think so. But Shireen was not the only one to perform this implausible act that day. The results of this exercise involving the students of Ramtha's School of Enlightenment violate the laws of empirical probability theory.

Apparently, humans are capable of communicating with matter intangibly. The exciting thing is that the hard science of modern physics is starting to lend proof to the existence of a ubiquitous energy field, which could offer an explanation for the miracle of a blindfolded woman who finds her drawing amidst 600 others.

In her book 'The Field', investigative journalist Lynne McTaggart provides an overview of recent scientific discoveries that demonstrate that there is an all encompassing energy field connecting man and matter.

In their search for the heart of the matter, for the smallest particle, scientists discovered the field's special characteristics and potential.

The so-called Zero Point Field (the name comes from the fact that even at absolute zero, minus 273 degrees Celsius, energy can still be measured) appears to provide the explanation for countless known phenomena and processes that had stumped the scientific community for generations.

Gravity, electromagnetism, clairvoyance, telepathy, and the spontaneous healing of wounds - the origins of these diverse phenomena can all be traced back to this quantum field.

McTaggart writes: Researchers discovered that the Zero Point Field contains the blueprint for our existence. Everything and everyone is connected with one another through this field in which all information from all time is said to be stored. Ultimately, everything, from man to matter, can be traced back to a collection of electric charges that are continually in contact with this endless sea of energy. Our interaction with this field determines who we are, will become, and have been. The field is the alpha and omega of our existence.

Health and Zero-Point Energy

Zero-point and Tachyon energy can be easily understood by anyone who realizes that all matter, from this page to the human heart, and to the cosmos and beyond, is made of energy.

Simply stated, everything in this universe of time and space is 'Source Energy', also called zero-point energy, from which everything is created. It is formless, it is everywhere, and it contains 'All That Is'.

Holistic health, harmony and healing on the physical, emotional, mental, and spiritual levels, are all based on an energy source that is integral to our existence. Therefore, healing at any level is very dependent on tapping into the primordial energy that is the source of existence. From maintenance and rejuvenation to the deepest levels of holistic healing, all are made possible by our ability to tap into the energy source that energizes and creates the form of all material existence as we know it, via the 'Energetic Continuum'.

The 'Energetic Continuum' is the continuous flow of the entire range of energies as they move 'down' from the Source, condensing into decreasingly slower rates of vibration. This process creates the dense, three-dimensional world in which we live.

Zero-point energy is considered to be the source, or starting point, of the Energetic Continuum. Every life form has its own, individual Energetic Continuum.

For example: A human has many different energy frequencies within its form; from the most subtle, spiritual energy fields down to the most dense, physical body. In the physical body, alone, there are many different frequencies. The cells, organs, tissues, blood, and bones all have their own energy and frequency, which all flow together to shape one human being.

While every life form has its own Energetic Continuum, it is connected to the Energetic Continuum of all other life forms via. 'Subtle Organizing Energy Fields' (SOEFs) assembling one big, Energetic Continuum. So, while we are each unique and individual, we are also interconnected. 'We are one'.

Some characteristics of Zero-Point Energy are:
1. It is faster than the speed of light.
2. It is omnipresent, and
3. While having no specific frequency or form, it contains all the potential necessary to create perfect form.

Zero-point energy does not interact directly with our slower-than-the-speed-of-light physical world. Through many energetic fields and levels, it condenses to a frequency rate that our bodies can comprehend and utilize.

First, it condenses into tachyon particles that have form. Like zero-point energy, tachyon moves faster than the speed of light and is omnipresent. Though it is not a specific frequency, tachyon is the source of all frequencies; it provides all potential necessary for creating, maintaining and evolving perfect form in our world.

The only difference between tachyon energy and zero-point energy is that tachyon has form and zero-point does not.

Some characteristics of tachyons are:
1. They are faster than the speed of light.
2. They are omnipresent.
3. They have form, yet contain, like the zero-point energy, all the potential necessary to create a three-dimensional universe.

Tachyon energy interacts directly with the slower-than-the-speed-of-light world through the SOEFs. Containing the blueprints for perfect order, SOEFs are the 'cosmic glue' that holds all forms together. They are the matrix upon which physical and subtle bodies are formed.

Tachyon, pure life-force energy, is converted by the SOEFs into the exact frequencies needed to maintain and restore perfect balance to a life form. No matter what the form, animate or inanimate, SOEFs hold all energy frequencies together.

Some characteristics of a Subtle Organizing Energy Field are:
1. It is almost at the speed of light, yet always below it.
2. It directly converts tachyon energy into the exact frequency needed to create and maintain perfect balance of the associated form.
3. A Divine feed back mechanism, it is the glue of the universe.
4. It can be depleted or destroyed by frequencies.

If a SOEF is blocked or depleted, the flow of life force energy through the Energetic Continuum can become deficient. The result is a state of disharmony and imbalance, i.e. chaos. This deficiency may present itself through symptoms; such as pain, fatigue, or disease.

If tachyon energy is applied to a deficient area where the SOEFs are blocked or depleted, it will immediately provide the SOEFs with all the potential to convert the exact frequencies needed to restore harmony and balance, making the area healthy once again.

If tachyon energy is applied to an area where the SOEFS are in perfect balance, then nothing happens. The SOEFs hold the intelligence to determine the exact frequencies needed for that perfect order. Tachyon Energy is the 'Source of All Frequencies'.

Tachyon energy is the elixir of body, mind, and spirit. In holistic medicine the primary objective is to heal the whole being physically, emotionally, mentally, and spiritually. The keys to that goal are the SOEFs and their proper functioning.

Tachyon, as the source of all energies, directly charges the blocked or depleted SOEFs in the physical, emotional, mental, and spiritual bodies. The SOEFs themselves create perfect order again. So tapping into tachyon energy affects our whole 'self'. The physical world of forms and frequencies is the end result of the Energetic Continuum.

To affect our slower than light world, tachyon energy has to be converted by SOEFs on all energy levels (subtle, physical, emotional, mental and spiritual) to keep the Energetic Continuum flowing.

1. Physically, it energizes the body's SOEFs so that health is maintained or restored.
2. Emotionally, it energizes the SOEFs of the emotional body so that unconditional love is restored.
3. Mentally, it energizes the SOEFs of the mental body so that wisdom and clarity is restored.
4. Spiritually, it enhances our connection to the Source - often called by other names such as Divine Intelligence, All That Is, God, or Higher Power.

Some characteristics of a Frequency are,

1. It is below the speed of light.
2. It is held in balance by a SOEF.
3. It has spin or oscillation and is affected by gravity.
4. It has no intelligence.

A Focal Touch Healer is able to channel tachyon energy through themselves. When their hands are placed on the body they energize the SOEFs, thus providing energy for the body-mind-spirit unit to heal itself.

Tachyon creates order out of disorder. Wherever it is applied (human, pet, plant, food, water, electro-magnetic fields (EMFs), soil, etc), it charges the SOEFs.

Everything that has lost order or balance can potentially be brought back into balance by tachyon because of the re-connection into the individual and overall Energetic Continuum.

Building up the strength and integrity of a weak area leads to natural healing by restructuring and/or releasing whatever has caused an imbalance.

This restructuring or release can result in symptoms that may seem to aggravate existing symptoms (healing crisis). As pure life-force energy is drawn into a deficient area (place of disorder), there also can be detoxifying symptoms.

These are positive indications that the body is releasing/restructuring in the process of healing. Truly, there are no negative side effects from using tachyon energy.

What can seem to be negative effects are always the symptoms of detoxification as the body heals. These are positive signs.

Remember:
- Tachyon brings order to disorder.
- It energizes the SOEFs, which allows the body to heal.

The Energetic Continuum

Disease or illness comes when a blockage occurs within our individual Energetic Continuum. It makes sense, then, that we must clear all the blockages to restore the vertical alignment of our Energetic Continuum. In essence, a blockage is defined as a disorder or chaos in the Energetic Continuum causing an energy deficiency.

These blockages in the continuum are in the form of particular frequencies that ultimately create disorder or disease in the physical body.

Tachyon Energy, because it is the source particle of energy that organizes and energizes the SOEFs, provides the potential to restore harmonious healing frequencies.

Tachyon Energy organizes that which is disorganized. It realigns and restores the SOEFs to their natural state of order and balance, thus creating a state of well being or health.

For example, if someone has experienced an emotional stress and continues to go through life without any release or balance, a blockage of energy will occur in the emotional body of that human being.

This blockage in the natural flow of energy (Energetic Continuum) in turn will cause an energy deficiency between the emotional body and a part of the physical body.

Let's say the blockage is causing a deficiency in the lower lumbar area of the back. This person may begin to experience lower back pain. If the stress continues, the situation may escalate into severe back pain, ruptured disk problems, or even degenerative disk disease.

Anytime part of the Energetic Continuum is blocked, the organ or system that is left in a deficient energetic state will ultimately succumb to one of this world's many degenerative diseases.

When focused into the specific deficient area, Tachyon Energy reorganizes and energizes the disrupted SOEFs, therefore allowing all the blockages to dissipate. The body is able to re-connect to its Energetic Continuum when the blockage is removed.

Connecting to the Energetic Continuum means increasing the flow of energy from life's source, Zero-Point Energy. As co-creators in our state of health, once we increase the flow of Life-Force Energy, we can then be relieved of the emotional stress.

In itself, Tachyon Energy is not a frequency; however, it contains the potential of all frequencies. This is important to understand because of the confusion surrounding the various frequency-energy therapies being used by some holistic healers.

Once it is understood that Tachyon (being the first particle of formless Zero-Point Energy) is the source of all frequencies, it is easy to place Tachyon in the energetic spectrum. All frequencies, such as photon, orgone or light waves, can become coherent and balanced when Tachyon is used to energize the SOEFs.

Through the Energetic Continuum, Tachyon interacts with the SOEFs, which absorb the potential needed for energizing them and strengthening their frequencies. The Energetic Continuum applies to everything we know of in our existence.

All forms in our world have vibrations. In the process, the frequency determines the character, the individual qualities of the vibration. It creates the difference between colours and sounds, as well as between brain cells and liver cells, between the rose and the bird - and all the rest of the participants in this universe.

Even the hardest material, such as a diamond, is nothing other than the dance of vibrations at a specific frequency and in a particular form.

The one thing that all physical forms of our universe have in common is that they move at less than the speed of light, which is the boundary within which our Creation takes place.

Please note that terms like Prana, Chi, Orgone, life force, Ki etc. cannot be equated with Zero-Point Energy since, without exception, these are energies that have already been manifested within a specific frequency range.

Tachyon energy is therefore the critical factor which energizes the SOEFs. So the more Tachyon energy we bring into our lives, the more energized and therefore organized are our SOEFs.

The energizing of the SOEFs is what creates health and rejuvenation because it reverses entropy, or aging. When tachyon energy is free flowing, we have an endless source of energy to rebuild and maintain our SOEFs, so we continually reverse entropy.

This explains how the body can, in effect, become a 'faster-than-light energy' conduit, since we are linked to the unlimited Zero-Point Energy as our ultimate source of energy.

As a result, the body-mind complex becomes more clear and balanced in spiritual evolution, and it becomes an increasingly better transducer and conductor of energy. As this happens, the body is able to store and transmit greater and greater amounts of this higher energy. This process can account for some of the many miracles said to occur in the presence of spiritual masters.

For example, spontaneous healing is reported to have occurred when people simply touched the robe of Jesus. We now understand that there was a flow of this pure cosmic or God energy into people that reorganized and reenergized their SOEFs, allowing the disease processes to be reversed.

People's faith allowed them to draw and be receptive to the healing energy.

Tachyon Energy and Focal Touch Healing are totally different.

With all the preceding background knowledge, the focus of the unique effect in the use of tachyons for healing and development becomes clear.

When tachyon energy is supplied, the disturbed SOEFs are strengthened. According to their very individual possibilities and dynamics, the SOEFs re-create the optimal balance for the forms that they have shaped and continue to maintain them.

Accordingly, tachyon energy is the most direct way of strengthening the SOEFs powers of self-healing. In contrast to the use of frequencies, there can be no overdose of tachyon, no application is too long, and we don't need to be concerned about using the right remedy.

This energy contains all the potential for everything in the universe and for all forms in an optimal manner.

On the basis of this abundance of tachyon energy, the SOEFs transform precisely the frequencies that enable an optimal functioning of the corresponding form (organ, gland, chakra, injured body part, etc.).

Once the balance (healing) has been attained, the subtle organizing energy fields ends this process on its own. A continued supply of tachyon energy has no further effect.

Without exception, all manifestations and symptoms in correlation with the use of Tachyon energy are the regulating, balance-creating action of the SOEFs ! We call the results of this cleansing process 'detoxification'.

Whenever a person using tachyon experiences detoxification, it should be welcomed as the necessary clean-up action. If this process takes place too vehemently, it usually suffices to reduce the amount of tachyon energy supplied, allowing the corresponding subtle organizing energy fields to complete their work in a slower and gentler way.

David Wagner explains that tachyon energy is Life force energy or Chi, Prana, Ki, Orenda or Mana, as various esoteric traditions have referred to it. Traditionally, it has been notably difficult to come by.

You're born with some obviously, some you get from your food, and some you get by breathing it in, but not much.

To get therapeutic or spiritually significant amounts of it requires years of meditation, exercises such as a breathing discipline called Pranayama.

Learning to tune into the Zero Point Energy field enables us to create consciously. We often get in the way of our ability to tune in.

Shireen says that there is a clear difference between concentrating and tuning in. If I concentrate, I try with all my might to achieve something with my thoughts. Usually you achieve just the opposite !

What we call 'thinking' is actually mainly about doubting. You wind up in all kinds of emotions, *"I can't do this, what am I doing here ?"* and you don't achieve your aim. Tuning in means not thinking and making contact with the information that's already there. You become one with the information and resonate with it.

"A Cry From The Womb"

By Gwendolyn Awen Jones

This book is a guide to Healing and helping Souls return to the Light after sudden death, miscarriage, stillbirth, or abortion.

Stunning case histories show why a child's Soul may not be able to reach the Light after a traumatic death or due to emotional entanglement with the grieving family. This may often be the case if the child was lost before full term and the needed transitional rites were omitted.

Even years after the loss the physical, emotional, and spiritual well-being of the parents may be undermined unless Healing and release work is completed - the needed rituals are explained and drafted.

Gwen carefully and compassionately teaches how to do this work, and tells why it is essential to lovingly communicate with the Soul of the child during pregnancy - especially so should the child be lost.

Unwanted pregnancies are discussed, and loving ways for a natural termination are suggested - which benefit all concerned without hurt or harm to anyone involved !

Gwen was born with a gift of being able to see into the spiritual realms. "As a child I saw many things that others did not see. Some things frightened me, others were beautiful, but I had no way of knowing what I was seeing as no-one around me could see as I did. I learned not to speak about what I saw as folks reacted strangely, especially when I spoke of visions that later came true. It was not until I went to Mexico in my early twenties and met a Mayan curandera (a native healer) that I began to understand that my unusual way of seeing was a gift that could be used for healing."

"As a medical intuitive I can see all levels of the human field and can see where the damage is that is causing illness. Often physical illness is caused by problems in the mental, emotional or spiritual realms. Because I can see those levels of the human field I can help a person resolve the issues."

"Over the years I have seen a repeating pattern of illness around men and women who have lost a child, especially if the child was lost before full term or was stillborn. Most often the grief has been pushed down to the 'core of their being' and no-one has helped them or counseled them after the loss. Without closure or guidance on how to heal, the parent's grief can hold the child's soul back. Often I find the child's soul still enmeshed in the energy field of the parent. This causes a blockage in the flow of life energy in the parent, which can result in serious illness."

The book is for anyone wishing to heal after loss. It is also offers important information for couples planning to conceive a child. Real life stories show how the child in the womb may be harmed by the environment the mother finds herself in. It shows how parents' thoughts towards a child during gestation can have an immense impact upon the growth of the child. A loving atmosphere is essential for healthy growth.

"The book is in five sections: the first is my story and explains how I came to do the work I do as a medical intuitive and healer; the second section explains all the levels of the human energy field; the third section has powerful client history cases; the fourth contains all the prayers parents may use for healing themselves and to assist the transition of the soul of the child into the light; the last section contains references and a final jewel - 'A Journey to the Moment of Conception'. Many who have read the book say this short chapter is the most powerful in the book. It explains the spirit's journey into physical incarnation."

"When a child dies we need to realize our work is not done until the child has been assisted back to the light with love and forgiveness in our hearts. No matter how the child died, forgiveness is essential for all involved. Most particularly we must forgive ourselves. Too often parents become ill because they blame themselves. Blame is another of those life-depleting energies that can destroy our health."

Reader feedback from "A Cry from the Womb" has been overwhelmingly powerful ! Men and women are telling how it has changed their lives completely. Women in particular have said after years of grief they have finally found peace by using the prayers in the book. They are buying many books at a time to share with their friends and family.

It is amazing how much sadness and ill-health (especially in women) has resulted from failure to work with Spirit to overcome the effects due to problems in pregnancies including miscarriages and abortions - and that these continue for a great number of years unless Healed with Love. These may well be the cause of many problems that are untreatable by normal methods !

"A Cry from the Womb" - ISBN 978-0-9740730-1-6

Website: www.angelsoflightandhealing.org

E-mail: gwen@angelsoflightandhealing.org

Some Further Thoughts

by John Living

Colours and Sacred Symbols

Over the years I have noticed that when locating 'black spots' in an aura these often form the points of the pattern of a six pointed star - the shape used by the 'Star of David' and by the Sign of the Heart Chakra - the Mark of Vishnu from India, and the Sign of Ptah from Ancient Egypt, used as the sign of the Holistic Intuition Society.

This symbol seems to surround an injury or site of disease - and when the points are 'exploded into Light' by the Ptah Pendulum, the colours associated with the star change.

The basis for the star is two triangles that are interlaced. It is possible that a three dimensional pattern is used, as defined by the sacred mathematical symbol of 'Interlaced Tetrahedrons', comprising two tetrahedrons of independent colours. If so, these would have even stronger effects. It is possible that octahedrons and other symbols are involved in a similar way.

These colours represent the vibrations attached to the symbol - and the meaning / effect of the symbol is dictated by these colours.

Since working with Bill Ellis on this book, I have realized the importance of changing these colours when Healing a Being - human or otherwise. Accordingly I have sought enlightenment on the variations that can be used - but have had great difficulty, since it seems to depend on the location of the symbol.

It seems that the safest and most effective Healing colours to be used are pink and green. Ensuring that any six pointed star pattern, interlaced tetrahedral, or other symbol that is found in or around a Healee is changed to vibrate with these colours will usually lead to a good healing.

I suggest that you first ask if any shape is involved - checking if it is a two dimensional six-pointed star, interlaced tetrahedrons, or other symbol.

If any shape is identified, ask for the colours involved, and whether they are beneficial or noxious.

Check also that the energies forming the colours are 'spiralling good' - in a clockwise spiral. Anti-clockwise spiralling may reverse a normal beneficial action to make it noxious.

If you are able to see them clairvoyantly, still ask, since there may be a pattern in a plane or dimension beyond your sight. If you are using a Ptah Pendulum, you will find that it is programmed to work with the colours in the most suitable way.

This investigation was a most exciting experience - I had never tried to communicate with the colours before, and some of the answers were completely unexpected.

My impression was that the colours themselves were excited at being recognized as 'Beings in their own right' - and that the communication with a human being was like an expedition into the unknown.

When contacting the colours, please treat them with love and respect. They do not like hurting, but some seem to have been given a bad job - a reason why they kept telling how they could be healed !

As a further thought, these are the colours that we see with our eyes - but it seems that these are repeated in octaves at various speeds, and probably in different dimensions. If so, then these results could have great impact in many other ways.

As usual, protection will need to be placed to prevent reversion to 'not good' colours, and the Healer should check that the colours remain pink and 'good green' - or the healing colours used.

After this change in vibration, a 'Brilliant Point of Good Gold Light' may be inserted into the diseased area, to expand outwards - Healing the injured parts as it expands, and perhaps to form auric protection.

Acupuncture

I had a thought ! Bill has explained some excellent ways of Healing the Chakras and organs in this book - could some of these methods be applied to the meridians and points used in Acupuncture ?

I did a Google search for acupuncture meridians, and came across Dr Halevi's web site and printed his diagrams of the meridians - go to www.acumedico.com/meridians.htm to do this yourself; they are the most detailed illustrations of meridians that I have seen.

Shmuel Halevi has over 20 years of clinical practice in Acupressure, being trained in North America and then in Taiwan, and his articles have been published in prestigious medical journals.

I then bought his book 'Chopsticks Acupuncture' (Trafford Publishing - ISBN 978-1-5539-5610-5) which is an incredible explanation of Chinese Healing and its history, with full details of Acupuncture and Acupressure, and loaded with information concerning the effect of the various points on health - and which points to investigate for various health problems.

Remember that Chinese Healing has been proven to work for many thousands of years - western medicine is relatively new, with its basic start in the mid 19th century (before that time it was mainly concerned with bleeding and cutting off rotten limbs !)

Shmuel's book goes way beyond normal Acupuncture - he explains how a person can Heal themselves by using chopsticks and lengths of broom handles to apply Acupressure to the needed points !

I have now used Dowsing to locate the problems in the meridians and the points to be Healed, and to then do the needed Healing using my Ptah Pendulum. It does work !

Sai Sanjeevini Cards

Coming westwards from China we arrive at the Indian sub-continent - the source of many Healing practices including these cards. They work as Radionic devices to load the needed Healing energies to water (and other substance).

There are 60 cards for the various parts of the body, and 186 for various health problems.

The complete set, with instructions, can be freely downloaded from the Sanjeevini web site: www.saisanjeevini.org - print out the complete manual

These have been successfully used world-wide to Heal health problems without resort to pharmaceutical drugs, so saving much expense.

Lulu

This is the name given to a sketched 'doll' used for Chiropractic type Healing - but you can make your own sketch of the bone structures in a body, or use diagrams in books such as 'The Anatomy Colouring Book' by Wynn Kapit & Lawrence Elson, ISBN 978-0-0645-5016-1.

You Dowse to find which bone structure is out of alignment, how many taps should be given and their direction, and then place the eraser end of a pencil onto the point indicated and give the required taps !

The idea is simple, and works ! Juanita Ott in Canada felt the change made by Joe Smith in the USA as he worked on her body !

Time Lines

Harry Chambers, who lives in Hawiai, has found a most interesting method of Healing:

"I have been doing a lot of energy discharge work on myself using a 1 foot ruler and with an ink pen drawing a 1 foot line in length on a piece of paper; with the intent that the length of the line represents a period in my life; as I draw the line I may think of some bad life experience that I had in the past.

I then take an aura meter (or very flimsy or sensitive dowsing rod) and scan slowly over the line. In the normal mode, the rod swing would be clockwise or counter-clockwise; when it begins to bob 'up and down' in a bobbing motion, it indicates an energy point on the line of discordant energy or thought trauma that is bothering me.

I may have more than just one point, so far, I have had 3 points on one line ! So the full length of the line should be scanned. When I am at a point on the straight line where a trauma is located I seek to release it.

I take my right middle finger hold it on the line at the point of the truama, and I take my left middle finger and hold it on my right eye.

This seems to create a circuited energy flow - so that the trauma is released from my body into the same area on the drawn line that my Dowsing tool indicated.

I may shake or yawn doing this energy release work - sometimes tears may form in my eyes.

After this is done, I take my rod and go back and rescan over the drawn line. If I get no bobbing 'up and down' over this same point this shows that the thought trauma has been fully released.

If I get a little bobbing motion over the same area, I go back and repeat the exercise; I recheck and recheck until the bobbing 'up and down' over the point ceases. I have found that if I am facing a certain direction the trauma is release more completely and faster ! I am able to dowse in advance to find the direction I need to face to get such a fuller and stronger release.

I have also found that taking a piece of metal and tapping the area on the line 3 times seems to better free up hidden energies that need to be cleared doing the treatment session.

A week later I rescan this line, to see if some of the old traumas have returned - if so, I repeat the exercise.

Inner healing may be needed to remove the root cause - to clear problems due to discarnate spirits, an inner child issue; or some soul parts missing - and the trauma may show itself as a personality disorder.

This method seems to have a broad range of applications ! I was talking on the phone with a guy and somehow we came to talk of how a person could be helped by being able to regain missing notes that the person's voice is unable to make. So I looked at each note and dowsed which one my voice may be missing - I got about 5 notes.

Then I drew a line when singing one note, and then scanned over that line; I found points where my rod would bob, so then I did the same method to discharge energy that is discordant on this line.

This may be a very simple way of releasing trauma that is in their body indicated by voice blockages."

Harry also suggests that this may work to identify root causes of phobias, allergies, etc., based on locating when they were first triggered.

It may be that a line could be drawn having points marked for conception and birth prior to the normal life line, to identify problems that originated in that time frame.

Perhaps such a line could be used to represent previous life times - recognizing that often problems that manifest in the current life may be rooted in past incarnations.

When using this technique, the line can be of any length providing that the intent when drawing the line is that it represents a time frame - and times can be marked.

The intent should also be that all problems that are found (and their causes) are Healed completely.

Distant Healing Manual

This manual has been compiled using material from many sources, with credit shown to those sources where applicable. Much has come from my own working with 'Upstairs' - my nick-name for the Angelic Beings, Leaders of Healing Energies, Guides, and others who are in non-physical dimensions - although they do work in all the dimensions of creation.

It is published in a protected .pdf format - you can print copies of pages for your own use, but not make changes to the original work or copy pages to other formats.

To use the techniques that are explained in this manual you must have gained efficiency and confidence in your Dowsing abilities.

It is intended to form a Healing Group on the Internet (with web page) to give people requiring Healing access to Healers who have proven abilities and are efficient in the techniques explained in this manual.

Fees will be chargeable for the time that Healers spend doing Healing - there is no charge for the Healing itself, which is done by 'Upstairs'.

You are welcome to apply for membership of this group - Dowsing methods will be used to check your abilities and the willingness of 'Upstairs' to work with you, and also to assign people who need Healing (the Healees) to you. Case records are imperative, and feedback from Healees will be obtained.

You are, of course, free to use these techniques as you wish on your own patients.

To obtain this manual, go to www.in2it.ca/Books.htm - it will be send to you shortly after receipt of your payment by PayPal.

A couple of sample pages follow !

Note that included in this manual is Distant Healing of Acupuncture meridians and points by Dowsing! A new adventure!

For full details of Acupuncture see 'Chopsticks Acupuncture' by Dr Shmuel Halevi, ISBN 978-1-5539-5610-5, which explains how people can easily do Acupressure Healing on themselves using simple tools. See Dr Halevi's web page: www.acumedico.com for more information about this marvelous book!

Master Chart

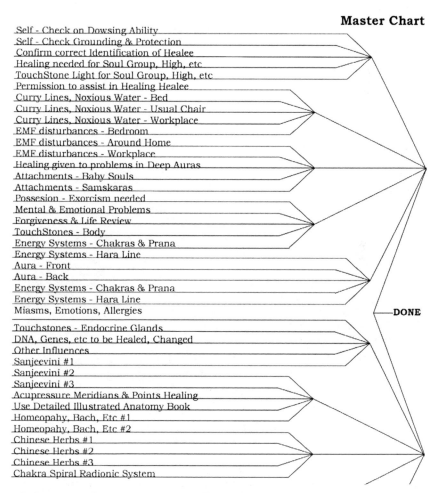

Self - Check on Dowsing Ability
Self - Check Grounding & Protection
Confirm correct Identification of Healee
Healing needed for Soul Group, High, etc
TouchStone Light for Soul Group, High, etc
Permission to assist in Healing Healee
Curry Lines, Noxious Water - Bed
Curry Lines, Noxious Water - Usual Chair
Curry Lines, Noxious Water - Workplace
EMF disturbances - Bedroom
EMF disturbances - Around Home
EMF disturbances - Workplace
Healing given to problems in Deep Auras
Attachments - Baby Souls
Attachments - Samskaras
Possesion - Exorcism needed
Mental & Emotional Problems
Forgiveness & Life Review
TouchStones - Body
Energy Systems - Chakras & Prana
Energy Systems - Hara Line
Aura - Front
Aura - Back
Energy Systems - Chakras & Prana
Energy Systems - Hara Line
Miasms, Emotions, Allergies

Touchstones - Endocrine Glands
DNA, Genes, etc to be Healed, Changed
Other Influences
Sanjeevini #1
Sanjeevini #2
Sanjeevini #3
Acupressure Meridians & Points Healing
Use Detailed Illustrated Anatomy Book
Homeopahy, Bach, Etc #1
Homeopahy, Bach, Etc #2
Chinese Herbs #1
Chinese Herbs #2
Chinese Herbs #3
Chakra Spiral Radionic System

—DONE

Master Chart of the Distant Healing Manual

(Note that this is not yet finalized - typical chart shown as example)
Similar letter-sized blank charts are provided for your own use
having 25, 50, and 100 entries per chart page.

The Chakra Spiral - with Safety Program

Taken from Christopher Hills' books 'Energy, Matter, and Form' and 'Supersensonics'
This is one of the most powerful symbols for both transmission and receiving.
It may be an excellent transmitter to use in a 'Paper Radionics' machine.
Place the descriptions of Healing to be sent on top of the spiral, then details of the Healee.

All Healing is sent to the part of the Being needing it with True Holy Love, Namaste and the Intent to Heal Good in a Good Way as required for Healing by the Wisdom of the Being, the Wisdom of the Body, and the Heart of the Healee, working with the co-operation of the 'Light of Light Angels', the 'Love Namaste Healing Team', and 'The System'. Ego is excluded.
The Healing sent may be pulsed, the frequency of pulses, duration and intensity to be as needed for perfect good health without any unwanted side effects or actions that are non-beneficial or cause harm or hurting. The Healing is then sealed and stabilized with Light Bluish White and White Light & any other needed protection to prevent any recurrence of the existing problems or any that are similar.

Key advantages of this diagrammatic Radionic Device are that whereas most devices need to be switched ON or OFF this is done automatically as needed, that a Safety Program is included, and that the Healing Energies and Vibrational Patterns are sent by Pulsing - which makes them more effective.

Books by John Living   www.in2it.ca/Books.htm

Earth Radiation - Käthe Bachler   ISBN 978-0-9686323-5-2

<u>2nd English Edition, with 'Further Thoughts' by John Living</u>

This is the classic record of the identification and location of energies from the earth which are noxious to human beings.

The book is a distillation of over 11,000 cases of investigation of these energies in more than 3,000 homes in 14 countries !

Originally written in German, it became a 'best seller' in Europe and was translated first into Spanish, and then into English. The first English edition has long been 'out of print', and existing second hand copies have been fetching prices of US$90 on eBay !

Illustrations show the location of 'Curry Grid Lines' and 'Noxious Water Veins' that radiate noxious energies, especially where they cross.

These illustrations are accompanied by records of the illnesses resulting from sleeping or sitting for a long time in the energy fields - and how great improvements in health occurred when the location of beds, school seats, etc., were moved.

Very simple, very cheap, and very effective !

"We do not claim that every zone of disturbance will result in cancer. <u>Rather, we have found zones of disturbance in every case of cancer.</u> ... Physicians ought to consider geopathic influences as one possible cause of illness, and recommend moving the bed on a trial basis"

Many other illnesses have also been observed to result from these noxious energies - pregnancy failures, infant mortality, insomnia, inattention at school, improper behaviour, rheumatism, multiple sclerosis, parasitic attacks, and more.

<u>Case# 660. The ten-month-old baby was tied to his crib.</u>

The parents were afraid he might fall out of bed, because he stood up again and again.

When in his playpen, he only occupied the half which was 'free of radiation', never the half above the curry strip. The father finally phoned me:

"Since we moved the bed, we have had no problem with his sleeping and he is healthy and robust."

Case# 403. She had a crying spell almost every day.

She and two other children had their desks moved, and the symptoms of all three children disappeared

(principal's confirmation available.)

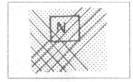

Many of the results are attested by medical doctors who found that cures were only effective after exposure to noxious earth energies ceased. Cases are quoted which include the use of these techniques by physicians for their own health.

Case# 1367. Physician Dr H required a gall bladder operation.

Ever since she moved to her present sleeping place she had been ill. She suffered from pain and anxiety attacks at night in bed.

Everywhere else she seemed to sleep well.

She changed the bed immediately - and slept better the very first night.

She said: *"I don't understand why conventional medicine does not acknowledge the value of dowsing. It seems to me they ought to be grateful for the help."*

One of the key points that this book makes is that many other problems, not just cancer, are attributable to some large degree to earth energies that are noxious to humans.

By eliminating the effects of these we can expect improvements in education and in behaviour, reductions in work losses and medical expenses, and better health at minimal cost.

Case# 1486c. A chemist from Salzburg

felt discomfort, registered slight fevers, and was nervous while working at his bench in his laboratory.

Many of his experiments failed and had to be repeated.   Whenever he worked at a place free of radiation, his experiments proved to be successful.

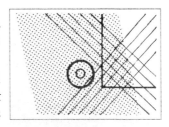

Intuition 'On Demand'   ISBN 978-0-9686323-3-8

We look at the way that our beings operate, including an overview of our 'energy bodies' and 'soul senses', and how to work with our Heart as our link to 'Upstairs', and examine the methods used to liaise with our sub-conscious self to improve our working relationship, and how awareness of our environment and expansion of our knowledge increase our abilities to work with our Intuition.

We are 'ruled' by our beliefs; some are based on things that we have been told by others - that may not be 'our truth'. But these become established as programs that we run automatically. Examples are given of ways to change now existing programs, and how to install new programs for our well-being.

Some very simple ways to improve our health are discussed, and methods of helping our Heart-Mind-Brain team to access our Intuition and to signal answers via our nervous-muscular system are examined, including the use of our real physical '6th sense' - the sense of balance.

We investigate methods of amplifying our Intuitive signals to enable more diverse use of our 'Power of Thought', including effective ways of improving life for all by adjusting the vibrational patterns of energy - including the use of thought to make simple medicine for oneself!

At the end of the book some interesting games are described which will help participants to improve their Intuitive abilities. The approach used in this book is to 'keep it simple'. There are a lot of little hints - if they suit you, then use them to improve your life.

Intuition Technology   ISBN 978-0-9686323-4-5

This includes most of the writings in Intuition 'On Demand' - but goes much further into details and uses - especially for Healing.

The skills taught in this book have been used for a great many years - mainly to help others. There are many wonderful teachers around the globe, and this book tries to collect their wisdom together.

The major use today is in health matters - locating noxious energies and Healing them; identifying health problems and finding ways to overcome them; and improving the well-ness of people by using our 'Power of Thought'.

Everything that exists is made of energy - and this applies to other dimensions as well as the physical dimensions. Knowing this, we can understand how the 'Power of Thought' and that 'We are all the same' gives us the ability to work with 'All That Is', including the 'Angelic Realm' - for Healing of ourselves and our friends, and for the general good of all.

Western medicine seeks mainly to stop the effects of a disease - rarely to uncover and Heal the underlying causes, which often are not in the physical dimension. Energy Healing, using Dowsing, can locate and identify these causes, and Heal them before disease manifests in the physical body.

Orders for these books can be placed with your local bookshop, or purchased directly from the society.

Sleep Well, Be Healthy   ISBN 978-0-9686323-2-1

This is a 64 page condensed version of 'Earth Radiation' - it has the introduction to feeling noxious energies and guide-lines on how to overcome their effects by John Living, with a good selection of the case histories reported by Käthe Bachler.

This booklet has been designed as a hand-out by Professional Dowsers to their clients, to help them to understand and recognize the problems involved and know that they can be solved.

It is also a means of explaining to Health Care Professionals that problems with these noxious energies exist - and that Dowsing may be required for their patients to be able to recover good health.

Your Pendulum   ISBN 978-0-9686323-6-9

This is a 48 page booklet that introduces people to the use of a Pendulum - keeping it simple, and giving hints for use.

These booklets are available only from the Holistic Intuition Society - which sells individual copies for $5 each - with bulk sales costing the purchasers between $2 and $1.20 each (plus shipping and handling). For detailed information see www.in2it.ca/Books.htm - bulk prices are listed separately.

The Holistic Intuition Society's 'Shop'

"Love Living" Bracelets

In the 1925 Georges Lakhovsky in France developed a coil for the protection of trees; copper wire was stuck into the ground, turns were made around the tree, and the loose end was pointed towards the sky as an aerial. In 1928 he formed a variation of this that was geared to improve the health of humans, which he called the 'multi-wave oscillator', based on his then new theory that cells are microscopic oscillating circuits.

This was successfully used in French, Italian, and Swedish clinics, and when Lakhovsky escaped to the USA in 1941 it proved successful in a major New York hospital. Among problems successfully treated were cancerous growths from Radium burns, goiters, arthritis, chronic bronchitis, congenital hip dislocation, and many others. (Tompkins & Bird: 'Secret Life of Plants').

John Living made a number of different rings, testing the effect on glasses of water showed that the water had a radiance of about 5KÅ (5,000 Ångstroms - the human body for a normal person is about 6.5 KÅ) which in 2 minutes increased to 20KÅ for the medium sized rings and 60 KÅ for the smallest ring - the effect is more concentrated.

They are sturdy, attractive, and within the reach of most purses. So which ring type is best ? This depends on the use !

The bracelets and smaller rings #1, #2, and #3 are of twisted copper wire, having a small gap; a vinyl tube prevents the copper from being in direct contact with your skin.

They increase the radiance of your blood so that diseases are repelled, and give the vibrational pattern of copper, like the way a homeopathic remedy works.

This waterproof casing design permits easy cleaning, prevents corrosion, and allows opening. The combination of vinyl with copper blends into the skin colour, so that the bracelet is less noticeable. A hardy bracelet, suitable for constant wear, even ideal for a man in the office or working outside.

You can expect all the water in your body (over 75% of you !) to become potentized with a high radiance. Germs and viruses do not thrive in such an environment, so your LOVE LIVING Bracelets helps to keep you healthy !

A number of successes are reported with the relief of headaches by placing a #2 Energy ring around the neck - if below a shirt or sweater, it is not noticeable.

It may be that some people who have other head problems, perhaps including Alzheimer's and Parkinson's diseases, benefit from wearing a neck ring. The cost of a trial is minimal, the possible benefits considerable, and there is no health risk involved

'L' Rods

These are made from welding rods, with a wooden handle having a plastic insert for low friction movement and a metal end cap.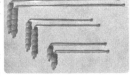

The rod arm has a metal end cap to enhance your Dowsing response and prevent damage to people.

Glass Bead Pendulums

The glass beads have been hand made by craftsmen, and come in various colours and configurations; they are held by a braided nylon string, the string colour being suitable for the bead.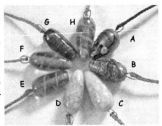

Bendable Bobber

This tool has pewter weights fitted to the end of a specially wound spring 'wand' inserted into a ball-point pen case. It give great sensitivity, and bends to fit in your pocket.

The Ptah Pendulum

John Living found that the Osiris Pendulum has a special ability to locate 'not good' energies in a person's aura, and when used in 'extraction mode' (an anti-clockwise circle) it removed such energies.

But there was a problem - they tended to go into the hand of the Healer/Dowser who was using the Pendulum !

To overcome this, John attached his Osiris Pendulum to the 'extract' end of one of the Healing Coils developed by Slim Spurling.

This converted the energies that were removed into being 'good' energies - and thus prevented deleterious effects from being experienced by the Healer/Dowser, giving instead a beneficial effect.

The next step was to attach one of Slim's Coils to a cord, so as to make a Pendulum. This was even more powerful in extracting 'not good' energies and converting them to being 'good', but did not have the ability of the Osiris Pendulum in locating problems in auras.

An effort was made to get the Osiris Pendulum, designed on geometric theory, to teach the 'Slim's Coil' Pendulum its skill in locating problems in auras - and this was successful !

The Isis Pendulum has the gift of putting 'good' energies into the recipient in a similar way, so a cord was attached to the output end of one of Slim's Coils to make a Pendulum that put 'good' energy into a person - and again this was a success !

Then the thought was received "Why not combine them into a dual purpose Pendulum ?" - and so the 'Ptah Pendulum' was developed.

John Living has tested this on himself and on a number of other people who needed Healing - with excellent results.

He has used it to locate and Heal 'not good' energies in the land, such as curses and other 'bad medicine', and understands that it is one of the most powerful Healing devices that exists.

When working with the Healing Angels and other Healing Energies John uses the 'Ptah Pendulum' to clear energies that are causing problems as a preliminary step to reduce the work needed to be done by the Healing Energies / Angels.

All the 'Ptah Pendulums' are blessed with the abilities of the Osiris and Isis Pendulums, and have been made with True Holy Love.

Signals

In all work with the 'Ptah Pendulum' a clockwise circle indicates YES and is the 'Input Mode'. An anti-clockwise circle indicates NO and is the 'Extract Mode'.

When asking a question it does not matter which end of the Pendulum is held.

The 'Ptah Pendulum' will extract or input, and then swing towards the next position that it needs to go - the direction could be one of two ways, since it is swinging, and your Intuition will guide you to the correct place.

If you go in the wrong direction, the 'Ptah Pendulum' will not circle (or make a very small signal) - so reverse the direction that you are moving the Pendulum. When in the correct place it will circle to do the needed work.

Holding your 'Ptah Pendulum'

In extract mode, the hand holds the shorter of the two coils. For input mode, the longer coil is held. To avoid bending the coil that is held, hold it at its bottom - the strain is not transmitted to the part of the coil above your hand.

Start at the head of the person or centre of the token, and make an anti-clockwise circle (extract mode, shorter coil in hand) around this point, widening in a spiral to enclose most of the Healee; then hold the 'Ptah Pendulum' stationary at the start point - it will start to circle on its own accord to extract 'not good' energies.

When the circling finishes, the 'Ptah Pendulum' will swing, pointing to the next location of 'not good' energies - move it slowly in the direction indicated until it starts to swing again. This is repeated until it remains stationary.

Now change to input mode - the longer coil is held in hand, making clockwise circles - again on its own accord - and this procedure is repeated.

Logically this should remove all 'not good' energies, and replace them all with 'good' energies. But the metaphysical world is not logical !

Perhaps what happens is that some 'not good' energies resist the extraction, but are weakened by the input of True Holy Love, so that by repeating this whole procedure again more 'not good' energies will be extracted.

To make certain that all has been cleared, keep on repeating the extraction mode and then input mode until no circling occurs. And as a final check, start again at the start point and make a spiral, then go to the start point and sees if any swinging or circling occurs.

If so, then repeat the whole procedure again - and keep on until there is not any swinging or circling.

Note that this is not just to Heal people - for 'person' you can substitute 'animal', 'bird', etc.

DVDs of Speakers and Workshops

We have recorded the lectures and workshops on Dowsing and on Healing at the conventions promoted by the Society, and have these available on DVDs that are playable world-wide.

The workshops were given by recognized masters of Dowsing to teach their skills - including the ability of Dowsers to use their 'Power of Thought' for healing the energies of humans, animals, and plants.

More Information

The Holistic Intuition Society sells more Dowsing and Healing tools - these are shown on our website at: **www.in2it.ca/tools.htm** together with prices and ordering information.

The key intent is to provide simple tools that can be easily used, at reasonable cost, and that do their job effectively and safely without any side effects.

The Holistic Intuition Society

c/o Executive Secretary: John Living, Professional Engineer

RR# 1 S9 C6, Galiano Island, BC, V0N 1P0 Canada

Telephone (250)539-5807

Toll Free Canada & USA: 1-866-369-7464

**Unfortunately we cannot process credit cards - except by PayPal
PayPal is set-up on our web site,**

A cheque or money order in Canadian or US funds is acceptable.

Lightning Source UK Ltd.
Milton Keynes UK
28 April 2010

153463UK00001B/198/P